ADOPTION:

International Perspectives

ADOPTION:
International Perspectives

Edited by
Euthymia D. Hibbs, Ph.D.

International Universities Press
Madison   Connecticut

Library of Congress Cataloging-in-Publication Data

Adoption : international perspectives / edited by Euthymia D. Hibbs.
    p. cm.
    Includes bibliographical references and indexes.
    ISBN 0-8236-0096-3
    1. Adoption. 2. Adoption—Psychological aspects. I. Hibbs, Euthymia D.
    [DNLM: 1.Adoption. HV 875 A239]
HV875.A338 1991
362.7'34—dc20
DNLM/DLC
for Library of Congress   91-7036
                                              CIP

Manufactured in the United States of America

Contents

Contributors

Maria Berkowska, Ph.D.   Lecturer, Institute of Social Medicine, Medical Academy, Poznan, Poland

Lucile A. C. Bunjes, Ph.D.   Clinical Pedagogue, Adoption Center, University of Utrecht, The Netherlands

Graziella Caiani-Praturlon, S.W.   Director, International Social Service, Italian Branch, Rome, Italy

Linda M. Claxton-Brynjulfson,M.S.W.,A.C.S.W. Post-Legal Adoption Services, Children's Home Society of Minnesota, U.S.A.

Ann Corcoran, Dipl.S.W.   Department of Social Welfare, Wellington, New Zealand

Richard A. Detweiler, Ph.D.   Professor of Psychology, Department of Psychology, Drew University, Madison, New Jersey, U.S.A.

Vera I. Fahlberg, M.D.   Clinical Director, Forest Height Lodge, Evergreen, Colorado, U.S.A.

John Fitzgerald, C.Q.S.W.   Director, The Bridge Child Care Consultancy Service, London, U.K.

Adriano Giannotti, M.D.   Director, Second Chair, Child Neuropsychiatry, University of Rome, La Sapienza; Supervising Analyst, Italian Psychoanalytical Association, (S.P.I.), Rome, Italy

Euthymia D. Hibbs, Ph.D.   Clinical Research Psychologist, National Institute of Mental Health, Intramural Research Program, Bethesda, Maryland, U.S.A.

René A. C. Hoksbergen, Ph.D.   Professor of Adoption Center, Utrecht University, Utrecht, The Netherlands

Tassoula Koussidou, M.S.W.   Supervisor of the Adoption and Counseling Sections, Metera Babies Center, Athens, Greece

Billy Maganiotou, B.A.   Head of Social Service, Metera Babies
Center, Athens, Greece

Kathlyn S. Marquis, M.S.W.   Psychotherapist, Richmond Memo-
rial Hospital, Staten Island, New York, U.S.A.

Jadwiga Migaszewska-Majewicz, Ph.D.   Head of the Department
of Child Psychology, Health Services, Poznan, Poland

Giuliana Milana Lisa, S.W.   Child Psychotherapist, International
Social Service, Rome, Italy

Paola Natali, Ph.D.   Psychotherapist, Second Chair, Child Neuropsychiatry, University of Rome, La Sapienza, Rome, Italy

Gerry O'Hara, C.Q.S.W. Dipl.S.W.   Regional Officer, Children
and Families, Lothian Regional Council, Edinburgh, U.K.

Elpetha Panera, S.W.   Principal of Social Workers, Department of
Social Welfare of Thessaloniki, Greece

William Pierce, Ph.D.   President, National Council for Adoption,
Washington, D.C., U.S.A.

Jane Rowe, M.A.   Research Project Director, British Agencies for
Adoption, London, U.K.

Ugo Sabatello, M.D.   Child Neuropsychiatrist, Second Chair,
Child Neuropsychiatry, University of Rome, La Sapienza, Rome,
Italy

Paul Sachdev, Ph.D.   Professor, School of Social Work, Newfound-
land, Canada

Dorit Sharav, M.A.   Clinical Psychologist, Jerusalem, Israel

John Triseliotis, Ph.D.   Director, Department of Social Policy and
Social Work, University of Edinburgh, Edinburgh, U.K.

John Tsiantis, M.D., D.P.M., F.R.C.   Director, Department of Psychological Pediatrics, Aghia Sophia Children's Hospital, Athens,
Greece

Robert J. Vitillo, A.C.S.W.   Priest, International Charities, Vatican

Richard A. H. White, L.B.   Solicitor, London, U.K.

Preface

Although the number of children in need of homes has diminished in the developed countries in recent years, adoption continues to be a major factor in child welfare, for there will always be some children in need of adoptive parents and adoption will continue to be an important means for child protection. Today, more than ever, adoption is an even greater challenge for social agencies and professionals, since, increasingly the children needing homes are special needs children—those who are older, abused, or handicapped.

Most developed countries experienced a peak in the number of babies adopted in the 1950s and 1960s, when adoption was considered a panacea for homeless children and childless couples. However, during the 1970s and 1980s, thinking on adoption changed, and today it has become a controversial issue. Clinical experience and research findings have shown that adoption is neither a perfect nor an easy solution, and in order to ensure a positive outcome, much specialized and individualized work has to be done with all parties involved prior to and after adoption.

The following questions confront many adoption agencies, professionals, and users of their services: Are services to single parents and disadvantaged families adequate to encourage them to continue caring for their children? How much time and what services should be given to the biological family with children in care to help them resume responsibility for their children before termination of parental rights is considered? Should traditional adoption be abolished in favor of long-term foster care or open adoption? What policies should determine the opening of records for adoptees seeking their roots?

Moreover, with the increasing number of international and interracial adoptions and the controversy surrounding them, adoption is no longer limited to local or national levels. It has become an international issue calling for the exchange and sharing of experiences, knowledge, and ideas among countries. I think that the papers in this volume by a group of international experts in adoption skillfully address these issues and fulfill this need.

Panos Palmos, M.D.
President of the Board
of the Metera Babies Center

Acknowledgments

This book was supported and financed by the Metera Babies Center, the leading adoption agency in Athens, Greece.

I wish to thank: Dr. Panos Palmos and Ms. Tassoula Koussidou, the professionals, and the Board of Directors of the Metera Babies Center without whose collaboration and support this book would not have taken form; the International Study Center for Children and Families, for its collaboration; the International Social Service, Greek Branch; the National Committee for Adoption, U.S.A.; the Greek Ministry of Health and Welfare, the Ministry of Culture, and the Youth Secretariat.

Special thanks to Mrs. Ellen Smith and Ms. Eleni Pallas who worked very hard on the preparation of the manuscript.

Introduction

Adoption has undergone a succession of modifications throughout the ages as societal attitudes have changed and scientific knowledge has increased. As early as the eighteenth century B.C., in the Babylonian codes of Hammurabi, adoption was both recognized and legally regulated. Several laws controlled adoption in ancient Greece, Egypt, and Rome as well. In ancient times, the apparent reason for adoption was to ensure an heir, the continuance of business, and the perpetuation of the family name of childless couples. The adoption rationale remained the same until the greater part of the early twentieth century, at least in the Western World, where adoption was seen as a way to provide babies for childless couples. Healthy, white infants were preferred, leaving other children, orphaned or unwanted, to institutions. Only in the last three decades has the best interest of the child been considered and legal provisions have been enacted to ensure a stable environment where the child's physical and emotional development can be enhanced. Today, on the threshold of the twenty-first century, new issues have surfaced on the adoption scene: open versus closed adoptions, independent adoptions versus those through specialized agencies, international and cross-cultural adoptions, and the adoption of children with special needs.

Disciplines such as child and human development, family systems, psychopathology, biology, and genetics examined adoption and explored the issues that are mostly encountered in the adoptive situation. How does one develop and function in society with the burden of early rejection? How does one form an identity when vital genetic and historical information and cultural continuity is missing? How does a couple who are unable to conceive raise a child that someone

xv

else gave birth to? How could the nuclear and extensive family reorga-
nize to include a non-blood relative into their family system? What
role does biology and genetics play in the individual's development
and how may they affect the adoptive family? What is the best way to
raise a child from a different culture or with special needs, and what
are the consequences of such an adoption on parents and child alike?

One question that defies scientific and regulatory solution is that
of secrecy in adoption. Although adoption professionals do their best
to educate parents about when and how to tell a child that he is
adopted, many children and adults in many countries today are unaware of their adoptive status. Some adults learn they were adopted
during a medical emergency situation and, frequently, this discovery
is devastating. Others learn about their adoptive status at the death-
bed of the last adoptive parent. In the latter case the adopted persons
are left in an even worse situation, since there is no one to help them
work through their double grief.

Why do parents keep the adoption a secret? Some "never found
the courage to tell," or better, they were "afraid to hurt the child's
feelings," or believe that the child "will be happier in believing that
they are the biological parents." Others keep the adoptive status secret
because the child was obtained through illegal means—abducted or
the parents were killed in a war and infants were taken away.

Another issue is that of the adoptive parents' age. It has been
established that the adoptive family should resemble that of the biological one, i.e., no more than thirty to forty years of age difference
between children and parents. Although this would be the ideal situation, today, even the biological family structure is changing. Women
in their early forties give birth to children and fathers are sometimes
even older. As John Fitzgerald (Chapter 13) suggests, the traditional
criteria for selecting parents should be modified to fit the realities of
our changing society in order to meet children's need of a home.

These multiple issues make adoption a distinctive domain where
societal changes must be taken into consideration, specialized techniques need to be updated in handling the adoption process, and
innovative intervention methods are required to manage problems
that arise from adoption.

In this volume professionals from many countries and different
disciplines share their expertise and experiences on the subject of
adoption. Areas discussed range from legal issues to the dynamics

of adoption, from the selection of prospective parents to programs facilitating adoption, from developmental concerns to adoption outcome. In addition, techniques are presented for evaluating the prospective families, preparing children for adoption, and working with special needs children. After reading through the variety of reports one cannot but emerge enriched with the knowledge gained in this sensitive field of adoption, but also feel the controversy surrounding it. Today when the issue of abortion versus adoption has become one of the most salient moral and political concerns, at least in the United States, it is important to examine all available information. This volume should help clarify some issues surrounding adoption and enhance understanding.

Euthymia D. Hibbs, Ph.D.

Part I

ADOPTION IN PERSPECTIVE

1

Perspectives on Adoption

Jane Rowe, M.A.

In a brief paper on perspectives, one has to examine the subject in broad sweeps. But generalizations need to be grounded in real, individual experiences, so I hope that some quotations from adoptees and adoption workers will serve to highlight the range of attitudes and experiences that must be encompassed.

> "Adoption is a selfish act people do because they want a little child in their home."
> "Adoption is the most satisfactory form of permanent care yet devised by Western society for children whose own parents cannot undertake it."
> "One might say that adoption agencies are a system for redistributing children from the poor to the middle classes."
> "I have no problems about being adopted. It's been a very happy life."
> "My adoption hangs like a great black cloud over everything and overshadows everything else."
> "It makes you feel great to know you were wanted so much."
> "It is a burden to be chosen. Its very specialness isolates one."

These quotations illustrate some of the polarized attitudes and strong feelings which adoption arouses. Even when it is quite "usual," adoption never seems to be an everyday matter but stimulates special

3

interest and concern. Many of the feelings that adoption wakens are quite basic and primitive. We may find their roots in the folklore: there is the good fairy and white magic that disguises the king's son as the child of the woodchopper. There is fear and suspicion of the outsider, the changeling—bad fairy, black magic. There is fear of the "bad seed" throwing up a noxious weed in the tranquil family garden. At a conscious, intellectual level we dismiss these primitive ideas, but their influence often remains at a subconscious level unacknowledged but still potent.

Attitudes toward adoption are also shaped by the vital elements of moral judgment and personal and social values which spill over into economic and political issues. The status of adoption in any society provides many insights into that community's beliefs and priorities. Laws and customs concerning adoption show us whether the society is based on the nuclear family with emphasis on individual rights and freedoms, or on the tribe or extended family with its intricate system of obligations and supports. These laws and customs usually define the status of women and children and indicate attitudes toward strangers, outsiders, or those who differ from the norm because of handicap or disfigurement. In some cultures, adoption of children of a different race is unacceptable and in others the adoption of a physically or mentally handicapped child would be unthinkable.

There are some less obvious value judgments which also need consideration. Often adoption is seen as an opportunity for a child to have a "better" life. But, what do we mean by "better"? By what yardstick do we measure the quality of life? There are the material indices, of course, adequate food, clothing, medical care, and education. It may even be a basic issue of survival—life or death. There are psychological indices of being wanted, loved, and respected rather than abandoned, rejected, or scapegoated. For some children adoption offers rescue from psychological damage that may be worse than death. But there are questions of identity, roots, and the ties of family, community, and ethnic group. We see these most starkly in relation to interracial or inter-country adoptions, but the same issues are present in less obvious ways in every adoption decision.

The heavy responsibilities of adoption work and the strong emotions roused by it make balance very important. It is easy to protect oneself by becoming rigid, putting on blinders, shutting out the negatives, refusing to examine alternatives and insisting that "our way is

best." To see things in perspective is to see them in the right align-
ments and in proportion. It is good to hear about attitudes and practices different from our own. It helps to look back and see how theory
and practice have changed and developed. It is salutary to recall and
acknowledge the undesirable side effects of some of our well meaning
but ignorant interventions and to realize that in future our current
practice will be similarly a cause for concern even though we are
doing the best we know how. Therefore, a sense of perspective should
open our minds to new ideas. I hope, too, that it will inhibit any
tendency to fall into the trap of thinking that adoption services as we
see them in Western Europe, North America, Australia, and New
Zealand ought to be considered as prototypes of good social welfare
provision to be replicated in a similar way in other countries. I hope
to show that while adoption often produces some positive results from
unhappy and damaging situations, it is a good *solution*, not a choice
in itself and is at its best when least needed.

In the second half of this paper I will address four areas: (1) the
social and economic background of adoption; (2) loss and pain as
integral and inevitable; (3) the benefits of adoption; and (4) the role
of adoption in child care.

SOCIAL AND ECONOMIC BACKGROUND OF
ADOPTION

A quick look back into history and around the world shows us
that some children have always been brought up in other than their
biological families, either because they were orphaned and needed
care or because their parents gave, loaned, or sold them to others
who needed them for economic support or to carry out religious
obligations. In just a few places, such as the Pacific Islands, such
adoptions seem always to have been widespread and usual, but in most
countries they have been comparatively rare. Either way, adoption in
the past seemed always to have been an open, public, and well-ac-
cepted affair.

It is only in the twentieth century that we encounter the highly
confidential, almost secretive transfer of infants to strangers through
the use of an intermediary (either an individual or an agency). For a
few decades this type of adoption occurred on a considerable scale.

For instance in England and Wales in 1968—the peak year for adoptions—more than 16,000 children were adopted, most of them infants (this excludes children adopted by stepparents). This phase of adoption has now virtually ended for it could only occur in societies which allowed, even encouraged, widespread premarital sex, did not make birth control easily available, and were unable to accept the illegitimate children which resulted, and were unwilling or unable to provide the housing and economic support which would have enabled their mothers to keep and rear them.

We have seen that as soon as social and economic pressures ease, single mothers stop placing their babies for adoption. The twin problems—illegitimacy and infertility—no longer cancel each other out. The result, of course, is the unmet demand for babies from infertile couples who see adoption as the solution to childlessness. Some of these would-be parents are able to stretch their concept of parenthood and go on to adopt handicapped babies who were previously considered unadoptable, or older children whose own families have failed them. Socioeconomic factors play a part in these older child adoptions, too, though this aspect is usually less obvious. In Europe, North America, and Australia the problem is not so much the lack of basic necessities. The psychological effects of chronic and generalized deprivation in the midst of affluence contribute in part to family breakdown and poor parenting which brings many children into public care, and some of them into new families through adoption.

With no available babies in their own countries, some couples turn to inter-country adoption as a solution to the pain of childlessness. Here the economic aspects of adoption are even more starkly presented. In the Third World legacies of colonialism run deep. "First you want our labor and raw materials; now you want our children" is a natural response from countries struggling to survive. Of course, it does not feel like this to the Western families warmly opening their hearts and homes to a needy child from overseas. Yet money does come into it. Often it is easier to raise money to transport children across the world than to maintain them in their home country. We see much the same picture within Britain and the United States. It is easier and cheaper to run a quality adoption service for a few children than to provide the community services of housing, recreation, and income support that would reduce the need for children to be taken into public care.

These economic issues are an important background to any serious consideration of adoption services, but as individuals or social agencies we cannot do much about them. This is a task for politicians and governments.

LOSS AND PAIN

Adoption grows out of grief and is never accomplished without pain. One of the most difficult questions I have ever been asked was posed by a three-year-old. Ellen asked me, "Do you think my Mummy Jo cries for me?" For complex reasons of her own, this little girl's mother had determined to give her up for adoption, and a few days before I had held them both in my arms as they said their goodbyes. Now Ellen was struggling to come to terms with this apparent rejection.

I am sure that all people who work in adoption carry in their memories some specially poignant moments. We recall the flowing tears or silent, stony-faced anguish of a birth mother holding her baby for the last time. We see again the grief of a childless woman being introduced to the child who is to be hers by adoption and facing fully for the first time the reality that she will never experience pregnancy and childbirth and bear her own baby. We live again through the pain and guilt that both precedes and follows an adoption breakdown when those who started out with high hopes have to say, "We can't cope; he'll have to go back." We think about the unhappy, rebellious teenager who cries, "Why did she give me up? What's wrong with me? Didn't she love me?" These memories are the antidote to any fantasies of "happy ever after" that may tempt adoption workers. But the risk is that in our efforts to cope with this pain we avoid or try to deny it. This can result in superficial or coldly professional work that has little to offer the families involved.

It is ironic that the era of large-scale adoption of infants is coming to an end just when, for the first time, there is a large number of adopted adults in the population able and willing to tell us what it is like to grow up adopted. Inevitably we hear most from adoptees who have suffered in some way. When all goes well, adopted people merge into their new family and get on with their lives like the rest of us. But as people such as Betty Jean Lifton (1979) tell us, there are some adoptees who, beneath an often apparently successful exterior, carry deep psychological wounds. They feel incomplete, unreal—living in an "as if" world. They doubt themselves and have trouble with relationships. These adoptees are a minority, but their pain is real. Some of it is unnecessary—caused by ignorance, unsuitable placements, or a combination of unforeseeable circumstances. Some individuals just seem to be particularly vulnerable. They have a particular need for their genealogical roots in order to feel whole.

BENEFITS OF ADOPTION

Study after study (see Triseliotis, Chapter 24, in this volume) conducted at different times and in different parts of the globe has come up with the same conclusion: the great majority of adoption placements turn out well and adopted children, as a group, do better than those in group care or in long-term foster homes. The picture is the same whether the placements were of infants or older children, same race or interracial, same country or across countries. After reviewing all the research on adoption outcome John Triseliotis (1983) concludes: "In effect, what all the studies in adoption outcome seem to say is that whether we talk about the placement of young white or black infants, or of older children, we can expect up to 80% of them to work out satisfactorily" (p. 30). And after a similar review, Martin Shaw (1984) reports: "The overall picture of the adopted child presented in recent research, unlike the rather fragile creature shown in early, clinical studies, shows a sturdy, thriving youngster holding his own in comparison with his non-adopted peers" (p. 119).

The comments of contented adoptees are apt to be very low key but they ring true. Rather more obvious and exciting is the transformation that often occurs when a deprived and disturbed child finds a permanent, loving family. Danny was eighteen years old when we interviewed him for a research project and had been nine when he joined his new family. He expressed his feelings about being adopted in these words, "It's like getting a second chance. It's like getting a kidney transplant. You are struggling with one kidney and then you suddenly get a transplant and you're full of life again."

For the past ten years I have been associated with Parents for Children, a small adoption agency which specializes in placing children once thought to be unadoptable—older, handicapped, and troubled children. We hold an annual picnic to which all the families are invited. There, helping out and running errands at our recent picnic was Martin, now about nine years old. He is one of twin brothers born totally deaf. When referred to Parents for Children they were virtually out of contact and out of control. They had spent their lives in a variety of residential nurseries and special schools. With no hearing and no speech, they could not communicate with caregivers who did not know sign language. They appeared to have little relationship with each other and none at all with any adult. When taken out they had to be on a lead for fear they would run into the street. The transformation wrought by their single adoptive mother—a teacher of the deaf—has to be seen to be believed. Of course, Martin and his brother are still handicapped physically and emotionally and always will be. But as I watched him at that picnic, it was clear that Martin is now a person and not just a little lost creature.

In some quarters it has recently become fashionable to stress the negatives of family life with its potentially destructive or smothering relationships. But if we listen to children we hear a different story. Even those whose foster or adoptive homes have not been entirely happy usually see them as preferable to life in an institution, and the theme of permanence, of not having to move again, recurs often when one interviews children in public care or those who remember the time before they were adopted. "Adoption is when you don't have to be moved. No one can take you away."

Children without families are usually acutely aware of their deprivation. Carol, aged ten, explained, "I did so want to be a part of a family and stay for good. . . . When I was adopted I cried with happiness. Now I feel safe. I can now stay with my family for as long as I please and that will be for as long as I live."

Even when the stress of adolescence leads to adopted children leaving home for a while, most reestablish a more satisfactory adult relationship with their adoptive parents. The opportunity to do this is in marked contrast to those young people who leave residential care at seventeen or eighteen to live alone in a room or apartment. A seventeen-year-old who had lived most of her life in a children's home and was now in a room on her own said, "It gets lonely; it's only when you leave care you know you've been dumped, and it's right lonely . . . you've got to cope, you've got to be independent. Not like living with a family."

LEARNING FROM ADOPTION

For professionals concerned with adoption some of the valuable lessons have come during the past few years when placement of children with special needs has moved from hope to reality. We have had the humbling experience of recognizing that others can want, love, and cherish children with handicaps, disfigurements, and behavior problems that we ourselves could never accept. We have learned that our earlier ideas of the ideal adopters—young, childless, happily married, and reasonably prosperous couples—do not match up to the realities of caring for special needs children. We have been awed and amazed by the parenting skills, determination, and self-sacrifice of apparently ordinary people tackling extraordinary tasks in caring for disabled children. We have had to stretch our ideas of suitable adopters to include older couples, people with marginal incomes, single people, those who are themselves handicapped, and those who may already have children. We have learned the lesson that David Kirk (1964) tried to teach us long ago—that preparation for adoptive parenthood is more important than selection procedures and that post-adoption support and counseling will probably be necessary.

Adoptive children have confounded the experts who feared that lack of early bonding and attachment would be found to wreak irreversible damage. They have showed an amazing capacity to overcome trauma and make up for the developmental deficits of their early years. However, the adoption experience does not disprove the importance of bonding and attachment. Follow-up studies clearly show that the older the child at placement, the greater the risk of breakdown. They point to the importance of careful preplacement work with both child and family and the need to take active steps to help the child make new attachments.

Another area in which adoption has taught us a lot is that of heredity, genealogy, and the blood tie. People involved in adoption tend to be firm believers in the power of nurture rather than nature. But twins separated in early life and adopted by different families frequently show remarkable similarities in personality, achievement, and interests. We find, too, that some of the most stressful adoptions are those where adopters have tried to mold their child into ways alien to his personality and the youngster has rebelled.

It is now abundantly clear that the great majority of adopted children consider their adopters as their "real" parents and see parenthood as raising rather than giving birth to children. But we have also learned that genealogy matters. Adoptees not only want but need information about their origins and must fuse the two strands of their inheritance if they are to come to a comfortable sense of themselves. Experience with opening adoption records shows that while most adoptees have no serious problems over identity and neither need nor wish to trace their birth family, for a minority, the problem is acute. It can be summed up in the comment: "When I look in the mirror I don't know who I am." We are also brought face to face with the question: "Is it really essential for children to lose all their ties with their natural family if they are to be adopted?" The interest in genealogy and roots that so many of us enjoy helps one to appreciate how some adoptees may feel like displaced persons. But then again I think of my American friend who came to visit me in London and set off on a trip to Wales to "look up my ancestors." Since she was an adoptee, I wondered which family she meant. When she returned, full of her adventure, all was made clear. She had wanted to meet the Welsh relatives and visit the place that her adoptive grandmother had talked to her about when she was a little girl. When she spoke of "my family" she was referring only to the one she joined through adoption.

In summary, how can we see adoption in the right perspective? How can we balance the pros and cons of a procedure so full of potentialities for good yet carrying such an element of risk, such a burden of pain? Looking back now, those thousands of infant adoptions seem like some form of crazy social aberration. Yet at the time they were necessary, and happiness, knowledge, and new insights came out of them as well as much sorrow. If it had not been for the experience of placing all those babies, we would certainly not today be able to find new families for the children of broken homes or those who have been abused or neglected or rejected because of their handicaps. Without that earlier experience, we would not now have the necessary courage or the knowledge and expertise displayed by professionals working in "special needs" adoptions.

The analogy of a kidney transplant quoted earlier is a good one and helps to put things in perspective. Adoption *is* like an organ transplant with the same serious risks as well as hope of full recovery. But, just as high-tech medicine can be seen as more exciting and prestigious than preventive medicine, so, if we are not watchful, adoption can come to be seen as more exciting and prestigious than preventive social work. If that happens we will have serious problems. No responsible physician would contemplate doing an organ transplant if other, less drastic, avenues of treatment could help.

I believe in adoption, but I am more cautious about advocating it than I used to be. It is not just because I have become more aware of the negatives and risks, but because of the danger that adoption can be used as an easier or cheaper alternative to providing services to children in their own homes. If our perspectives are right, I think we will see that one part of our responsibility as adoption workers is to press for services to families and communities that will diminish the need for children to undergo such a radical transplant.

REFERENCES

Kirk, D. (1964), *Shared Fate*. New York: Free Press.
Lifton, B. J. (1979), *Lost and Found—The Adoption Experience*. New York: Dial Press.
Shaw, M. (1984), Growing up adopted. In: *Adoption, Essays in Social Policy, Law, and Sociology*, ed. P. Bean. London: Tavistock.
Triseliotis, J. (1983), Identity and security in adoption and long-term fostering. *Adopt. & Foster.*, 7:22–31.

Part II

Developmental Issues of Adoption

2

Parental Responses to the Developmental Stages of Adopted Children

Euthymia D. Hibbs, Ph.D.

Adoption studies have sought to sift out genetic versus environmental influences on the personality, to investigate outcomes of adoption, and to devise specialized clinical interventions for adoptees. In contrast, adoptive parents remain a relatively neglected population. They are first evaluated to find out if they are good enough to become parents of a given child and later they are interviewed for research purposes or seen in therapy mostly in relation to their adoptive children; in the latter instance either because they cannot cope with the demands of their adoptive child and/or because of the child's presenting problems. However, in more than a few ways they undergo the same experiences as biological parents. They experience the same happiness, contentment, difficulties, and disappointments, have hopes and dreams for their adoptive children, worry when they get sick, and want them to succeed in life as much as the biological parents do. But, at the same time adoptive parents may be more insecure and tentative in their role. They may misinterpret some of the child's negative expressions toward them at certain developmental stages, and may feel hurt when the child mentions or shows curiosity about his natural parents. In this chapter, I will first discuss the principal reason which leads people to becoming adoptive parents—infertility—and then discuss the developmental stages of children and examine some of the problematic responses of adoptive parents.

INFERTILITY

Since ancient times many cultural, social, and religious rites included honoring the phallus as the symbol of fertility. The Dionysiac celebrations had fertility as their aim, and were marked by processions where the phallus, the symbol of male fertility, was conspicuous. Infertility was considered a curse of the gods, condemning a family by ending its lineage (Darlington, 1969). Sterility was looked upon as disgraceful: "He whose testicles are crushed or whose male member is cut off shall not enter into the assembly of the Lord" (Deut. 23:1). Today, there is an attempt to be more broadminded, but infertility remains a major crisis for those who wish to have children. It is a personal crisis for the infertile individual, as well as a hardship on the marital relationship, and in some cultures a plight for the extended family. Most infertile couples discover that they cannot bear children only after they enter a marital relationship. Upon discovery, there is an initial feeling of desperation, helplessness, and hopelessness, and they feel as if they have lost control over their life decisions and life plans. Usually, the couple's next step following the discovery of infertility is the "doctoring process"—the humiliating exposure of their private life and private parts, their hopes and fears, their vulnerable selves into the hands of another person—the doctor (Kraft, Palombo, Mitchell, Dean, Myers, and Schmidt, 1980).

Infertility is dealt with differently by each individual, but a common reaction is to question one's sexual identity. The fact that 8 to 14 percent of adoptive parents have biological children of their own after adopting a child may suggest some early unresolved psychological conflicts about sexuality, reproduction, and parenthood. In general, men may perceive infertility as an insult to their masculinity and women may feel incomplete and unfeminine. An example of the latter is a twenty-six-year-old single woman who was born with a congenital uterus defect and knew that she could not bear children. She always sought out the Adonis-type male with a perfect physique. Once she met such an Adonis only to find out later that he was cryptorchid. Upon this discovery, she lashed out at him, humiliated him, and dropped him. It was very hard for her to relate to someone who reminded her of her own incompleteness.

Some individuals resolve the predicament of their infertility appropriately, that is, they are first sad, then angry. They grieve the loss of a faculty and finally accept the fact with resignation. For others, it is added to old narcissistic wounds and becomes unbearable. How one deals with the crisis depends on the individual's experiences as a child, how one was treated by one's parents, and one's sense of self. The decision to adopt and the quality of parenting is also very much related to these factors. Adoption may become a self-prescribed treatment and a second-best solution; or, it may provide couples with the opportunity to experience parenting by sharing love with a child.

As with the biological moment of conception, the adoption decision is also based on a moment of conception—the conception of the idea to adopt (Doxiadis, 1987, personal communication). Why does a couple decide at a specific moment to adopt? There are couples who discuss adoption for many years, then suddenly activate the decision. What is the precipitating event? To some, the idea may become reality after the death of a parent, or the loss of a loved one; for others, the decision may be made after the birth of a niece or nephew. When interviewing potential parents, exploring the dynamics of the conception of the idea to adopt and the activating event may provide understanding for some of the more unconscious motives behind the wish to adopt.

THE ADOPTION PROCESS

Adoption can take from a few months to a couple of years before it becomes final. Some prospective parents consider the waiting time as "expecting" a child, while for others with low self-esteem waiting may be viewed as being on probation (Brinich, 1980). In the latter case this "expecting" time may be filled with anxiety, impatience, and a fear that the unconscious underlying reasons for wanting a child might be discovered. Thus, as a response to this uncomfortable state they may project their feelings of inadequacy and anger onto adoption agencies, doctors, and whomever is involved in the adoption process.

In addition, the longer the wait before parents and adoptive child become a family and the older the child becomes, important early bonding and attachment are missed. This creates another burden for the triad; that is, to catch up on precious time lost and to get to know each other after some growth has occurred in all parties involved. If the child is placed immediately with the prospective adoptive family while awaiting completion of the legal work, there is apprehension and fear of becoming emotionally attached to a child who may be taken away if the adoption does not materialize. This fear of possible loss of the child and the holding back of emotional involvement has, of course, great implications for both the child and the parents.

Another set of problems may arise in independent adoptions, where the "expecting" or waiting time to get a child is minimal, and where there is no preparation or counseling for the prospective parents to help them examine their feelings about their decision or the circumstances under which they located the child. The adoptive parents may find themselves suddenly responsible for a child before they have dealt with their own feelings of loss of fertility. They might be inexperienced in giving to another human being, since until that time they have been preoccupied with their own misfortune and were immersed in the pain of being unable to procreate. The sudden arrival of a third party, as much as it was wanted, may be detrimental to the couple's homeostasis.

The adoption process is delicate; many things can go wrong. I believe that preparing a couple to assume the role of parent to a nonbiological offspring might be the key for a successful outcome of the adoption.

DEVELOPMENTAL STAGES OF THE ADOPTIVE FAMILY

Like biological parents, adoptive parents respond in different ways when a baby is placed in their arms. Some brighten up and glow with joy; others are more distant and need time to get to know and warm to the baby. A mother who was very nervous before she went to the hospital to pick up her adoptive child (although this was not the first meeting with the baby) said to me, "I feel very nervous. I know I have to bond with the child, but I do not know how to do it."

My advice to her was to isolate herself with the baby and talk to him. She protested saying, "But what should I tell him? He doesn't understand." I suggested that she tell the baby her life story, her difficult and happy moments, that she cry and laugh with the baby, that she tell him her plans and aspirations for him.

Although it is normal for the biological mother to cathect her infant with a great deal of narcissistic libido, it is harder for the adoptive mother to do so. The biological mother "had" a baby; the adoptive mother "got" a baby (Reeves, 1971). In other words, the biological mother created the baby within, while the adoptive mother acquired it from without. In addition, the adoptive baby may be a constant reminder of the adoptive mother's infertility, if she is the infertile partner, or a reminder of her unfulfilled wish to give birth to a child, if the husband is infertile.

THE FIRST YEAR

The first year of life following the adoption (assuming that the child was adopted soon after birth) can be a honeymoon period with the infant, that is if some feelings have been examined and the decision to adopt was based on a mature resolution. This may be because the infant is completely dependent on the adults for its survival, which has a quieting effect on their anxieties. After all, the infant does not know it is adopted, and behaves the same with adoptive or biological parents. However, in my clinical experience I have detected that a subtle competition begins between the parents. "Who's child is he?" Was he adopted to satisfy the sterile parent or the one who was deprived of procreating because of the infertility of the partner?

In the case of one couple, both husband and wife ran to the adopted infant's room when she woke up at night. They were unable to formulate a schedule of alternate care of the baby for fear that the baby would bond, recognize, and love one partner more than the other. One night when the baby had a fever and cried, they both, as usual, ran to the crib. Each wanted to hold the baby and console her. When the wife took the baby, the husband, who was the infertile partner, slapped her in the face. He wanted to claim the baby. The significance of this event lies in the unprecedented nature of his action. Usually, the couple was very tender to each other, functioning at high developmental levels.

Another very subtle phenomenon may occur when the child is at the phase of stranger anxiety. The adoptive parents feel very content when the child recognizes them and clings to them while refusing to go to strangers. For most parents and especially adoptive ones, this is tangible proof that they are not strangers to the child, as they secretly fear. Because of the unconscious wish to hold onto this reassurance, there is sometimes danger that parents will encourage this stage of development to last longer than necessary.

THE SECOND YEAR

The second year of life is often the most traumatic for biological parents and even more so for adoptive parents, who have to deal with the child's first experimentation with separation and autonomy. This is even more difficult for parents who adopt children who are in their second year of life. Many times adoptive parents cannot accept the child's autonomy. They barely have enough time to develop an attachment and a bond with the child before this little creature walks away, provoking the naturally insecure parents.

In addition, the child begins to have a mind of its own, says "no," and refuses to do certain things. Although this behavior is developmentally appropriate for the child, greater significance is attributed to it in the adoptive situation. At this point, especially when the child is difficult to handle, questions of genetics and illegitimacy emerge. Adoptive parents wonder: "Is this characteristic inherited? Had I given birth to this child would he do these things?"

I have heard many adoptive parents say: "He has had this difficult personality since infancy. It must be behavior inherited from his delinquent mother." In a way adoptive parents are fortunate because they can blame someone else when problems arise.

In the case of adoptive parents who feel as if they have stolen the baby, or feel that they did not deserve to have a baby, this is the time when they begin to fear that the child will leave them for someone else. Sometimes they may become overprotective to prove that they are better parents than the biological ones. Or, they may split the child into "our good child and their bad child."

For others, who have a hard time with intimate relationships, the separation–individuation stage may be a blessing. Finally this dependent baby stops clinging and demanding. However, this need for distance does not prevent or alleviate the fear of abandonment that parents experience at this stage. In general, people feel more in control when they abandon than when they are abandoned. Parents at this point feel powerless because they are somehow abandoned.

THE THIRD TO SEVENTH YEARS

The third to seventh years of life may be most difficult for parents, especially for those who have not resolved their own oedipal conflict. In such cases parents become anxious and try to repress the child's instinctual urges. Some have fantasies of incest which are expressed in projections. One mother, for instance, strongly believed that the baby-sitter was molesting her adopted child while she was at work. Others cannot deal with the youngster's sexuality and they resort to extramarital affairs. One may speculate that while such fantasies and acting out are common to all parents, they are more easily evoked in adoptive parents.

It is usually between the ages of three to seven that the child learns about being adopted. This poses great difficulty for both the parents and the child; the latter begins to wonder why his other mother rejected and gave him away and may have a hard time reconciling the fact that someone who gave birth to him did not want him. When difficulties arise between the child and his parents, the child often wonders if his biological parents would have behaved the same way (i.e., would have punished him). Eiduson and Livermore (1953) said of a group of adopted children they had treated, that "None of these children had accepted the fact of adoption in the sense of facing that these adoptive parents, with their good and bad sides, are his parents, the ones with whom he is going to have to work out his inner feelings of both love and hate" (p. 800). There are accounts from adopted children for whom the image of the idealized biological mother guided their lives: they did well, so she would be proud of them if she appeared at their door to claim them back; or, they did badly in order to punish her.

The children may act out on their parents their ambivalence toward being adopted, their fear of rejection, and their oedipal strivings. Again, depending on their psychological functioning, parents may facilitate the resolution of the adoption conflict or may feel scared, inadequate, and narcissistically hurt, and reject the child. It is at this age that we see most of the adopted children in treatment. It seems as if the parents relinquish their duties to the therapist. This is also seen in the transferential fantasies of the child who pretends that the therapist is the ideal real parent who comes to rescue him.

THE SEVENTH YEAR TO PUBERTY

From the seventh year to puberty, children learn more about the meaning of adoption, continue to challenge and test the parents to see if they are going to reject them, and some (mostly those we see for treatment) may engage in lying, stealing, or doing poorly in school. During this period, identification with the parent of the same sex should take place. Its success depends on how parents reconcile the perceived resemblance the child has with his biological parents and the reality of the adoptive situation.

Tooley (1982) suggested that parents:

> [G]ive bits of information that the child can weave into day-dreams. For example, national origin and any achievements of natural parents may be shared, if thoughtfully censored. An edited story would describe a natural father as mechanically skillful, but conceal the fact that he had been a safecracker. While on the subject of characteristics, it is wise to comment on the child's own talents and promise, supporting future-directed thinking and fantasizing [p. 58].

However, many parents who have problematic children may not think as clearly, especially the rejected parent of the opposite sex. They may feel hurt and wish to hurt in turn the child who rejects them by exaggerating the negative aspects of his biological parents. An example is that of a nine-year-old girl whose father was very seductive. The daughter was not able to resolve the oedipal attachment and identify with the mother for fear of interrupting the comfort she found with the father, and she also acted seductively toward him. The mother felt completely left out and lashed at her daughter several times: "It is in your genes. You are a whore like your mother." Comments like the latter can serve only as a wish fulfillment. A young boy said to me: "Anyway, my parents do not believe that I do not steal, so why not do it?"

ADOLESCENCE

All families with adolescent children undergo a stressful period, but for adoptive families adolescence may be even more strained. From the onset of puberty and the second separation–individuation stage, adopted children begin searching for clues about their genealogy because they feel rootless. Although they have been curious and spent many hours thinking about the adoption over the years, now they begin searching more systematically for information about their biological parents. Sometimes, mostly in late adolescence, they search until they find them, in order to formulate their own identity.

This period revives the adoptive parents' doubts about their adequacy as parents, their fears that the adoptive child will seek out the "other mother" and will love them less. Their own fantasies about illegitimacy, the lower socioeconomic level of the biological parents, and the projection of their self-perception of being deficient may lead to inhibiting the child in many aspects of his life, including learning. They may be possessive and impede the child from achieving independence and may show dissatisfaction with his achievements and friends.

The ambivalence of adoption is resolved when the child abjures the biological parents after mourning their loss, frees himself from the self-accusation that he was a bad person and that is why he was not wanted, and adopts the adoptive family. It is at that point that the adoptive parents may also feel more secure and confident about their parenting capabilities and the love of the adopted child.

CONCLUSION

In this paper I briefly discussed the primary reason for adoption—infertility—its dynamics and impact on the couple. I traced the developmental stages of adoptive parents as they parallel those of the children. The emphasis of this chapter was on the problematic aspects facing the adoptive family. The aim was to sensitize professionals and others about the major problem areas that might arise in the developmental growth of the family. There are many successful adoptions, and in most cases adoption is a better solution for the children in lieu of multiple foster care homes and institutionalization. The study of Larson and her colleagues (Larson, Bohlin, and Stenbacka, 1986) in Sweden indicated that in their sample adoptive children fared better than those who were placed in multiple foster situations. They also fared better than those who were unwanted but forced by court order to remain with the biological parents. Adoption is also a better solution for the adults who would otherwise be deprived of experiencing parenthood.

However, adoption remains a delicate matter and must be dealt with as such. In selecting adoptive parents it is imperative to carefully assess their conscious and unconscious reasons for adoption, their emotional attitudes concerning morality and illegitimacy, and their fears and difficulties in relating to the psychosexual development of the child.

It is also important to educate parents and encourage them to join parents' groups and to seek counseling at certain critical periods of the child's development.

Group counseling when children reach adolescence is also of great importance in order to facilitate as much as possible the family's smooth transition. Adoptive parents should be reassured by research findings that adoptive children, even when they meet their biological parents, nearly always return and choose the adoptive family as their true family.

REFERENCES

Brinich, P. (1980), Some potential effects of adoption on self and object. *The Psychoanalytic Study of the Child*, 34:107–133. New Haven, CT: Yale University Press.

Darlington, C. (1969), *The Evolution of Man and Society*. New York: Simon & Schuster.

Eiduson, B. N., & Livermore, J. B. (1953), Complications in therapy with adoptive children. *Amer. J. Orthopsychiat.*, 50:618–628.

Kraft, A. D., Palombo, J., Mitchell, D., Dean, C., Meyers, S., & Schmidt, A. (1980), The psychological dimensions of infertility. *Amer. J. Orthopsychiat.*, 50:618–628.

Larson, G., Bohlin, A. B., & Stenbacka, M. (1986), Prognosis of children admitted to institutional care during infancy. *Child Abuse & Neglect*, 10:361–368.

Reeves, A. C. (1971), Children with surrogate parents. *Brit. J. Med. Psychol.*, 44:155–171.

Tooley, K. M. (1982), Therapy of adoption-related or alienation depression. In: *Therapy for Adolescents*, ed. M. D. Stein & J. K. Davis. San Francisco: Jossey-Bass.

3

A Developmental Approach
to Separation/Loss

Vera I. Fahlberg, M.D.

From a developmental viewpoint, as the child grows up, he must accomplish varying tasks related to psychological maturation. The child cannot accomplish these tasks on his own nor can his parents accomplish them for him. The tasks are achieved only in the context of the parent–child relationship. Therefore, we can expect that parent separation or loss via foster care, adoption, or the death of one or both parents will have a major impact on the child's psychological development.

The impairment of the psychosocial development of a child may be due to one of the following: the child may have lost either all or a major part of his parent–child relationship and his energies may be going into coping with feelings related to the loss and are not available for coping with more age-appropriate developmental tasks; at times of stress, humans tend to regress to earlier levels in order to regroup their strengths, and children are not immune to regression; after the loss of a spouse through separation or death, the remaining parent must cope with his or her own psychological stress, and is emotionally unavailable to help the child accomplish the developmental tasks at hand.

The order in which the psychological maturation process takes place is quite consistent. Therefore, if the age of the child at the time

27

of the parental separation or loss is known, we can usually predict the psychological areas in which the child will be particularly vulnerable. If, subsequent to the loss, the child does not live in an environment that helps him regroup his strengths and cope with feelings, thus reestablishing psychological equilibrium, we can expect serious long-term effects secondary to the parent separation or loss. Indeed, many children who are in today's foster care system, or who have been adopted, are, to one degree or another, psychologically "stuck" at the age of the initial parent separation.

DEVELOPMENTAL TASKS RELATED TO THE EFFECTS OF LOSS

First Year of Life

The primary tasks to be accomplished within the parent–child relationship during the first year of life are threefold: (1) the meeting of dependency needs; (2) the building up of feelings of trust, security, and attachment; and (3) the beginning of sorting out the significance of various external and internal stimuli. Frequently, children who enter the child welfare system during their first year of life do so because these needs are not being met by the parents. These children may not show such severe effects secondary to separation and loss and may instead blossom in a new environment which provides and facilitates the development of the above-mentioned areas. However, other children whose needs are being met, but who still face parent loss, may show the effects of such loss in these three areas. There will likely be a regression to earlier levels of dependency. Feelings of trust, security, and attachment will be undermined and subsequent to the apparent loss, remedial measures will have to be taken to meet dependency needs and to facilitate attachment.

The third task relates to the child learning how to learn (Gesell, Halverson, Ilg, Thompson, Castner, Ames, and Amartuda, 1940). The beginning of learning how to sort out external and internal perceptions also depends on the parent figures who become mediators between the child and his environment. Even infants pick up the rhythms of a household and begin to develop a primitive sense of cause and effect. A hungry three- or four-month-old child starts to calm down when he sees the parent figure who usually provides physical nourishment (Spitz, 1965). A child who is fed only when hungry but not at other times starts to connect the internal sensations of hunger with the relief supplied by the externally provided food and starts to recognize this as a discrete form of discomfort associated with a particular form of relief. A seven- to eight-month-old child living in a family in which the father consistently comes home from work at the same time each day will show anticipatory excitement in response to a car at that time of day. With parent loss or separation, there are usually concomitant changes in the daily routine; thus, cause and effect acquisition is interrupted.

THE TODDLER YEARS (1–3)

The primary task for the toddler is mainly the switch from dependence to independence with increasing autonomy. Concomitant with the autonomy issues are those of identity. This is the time of life when the youngster becomes aware of himself as a person separate from his primary caretaker, and the time when true ego development begins. There is continued noticeable growth in terms of the awareness the child has about the implication of various sights, sounds, and smells, as well as increasing awareness of internal body states, such as a full bladder. This, too, is a time of very rapid language acquisition.

These, then, will be the areas of development most affected by parent loss or separation at this stage. It is quite common for children who experience parent separation at this point in their lives to have difficulty in developing an appropriate balance between dependency and autonomy. One child may withdraw and become more dependent as if he is saying, "It is not safe for me to become independent." Another child, with a different temperament, may go to the other extreme, becoming too independent. Such a child is apt to parent himself. He may withhold affection and seem stubborn and resistant in all areas for a prolonged period of time (Fahlberg, 1982).

Identity formation at this age seems to be related to several factors including the sex of the child, the child's position in the family, and the child's name. Obviously, the child's sex does not change with parent loss; however, his position in the family may change radically, particularly if by losing the parent the child has to move from one family to another. Position in the family not only relates to the child's birth order but also to other factors. That is, a first male child born into an extended family in which there have been no male children for several generations will have a different position from a female child. The child's position in the family is, to some degree, determined by the child's temperament. For example, in one family, the comment, "This is our active child" may carry a positive connotation; while in another family, that trait may be viewed as a negative. A child usually recognizes his name by the age of one year, and the given name becomes a part of his identity. Change of first name, especially at this particular stage of development, poses an extra burden for the child in terms of developing a strong sense of self.

Young children who are in a period of rapid language acquisition are usually dependent on a family member to initially be the "interpreter" for others. Loss of this person may have a significant impact on language development. Although the actual vocabulary used with children this age may not vary so much from one family to another, the rhythm of speech, the pronunciation, and the way words are connected seems to vary considerably.

PRESCHOOL YEARS (3–6)

The hallmarks of this age are continued individuation with increased independence and proficiency in the self-care areas, along with continued growth in the area of language development. However, two internal psychological struggles and the particular thinking characteristics of children of this age pose the biggest problems in resolving separation–loss issues.

Play is usually the medium used for the resolution of two major internal psychological issues: the big versus little struggle, and the good versus bad struggle. A child of this age receives many conflicting parental messages. He hears comments such as "Big boys don't wet their pants; they use the potty" combined with messages such as, "No, you are too little to be outside the fence." Thus, a child has to come to grips with the fact that he is neither big nor little but rather a combination of both. This is when the first real balance between dependency and independency is achieved. The infant was primarily dependent; the toddler's independency needs are strong in the service of individuation and ego development, but the preschooler is truly a combination of both. A child who successfully accepts this psychological position, that it is okay to be both dependent and independent, is well on his way toward having a healthy balance between these two factors to fall back on the remainder of his life.

The other internal psychological struggle has some similarities. The child must learn to accept himself as a good person who sometimes does naughty things, not as a person who is *either* good *or* bad. Indeed, these two issues are reflected in the majority of the preschooler's play (Hymes, 1969). Preschool children are involved in a variety of independent versus dependent play, such as playing house, school, doctor. A psychologically healthy preschooler goes back and forth between dependency and independency roles, enjoying each. "Good guys" versus "bad guys" is a recurrent theme in play, and most preschoolers relish both roles.

Children this age have characteristic thinking patterns as well. Egocentricity and magical thinking are especially prominent at this stage, as well as fear of parental abandonment. These particular characteristics combine to pose some predictable reactions to parental separation or loss. In the preschooler's attempts to make sense of the events in his world, the child nearly always perceives the events as occurring because he was "bad" in some way. It becomes very important, in trying to correct this misperception, to decode the child's particular brand of magical thinking. It is common for children of this age, when angry with a parent, to either verbalize or at least think "I hate you" or "I wish I had a different mommy (daddy)." Then, if a loss occurs, the child may attribute it to his "bad" thoughts, thus reinforcing the perception of himself as the cause. Another form of magical thinking needs to be closely watched for. This relates to the child's thinking that something he does or says can change the loss. And, just as the child perceives himself as responsible for the loss, he may also perceive himself as responsible for either regaining, or not regaining, the parent.

Children who have very high expectations for themselves and who see themselves as really "bad" whenever they make a mistake or are naughty, and who then subsequently "dump" on themselves, frequently have experienced parental separation at this particular stage of their life.

The child's magical thinking may also relate to "big" versus "little" issues. This is especially likely to occur if a child leaves a family and other children remain in the family. Then, the child's magical thinking may explain the loss in ways such as, "The baby stayed; babies are preferable. It's not safe to grow up."

Because this is also an age of heightened sexual awareness and of the young child's "falling in love" with the parent of the opposite sex, the child may attribute loss of either parent to his own thoughts and feelings in this area.

Even though it is very difficult, if not impossible, to overcome the child's egocentricity and magical thinking at this age, it is important to understand and decode the child's thinking so that at subsequent ages, as the child develops better conceptual skills, he can be helped to give up the old thinking. Unless one knows the particulars of the child's magical thinking, it is very difficult to aid in changing the perceptions even in later years.

GRADE SCHOOL YEARS (6–12)

The latency-age child is dependent on the security of the family relationships to provide him with the psychological energy to master family issues. The child's energies at this age go into mastering problems and relationships outside the family unit, while during his earlier years, most of the energy was expended on in-family skills and relationships. Most of the child's energies go into academic learning, improving gross and fine motor skills, and peer relationships, primarily with peers of the same sex. Clearly, repeated moves or separations are likely to have a negative impact on the child's academic and peer socialization skills.

Another major area of psychological growth occurs in terms of conscience development. Conscience development starts prior to this age and continues long after, but it is during this period that the biggest growth in this area occurs as the child moves from fear of displeasing adults to an internalized sense of right versus wrong that is no longer dependent upon an adult's presence.

During these years, there are major changes in the child's ability to think and conceptualize. Adolescent development becomes easier if the child has a stable parent pair to come up against, push off from, and individuate from. It is very difficult for the preadolescent to accomplish the normal tasks of this stage if he is having to cope with both physical and/or psychological separation or loss.

The primary task of the adolescent is to separate and individuate, which becomes particularly difficult if at the same time he must work on becoming a member of a new family unit. This is particularly true during early adolescence when the psychological tasks are most prominent. It does become easier in later adolescence when the physical emancipation, as opposed to the psychological emancipation, is most prominent.

CONCLUSION

By understanding the developmental tasks to be accomplished at varying ages, it becomes easier to understand both the short-term and the long-term effects of parent separation or loss. Since all adopted children have faced parent loss, and many have faced repeated losses, these are particularly important areas to be addressed by the clinician working with such children. Once it is understood which current issues may relate to early loss issues and how they relate to the separations, the task in helping young persons resolve these problems and change their behaviors becomes much easier.

REFERENCES

Fahlberg, V. I. (1982), *Child Development*. London: British Agencies for Adoption & Fostering.

Gesell, A., Halverson, H. M., Ilg, F. L., Thompson, H., Castner, B. M., Ames, L. B., & Amartuda, C. S. (1940), *The First Five Years of Life: The Preschool Years*. New York: Harper & Row.

Hymes, J. L., Jr. (1969), *The Child Under Six*. New Jersey: Prentice-Hall.

Spitz, R. (1965), *The First Year of Life*. New York: International Universities Press.

4

Identity and Genealogy in Adopted People

John Triseliotis, Ph.D., O.B.E.

Some writers have attempted to trace the origins of the self back to the prenatal period, others to the quality of the baby's earliest experiences in relation to its parents (Klein, 1932, 1960). There are those, for example Mead (1934), who place importance on ongoing life experiences, putting more emphasis on the interactions between people and their social environment. Identity and the sense of self are very difficult concepts to define or measure. Equally problematic is the attempt to identify the qualities and situations that contribute to a positive self-image.

In my view, identity is the result of multiple emotional, social, and cultural influences which contribute to the building of an integrated self. Personal and social identity denote the kind of consciousness that we all carry within us about who we are. Depending on its quality and strength, this sense of identity conveys a feeling of separateness from others, while at the same time it enables us to enter into daily social interactions and relationships with a degree of confidence. A secure identity is characteristic of deep feelings of security and belonging and of being conscious of oneself as an individual uniquely different from others, yet at the same time part of one's environment and of the human community.

35

My own understanding of the development of identity started through my studies (Triseliotis, 1973; Triseliotis and Russell, 1984) of the personal experiences and circumstances of separated children who had to be reared by adoptive or foster parents or, in many cases, had to grow up in residential institutions. How the multiple emotional, social, and cultural influences affect the person is illustrated by the diagram in Figure 4.1, which portrays the influence of the substitute family on an individual's personality. Obviously the self is not a passive recipient of influences for it also has the capacity to exert influence.

Through our studies (Triseliotis and Russell, 1984), we identified three important ingredients contributing to the development of identity: the quality of a child's experiences within his natural or substitute family; knowledge and understanding about his background and genealogy (particularly important for separated children); and community perceptions and attitudes toward the child. The nature and quality of these experiences will be influential in determining the individual's personality.

Erikson (1968) places emphasis on building identity through personal and internal experiences, while Mead (1934) stresses the part played by social influences, particularly those of the community. In my view the two types of experience are not separate but part of the same developmental continuum.

Erikson described a positive identity as "a sense of psychological well-being, a feeling of being at home in one's body, of knowing where one is going, an inner assuredness of anticipated recognition from those who count" (p. 165). Mead, in turn, remarked on how identity begins by what he calls "role-taking," namely, taking the attitudes and views that others have of us as our own, by learning to see ourselves through their eyes and acting according to their standards. Other social psychologists, such as Goffman (1960), agree with Mead that as a result of this process we may come to perceive ourselves as "best" or "second best," or "bad" or "dull." A sense of spoiled identity develops from receiving consistently negative messages, such as when the word *adoption* is loaded with negative connotations. Though in some respects we can intervene in the process of self-building and resist attempts by others to affix to us a certain self, nevertheless children in a formative stage of development have less power to resist consistently negative messages. We know, for example, that many children who

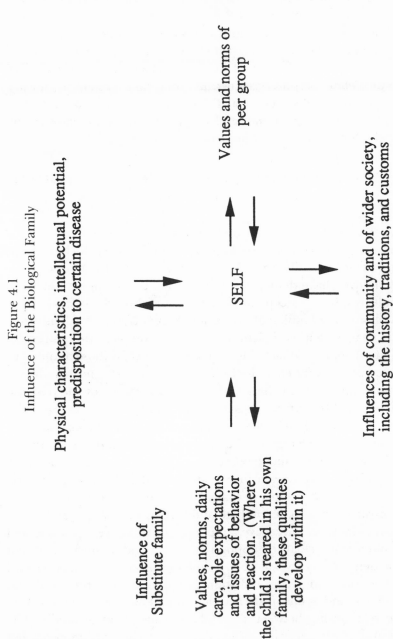

Figure 4.1
Influence of the Biological Family

Physical characteristics, intellectual potential, predisposition to certain disease

Values and norms of peer group

SELF

Influence of Substitute family

Values, norms, daily care, role expectations and issues of behavior and reaction. (Where the child is reared in his own family, these qualities develop within it)

Influences of community and of wider society, including the history, traditions, and customs of one's racial and ethnic group

Note 1: See also C. Picton (1980).

grow up in group homes, and even in foster care, tend to feel stigmatized because the community, in their view, looks upon them as "bad"
or "different" (Triseliotis and Russell, 1984).

The uncertainty and confusion some separated children feel
about their families of origin—who they are and why they were given
away—increases their sense of insecurity. This also reinforces their
sense of feeling "second class" because they fail to sustain the norma-
tive expectations of society. The following is a typical example: "You
go out with your girl friend, and you worry all the time about how
she will react when you tell her that you are adopted."

THE IMPORTANCE OF GENEALOGY, BACKGROUND, AND HISTORY

A small but vital part in the jigsaw puzzle of identity formation
is knowledge about one's background and forbears, including the
history of one's family, race, and ethnic group. Our studies of separated children have demonstrated to us that people, at least in Western cultures, have a deep emotional and social need and curiosity to
know about their families of origin and their ancestors. Such information is vital to help complete one's self or complete the pattern of
one's life. People who lack this information, such as those adopted or
in foster care, experience the lack as a deprivation, and may find it
stressful. Among other things, continuity is a carrier of the past and
of the hopes of the future. A sense of continuity with the past provides
some cushioning against crises or disappointments, even against anxiety generated by change or the fear of it. The need for continuity
and for a narrative about ourselves is well illustrated by Barbara
Hardy (1968): "We dream in narrative, daydream in narrative, remember, anticipate, hope, despair, believe, doubt, plan, sense, criti-
cize, construct, gossip, learn, hate and love by narrative" (p. 6).

Over the years successive adoption laws in Western Europe and
the United States cloaked adoption in secrecy and mystery. No doubt
the element of secrecy was partly aimed at protecting single parents
and their offspring from the stigma of unwanted parenthood and
illegitimacy, and at ensuring that natural parents would not interfere
in the relationship between the child and his adoptive family. The
1920s and 1930s were also a time, like today, when adoption was not

particularly popular, and it was thought that the guarantee of secrecy would encourage potential adopters to come forward. This attitude led to laws that unintentionally conveyed attitudes of secrecy and evasiveness and possibly of shame and stigma about adoption. The same secrecy and sometimes "economy with the truth" concerning some children's background was to extend beyond adoption to most children growing up outside their own families, including children in stepparenting relationships. Janet Hitchman (1966) in her autobiography writes with sadness on this subject: "No one thought of giving explanations to small orphans any more than to market bound pigs."

Since 1929, Scottish law (and also Finnish law) provides that on attaining the age of seventeen an adopted person can apply to Register House in Edinburgh for information from his original birth records. This is not out of consideration for the adoptees' psychological needs but for matters of inheritance. Nevertheless, this provision in Scottish law offered us the opportunity to study the importance of genealogical information to adoptees and subsequently to other people (Triseliotis, 1973; Triseliotis and Russell, 1984). We would like to think that as a result of our studies the consciousness and work practices of professionals, such as social workers, psychologists, and psychiatrists, have changed to recognize the meaning and importance to all children and adults of the truth about their genealogy and circumstances of upbringing. The sharing, in a positive way, of genealogical information is now seen as a step that promotes a sense of identity, aids in personality development, and satisfies curiosity.

We have found that the truth about backgrounds and the sharing of information not only does not undermine relationships with parents or substitute parents, but to the contrary it seems to strengthen and cement them. Children respect their parents and caretakers for telling them the truth and trust them even more. The truth, as many have told us, helps them know who they are and where they stand. In contrast, evasiveness, secrecy, and avoidance generates mistrust and increases curiosity and unhappiness. As some adopted children put it: "Trust is always better than deception. No one should have the right to erase part of another person's self, even if it is only a very minor part"; or "It is the adults who should take the initiative and explain things without waiting for children to ask. Often children don't know what to ask." Repeated questions voiced by most adoptees were: "Who are my first parents?" "What were they like?" "Why was I given up?" "I wonder if I have any brothers or sisters?"

Our own studies (Triseliotis, 1973; Triseliotis and Russell, 1974; Triseliotis and Hill, 1987) have also shown that the people who matter most to children are those who care for them and not necessarily those who gave birth to them, unless they happen to be the same persons. In this respect blood is not always thicker than water. The wish of children reared by substitute caretakers to know about their history and sometimes meet a biological parent is not a wish to give up or abandon their psychological parents. Children and adults can continue a good relationship with one set of parents while also having contact with the other parents. After all, human beings are capable of sustaining more than one relationship at the same time.

THE MEANING OF THE FAMILY OF ORIGIN AND OF ANCESTORS

The family of origin and the history of our forbears may represent only a small part of our identity, but it is a vital part which has to be satisfied, as some of our respondents told us: "If you don't know, it is like a loose end that needs tying up." "It is part of the tableau of your life." "You have to know the roots you came from to understand yourself." Curiosity about our immediate and more distant ancestors is natural. The less people know about their ancestry, the more likely it is that they will want to set out on a quest to satisfy their curiosity. The meaning of such a search cannot be overstated. Continued ignorance of vital information about one's background or the sudden discovery in adult life that one is not the child of people one had come to look upon as "parents" can be extremely distressing. The term *genealogical bewilderment* is used to convey the distress displayed by people who are ignorant or confused about their origins.

Uncertainty about one's origins is assuming more importance now compared to the past. Because of the diversity of life-styles and different methods of "conception" an increasing number of children are now being reared in families where one or both parents are not biological parents. For those children clarity about their past, the circumstances of their births, will be important for their self-concept and sense of general well-being.

Though many adopted people simply want information about their origins, some are also interested in establishing links with a biological parent or simply want to observe the parent from a distance. Perhaps a full body-image cannot be achieved without knowing what our parents or forbears looked like. It is a sad fact that in most of the recent discussions on issues such as surrogacy and in vitro fertilization, the needs of the children to know the truth about themselves have not yet surfaced.

Many of us take for granted our ability to answer without much difficulty questions such as the place of our birth, names of our parents and grandparents, or what our parents or grandparents did for a living, and whether they are alive or dead. Yet there are people in our society who, for a variety of reasons, are unable to answer such basic questions, and this fills them with embarrassment. The comments of some of our respondents who could not answer basic questions about themselves and their origins are indicative of the strength of the feeling: "I am a stranger to myself. I look into the mirror and ask: Who am I? and I have no answer to it. There is no one to compare myself with." "I have been living right through with a feeling of unreality about myself. I feel empty inside, like a big vacuum. I feel as if I am only half a person with the other half obscured."

In contrast to the above is the satisfaction and relative contentment often felt by those who are able to establish some of the facts about their family and life history: "It has been a great help to be able to know something exact about my roots"; "At last I can tell people where I was born."

It is a natural curiosity to want to know whether aspects of the past are reflected in one's children. Continuity with the past is usually preserved by conveying ideas and themes from one generation to the next. This is why many people like to have details about the personality, habits, character, hobbies, and interests of their ancestors. Frustration can arise from having some of the basic information but none of the more personal details.

Interest in the work of the genealogical societies has increased in the last fifteen years, mainly because of a greater interest in the past, in history and ethnicity. This coincided with minority groups insisting on equal rights; and with ethnic minorities insisting on observing their customs and traditions. The search for ethnic identity is only one step removed from the search for personal and social identity. Our studies of the early 1970s, in Scotland where access to birth records has been available since 1930 and in England since 1976, contributed in some measure to this increase in searching for information about one's ancestors, especially by children who had not been reared by their biological parents. The issue of origins is now featured regularly in plays, novels, television documentaries, and soap operas.

Of equal importance to genealogy searches is the official opening of records to people who were previously denied vital information about their background. Most social work agencies in Britain, for example, will now go to great lengths to search for information on behalf of people who were previously in their care and, if desired, try to link them with a member of their biological family.

New ways of working with children separated from their natural families now involve the preparation, from early on, of detailed Life Story books for each of them. These books include details about the child's past and his family tree, information about his circumstances, and life events important to him. The Life Story book is consistently updated to include new information or new events. The book belongs to the child, and he takes it with him should he move to a new family. Another way to help promote a child's identity is by taking him to visit the place he was born and where his parents or grandparents lived.

Both adoptive and foster parents are now given written details about the background of the children, along with explanations of why it is important to share this information with the child. Even unpalatable information has to be shared, provided it is done sensitively and within the child's capacity to understand. Children growing up with their own parents do not have the same need for Life Story books, since the parents usually act as living links between the past and the present. Even here, though, it is amazing how many knowledge gaps are discovered when people are asked to draw their family tree beyond the first generation.

SUMMARY

Growing up adopted need not be experienced as problematic or unusual, except that those adopted, like other separated children or children born through artificial insemination by donor or in vitro fertilization, have some additional tasks to perform. Our studies do not support the contention that adoption is inevitably accompanied by identity problems. Adopted people are neither more nor less likely to experience life's joys and upsets than other people. People reared by their biological parents often have to come to terms with aspects of life, for example, loss of a specific role, that can have an impact on their identity. We have found the following qualities (listed in order of importance) contribute to a secure identity and to a positive self-image in adopted people: the quality of their family relationships; awareness about their origins and the circumstances of their adoption; and absence of societal discrimination.

Now that most adoptions involve older children who have strong memories of and perhaps bonds and ties to important people from their past, social workers have the task of helping adopters maintain the children's continuity with the past, including, where appropriate, keeping the links with members of the biological family. Adoption with contact and "open" adoption should now be an option.

Similar and more demanding tasks are involved in inter-country adoptions—aside from the serious moral and empirical issues that surround them. If those adopting children from their own race or ethnic group have the tasks of helping them to know their roots, those adopting children from a different race or ethnic group have the double task of helping them also to develop awareness of their racial and ethnic origins.

REFERENCES

Erikson, E. H. (1968), *Identity: Youth and Crisis*. New York: W. W. Norton.
Goffman, E. (1960), *The Presentation of Self in Everyday Life*. London: Penguin.
Hardy, B. (1968), Towards a poetic fiction. *Novel*, 1:5–14.
Hitchman, J. (1966), *The King of the Barbarians*. London: Peacock.
Klein, M. (1932), *The Psycho-analysis of Children*. London: Hogarth Press.
——— (1960), A note on depression in the schizophrenic. *Internat. J. Psycho-Anal.*, 41:509–511.
Mead, G. H. (1934), *Mind, Self and Society*. Chicago: University of Chicago Press.
Picton, C. (1980), *Persons in Question*. Melbourne: Monash University.

Triseliotis, J. (1973), *In Search of Origins*. London: R.K.P.
────── Hill, M. (1987), Children and adoption allowance. *Adopt. & Foster.*,
    11:35–39.
────── Russell, J. (1984), *Hard to Place*. London: Gower.

Part III

Assessment of Prospective Parents

5

Preadoptive Diagnostic Work for Prospective Parents: Modality of Intervention

**Adriano Giannotti, M.D., Paola Natali, Ph.D.,
Ugo Sabatello, M.D.**

In this chapter we will discuss our experience in preadoptive diagnostic work as a modality for selecting couples who wish to adopt children.

At the Institute of Child Neuropsychiatry in Rome, we see many adopted children who come for consultation and who have multiple problems, such as learning difficulties, hyperactivity, and conduct disorders. Gradually, as we acquired diagnostic and therapeutic experience working with adoptive families, we began to notice that the adoptive situation itself was the cause of some specific conflicts both for the child and his parents. Consequently, we felt that consultation with the adoptive families ought to be modified and take into consideration clinical diagnostic and therapeutic points of view regarding the specific problems of adoption.

While we were treating "problematic" adoptions, the International Social Services Department asked us to consult with them in evaluating couples who wanted to adopt. Shortly thereafter, the Juvenile Court of Rome began referring adoptive parents to us for further evaluation.

Since we became consultants to the International Social Services Department we have evaluated approximately 100 couples who had multiple problems, were high risk, or cases of couples adopting a second child.

Our psychodynamic training led us to develop the following diagnostic approach, applying it to the needs and realities of working within an institutional setting "an internalized setting which may isolate certain invariable factors and through these formulate more general hypothetical interpretations" (Vetrone, 1986, p. 3). Our experience led us to conclude that preadoptive diagnostic work should integrate the crisis situation (infertility and/or decision to adopt) in addition to addressing the couple and the state of their marital relationship.

THE SETTING

We followed the model of "setting" as formalized by Dicks (1967), Giannakoulas (1978), Giannotti and Giannakoulas (1985), Eiguer and Ruffiot (1986). The couple is seen conjointly by a male and a female therapist. This specific setting considers the couple as a dyad in which the "choice of partner" (Dicks, 1967), that is, the choice of each other, is seen as being transferential and based upon the unconscious projection onto one's partner of the internalized image of the parent of the opposite sex. Both husband and wife attempt to recreate with the partner that illusory union with the father (for the woman) or with the mother (for the man)—"choice of complementariness"; or sometimes strive to keep themselves as distant as possible from such a union, if the relationship with the parent was perceived as deceptive or traumatic—"choice of contrast."

Based on this theoretical concept, the aim of meeting with therapists of each gender is to introduce the adoptive couple's internalized parents and to recreate their prosecutory attitude or absence of it. In this way, the dynamics of identification and projection of each party manifest themselves in the diagnostic work, while providing a warm reception for the couple in an attempt to be a means both of psychoanalytical assessment and support. Because we consider this period to be a critical and difficult time for the people involved in the adoption process, the team of therapists is available for further help and support, both prior to and following the adoption, upon request by the couple, although the diagnostic work is mainly performed to facilitate the court's decision.

THE DIAGNOSTIC PROCESS

Our diagnostic process is based on the premise that adoption is an "emerging problem" and that it provides the "emotional core" (Strachey, 1934; Ezriel, 1960) and the "peak" of our observation. The process has as aim: (1) to search into the specific anxieties that sometimes prevent the adoptive parents from providing the child with the necessary "mental space" for his development, while at the same time respecting his history and constitutive pride; (2) to help the couple via introducing ourselves into the potential development of a crisis, so that uninhibited forms of affection and thought may emerge instead of the consequences of the preexisting disposition (Bion, 1976); (3) to evaluate the couple's capacity to elaborate the narcissistic outrage linked to sterility, by evoking the internal prosecutory and "unknown" objects that the adopted child will awaken. This evocation seems to be mostly related to "the terrible mother of the primal scene . . . the image of the parents united in the sexual act" (Giannotti, 1980); (4) to avoid collusion with the couple regarding the concrete aspects of adoption (country of origin, gender, age, etc.), elements of reality, and the real persecutory attitude of controls established by the court. The couple may indeed use the same processes as the diagnostic technique to reinforce the split between idealized and persecutory aspects rather than increasing "insight." The split between good and bad, victim and persecutor seems to derive from some form of primitive spectra against those who are capable of conserving a child within themselves and those who, on the contrary, abandon or neglect the child.

Such forms of splitting between mind and body which adoption reenacts, "mental filiation," may be restored through the diagnostic process. The latter becomes a kind of therapeutic consultation and a point of reference, especially for couples who, having already adopted, need help and guidance. The work with the two therapists (three to four sessions in all) may offer an important opportunity and a way of exploring the "agony" linked to the adoption process. This becomes possible by providing the couple with a model for introspection and, at the same time, a real institutional point of reference in order to prepare them for future changes full of hidden challenges.

In our work with the prospective parents we share the same situation. That is, we do not know anything about the child: We do not know whether the adoption will take place, or whether the child has the capacity to integrate, develop, and adapt to a different reality. However, as Grimaldi (1983) said, the diagnostic process is not the forced simulation of a meeting with the "unknown," it is not carried out as an imagined psychodrama in which words evoke actions and situations, but on the contrary, the roles of parents and children are still "to be accomplished."

Preadoptive diagnosis focuses on what has already happened, a "catastrophe" conceived as an interruption and severing of a temporal continuity, a "double privation" presented in the same way both in the child and the adoptive parents seen by us.

For the child the "catastrophe" is the "lack of roots" (Fenu, Federici, and Chiarelli, 1985), the absence of his own genesis, the lack of a model which may contain the self. Even in the absence of a possible trauma, the initial abandonment is reexperienced by the child. He is faced with the necessity of leaving a habitual reality, which may be lacking in many ways but is familiar. Adoption symbolizes rebirth in that the child will need to establish new object relationships (with the new parents) even though it is due to necessity rather than biological continuity.

For the couple, the process of adoption is never comparable to the psychosomatic path of conception–maternity–birth, which holds the roots of the initial object relationship between children and their parents. The most persistent and central theme that we encounter in our parents is that of sterility. It often causes them to express great unconscious conflicts which cannot be easily explained, except in cases where the etiology is organic.

The need to repair the defeated creative capacity often causes defensive Messianic expectations (Bion, 1976), so as not to allow the integration between reality and fantasy. If such anxieties are present, the adoption may symbolize an "Immaculate Conception" for the adoptive couple, permitting them to have a child despite the biological necessity of conception and maternity. In addition, we find that the "genetic anxiety" (Bertolini, Balgera, Neri, and Peretti, 1986), that is separation anxiety due to birth, often prevents the couple from comparing themselves to internalized parental figures and thus from becoming parents themselves.

COUPLE A

"Why didn't I give up the idea of adoption when I became pregnant [later, she had a miscarriage]? Because in my opinion, according to my way of thinking, adoption is the right thing for me, it is a test, a way of measuring myself, while having children is such a natural thing, it's too simple. . . ."

Even if adoption is an act of volition which excludes the body and sexuality, the child still remains the fruit of a generative sexuality for the adoptive parents. It represents the return of a repressed past which is related to the most instinctive aspects linked to the couple's creativity, aggression, and the sexuality of the mother–child relationship.

As we mentioned earlier, the couple's relationship recalls in both partners the relationship with their own parents. Moreover, the couple's sexuality and generative capacity involves instinctual and primitive aspects which are linked to the primary scene and the relationship that each of the partners had with their mothers, whether the relationship was "good enough" (Winnicott, 1974), capable of containing and neutralizing the overwhelming perceptions (of hunger, thirst, illness, a sense of emptiness) of the child, or, on the contrary, intense and frustrating.

From our clinical experience we learned that very often, sterility, not due to organic factors, is rooted in the conflictual relationship with the parent of the same sex. For instance in cases of non-organic female sterility, we very often found that the woman is unable to identify with the creative mother and to form a relatively unconflictual feminine identity.

If elements such as aggressiveness and identification with the primary objects are not worked through they are often projected onto the child; the child of strangers "perhaps ill or perverse" so as to make him feel attacked by his adoptive parents, and the receptacle of all kinds of ambivalence.

COUPLE B

> She says, "of course, I used my imagination a lot regarding the child, for example, thinking what if he fell ill and died? If he died being the child of some alcoholic or prostitute . . . and not our child?"

Even if adoption presents itself as an act of reparation, it is all too often structured as a reiteration of the traumatic situation of the inability to conceive. Adoption may give the illusion of being in control and able to reverse sterility into an experience which may be conquered when it becomes "history." Presymbolic history, which precedes rational capacity, is the very thing which is often missing from the adoptive parents and their children. Presymbolic history is the adoptive parents' tie with their internalized parents, with their reciprocal, evolutive, and emotional background, and the relationship of the couple is seen as a realization of an unconscious need in the common project and experience of a child.

Even when there seems to be no precise psychopathology linked to the adoption (Blum, 1983), we believe that the problem of origin reunites both children and their parents. As the adopted child is always searching for his roots, as he is reborn through adoption, so his new parents will also very often manifest a conflictual relationship with their own parents, especially in their ability to overcome the envy toward their fertile parents.

Indeed, on becoming a mother or father, adoptive parents feel deprived of the period of gestation and the slow and reciprocal adaptation toward having a child. Instead of "primary maternal preoccupation" (Winnicott, 1958), there is an almost pathological desire experienced as global and caused by the negative elaboration of sterility.

In the pathological couple there is no place for curiosity toward the child (Shapiro, 1985), but rather "l'epoke" (suspension of judgment) as a defense against imagination or a conviction of "already knowing."

Paradoxically, curiosity toward the child as "another self" is possible in a biological dyad because the child is part of the mother and cannot, for this reason, be considered either as a total stranger or as absolutely naughty because he has something in common with his parents: he is a "witness" to their union.

The absence of curiosity toward the child to be adopted may be a defense against being disappointed by reality and a denial of the extraneous quality of the child. Not questioning themselves about the child's conception or birth facilitates the management of their real or imaginary relationship with their own parents. The child therefore becomes an unreal fantasy in which his state of need is felt deeply by the adoptive parents due to a projective identification with their own state of inadequacy and desire. The desire to have a child is a "desperate desire" lacking in creative representation which is colored by tones illuminated by idealization. On the other hand, the adoptive couple is entrusted with a difficult task: to give birth to the child as a fruit of their expectations, hopes, and fears, all the while repressing their desire so that the ideal child does not hide or depersonalize the real child. If such a desire is dangerous, it is also the only way to face up to the disillusionment which forces the parents to accept children who are often in a very deprived state.

The desire to have a "child" is often so strong that at a conscious level prospective parents cannot tolerate awaiting a child that might not arrive. It is an overwhelming emotion which may be explained, as we have already seen, by a narcissistic outrage, a deficiency comparable to a true mutilation of the self. The catastrophe, as we have just explained, has already happened, but in biology this term has another significance; that of a brutal discontinuity within the structure capable of giving rise to differentiation.

It seems to us that in clinical terms adoption symbolizes precisely the duality of being creative or destructive. The destructive aspect is realized through the compulsive reiteration of the unthinkable experience, for example, the abandonment for the child and sterility for the couple. In the pathology of adoption this is sometimes clinically manifested by the lack of empathy in the couple toward the child and the hyperactivity of the child (Grimaldi, 1983).

The creative aspect is, on the contrary, represented by the couple's wish to reestablish a link with their own childhood origins through adoption, repairing in this way the infirmity of the self, making an evolutionary leap, and causing the normal narcissism of the couple to recuperate.

In summary, we described the theoretical background and the modality of intervention in the preadoptive diagnosis for prospective parents, as it is formalized at the Institute of Child Neuropsychiatry, University of Rome, La Sapienza. We focused on the general problems linked to adoption and to the diagnostic setting utilized.

REFERENCES

Bertolini, M., Balgera, A., Neri, F., & Peretti, A. (1986), Identificazione ed identita: Strumenti semiologici per una prognosi sulla adozione (Identification and identity: Semiologic instruments for a prognosis on adoption). Atti XII Congresso Nazionale della Societa Italiana di Neuropsichiatria Infantile "Affidamento ed Adozione." Cefalu 1–4 October, pp. 101–105.

Bion, W. R. (1976), *The Catastrophic Change. Group and Organization Studies.* Colchester, UK: University Associates.

Blum, H. P. (1983), Adoptive parents—generative conflicts and generational continuity. *The Psychoanalytic Study of the Child,* 38:141–163.

Dicks, H. (1967), *Marital Tensions.* London: Routledge & Kegan Paul.

Eiguer, A., and Ruffiot, A. (1986), *Terapia Psiocoanalitica della Coppia.* Roma: Borla.

Ezriel, H. (1960), Le role du transfert dans le traitement psychanalytique de groupe (The role of the transference in the psychoanalytic treatment of the group). In: *Pratique de la psychotherapie de groupe,* Vol. 2, ed. P. Schneider. Paris: Presses Universitaire Français.

Fenu, M. A., Federici, C., & Chiarelli, R. (1985), Il se del bambino adottivo (The self of adopted children). *Psichiatria dell'Infanzia e della Adolescenza,* 52:421–428.

Giannakoulas, A. (1978), *Teoria e Terapia della Coppia. Seminari di formazione psicodinamica (Theory and Therapy of the Couple. Seminars of Psychodynamic Training).* Rome: Instituto di Neuropsichiatria Infantile.

Giannotti, A. (1980), Lo sviluppo psico-sessuale nella prima infanzia (The psycho-sexual development in infancy). *Rivista di sessuologia,* 4:28–41.

——— Giannakoulas, A. (1985), Il processo psicoanalitico negli adulti e nei bambini (considerazioni sulla relazione coppia genitoriale-patologia del bambino) (The psychoanalytic process in adults and children [considerations of the relationship between parental couple and child psychopathology]. *Prospettive Psicoanalitiche nel Lavoro Instituzionale,* 3:68–82.

Grimaldi, A. (1983), Accogliere lo sconosciuto. Appunti sull'adottare (Welcoming the stranger: Notes on adoption). *Prospettive Psicoanalitiche nel Lavoro Instituzionale.* 1:207–211.

Shapiro, E. R. (1985), Sulla curiosita: Formazione dei confini interpersonali nella vita familiare. *Prospettive Psicoanalitiche nel Lavoro Instituzionale,* 3:51–67.

Strachey, J. (1934), The nature of the therapeutic action of psychoanalysis. *Internat. J. Psycho-Anal.,* 20:92–127.

Vetrone, G. (1986), Introduzione. *Prospettive Psicoanalitiche nel Lavoro Instituzionale,* 2:1–10.

Winnicott, D. W. (1958), *Collected Papers: Through Pediatrics to Psychoanalysis.* New York: Basic Books.

—— (1974), Fear of breakdown. *Internat. Rev. Psychoanal.,* 1:103–107.

6

Assessment of Parental Care Capacity

in the Context of Adoption

John Tsiantis, M.D., D.P.N., F.R.C.

In the last twenty to thirty years the desire in Western countries to adopt children has in general outstripped the number of children available. In addition, adoption has ceased to be a rescue operation for children of all ages and especially for those from poor and disorganized families. Today, the goals are to ensure that the children adopted correspond to the desires and expectations of the adoptive parents and that the normal development of the child's personality is safeguarded.

At the same time, adoption has triggered a considerable amount of interest among researchers concerning the effect of heredity and the environment on the normal psychosocial development of the child. The expansion of research into the reassessment of concepts such as the "critical periods" in the development of the child, the "blood bond," and "maternal deprivation," together with technological developments in dealing with sterility by such means as artificial fertilization, has helped change the public's attitude toward adoption. These changes, together with the attitudes and personalities of the adoptive parents—which create the child's environment—are of the greatest importance in successful adoptions. Consequently, not only small children but older children and those with special needs and of a race and color different from that of the adoptive parents have been able to find homes through adoption.

DEVELOPMENTAL PROCESSES—BIOLOGICAL AND ADOPTIVE PARENTS

It is a matter of common knowledge that the role of parents is of immense importance in the upbringing of children, and work such as that done by Bowlby (1951), Winnicott (1958), Mahler, Pine, and Bergman (1975), Spitz (1965), and A. Freud (1965) has stressed the significance of early experiences in the smooth and normal development of the child's personality. In this chapter I will not refer to positions with which we are all familiar, but I will go a little further into the thinking surrounding the assessment of the ability of potential adoptive parents to care for a child. More specifically, we shall be examining issues involving proper and sensitive responsiveness on the part of the adoptive parents toward the needs of the adopted child during his or her development. I shall examine the special anxieties and conflicts created in the adoptive parents themselves, in their families, and in the child as a result of the adoption. I should state at the outset that assessing potential adoptive parents is an extremely difficult and complex task, and when I am occasionally asked, as part of my clinical practice, to make such an assessment I feel very acutely the burden of such an undertaking. I ask myself who am I and what authority do I have to decide whether specific people are in a position to bring up children and care for them. I also take into account the fact that we are dealing with the life of an infant, a small child, and that infants and young children need people who will try to respond to their needs. People are not perfect, and are incapable of functioning with the mechanical refinement of a computer. In short, what I want to stress is that infants and young children need people and not machines.

Another point I would like to make is that I do not regard myself as an expert on adoption and that my views are those of a child psychiatrist who has worked for some years with children and parents. It is essential to remember, however, that when thinking about infants and young children there are some fundamental factors to bear in mind. First of all, we have to remember that an infant enters the world with a biological potential for development and very soon develops the ability to form relationships with its mother and father and, later, with its siblings.

In reality, what we are talking about is an initial dynamic dyad or triad, each of the members of which reinforces, positively or negatively, the behavior of the other(s). The infant or young child is, of course, the most sensitive member of the group. He or she has extensive needs that are not confined to the biological sphere, in the sense of the need for food and physical care, but encompass also the following psychological needs:

1. The need for love and affection, which, apart from anything else, will help the infant express its own emotions.
2. The need for stimuli from the environment, which will help the infant manifest its own innate potential.
3. The need for uninterrupted continuity in its life. In this way it will be possible to avoid the damage and traumas to the child's personality which are brought about by loss of and separation from the love objects.

We must be careful when using the word *needs*, though, for needs vary according to the young child's developmental stage. Allow me also to recall the words of Bowlby (1951): "What is essential for the mental health of infants and young children is the existence of a mother or a mother surrogate" (p. 13).

Since then, of course, other researchers have added the importance of the father and the siblings. The parents who are going to adopt become surrogates for the biological parents. Before going on to examine the question of the adoptive parents, I think it would be useful to give a brief summary of what happens to the biological parents from the moment they make the decision to have a child: what anxieties they are subject to, what are their hopes and fears, where their expectations lie.

FROM PREGNANCY TO MOTHERHOOD

As we know, the mother during pregnancy is in a special psychological state in which she experiences the child as if it were an integral part of herself. In pregnancy, that is, there is a transfer of the libido from external reality into the self. This narcissism invests the mother's extended self representation and helps her feel the baby growing within her as a part of herself. At the same time and in addition to the sense of oneness with the child, the mother also weaves fantasies about the baby and molds it in accordance with the desires and aspects of her own ideal self. In other words, the mother has a sense of unity with the child, a state of mind which is characterized by a conscious but simultaneously profoundly unconscious identification with the baby.

According to Winnicott (1958), primary maternal preoccupation "Gradually develops and becomes a state of heightened sensitivity during, and especially towards the end of, the pregnancy and it lasts for a few weeks after birth of the child" (p. 302). In his view, it is a form of "normal illness" and it is as essential as providing a framework for the biological potential of the child to manifest itself and for its innate trends to develop. Thus the infant will experience his or her movements and feelings and the mother will respond appropriately and sensitively to the child's needs. It obviously follows that the infant's mother is the most suitable person to care for it. She is the person capable of reaching the stage of primary maternal preoccupation. It should be mentioned at this point, of course, that the mother is sometimes unable to reach this stage for a number of reasons, even though she may be a highly creative individual in other fields. In these cases the infant will experience deprivation, and mother must make reparations later in the life of the child, or if deprivation is severe, the work will have to be done by therapists. By the same token, a woman who is about to adopt a child will be able to enter this stage of primary maternal preoccupation and adapt well to the needs of the infant by virtue of her ability to identify with the infant. This will help the baby to acquire the feeling that it is beginning to exist, to have experiences, to begin to build its own ego, to confront the difficulties of life. When, on the other hand, this initial care is not available the baby develops primitive defense mechanisms and a false self and will feel the threat of nonexistence (Winnicott, 1958).

What we have said thus far emphasizes the tremendous importance of prospective adoptive parents acquiring an infant as soon after the baby's birth as possible—straight from the maternity hospital, if this is feasible.

In this way the adoptive mother, who has not had the experience of pregnancy, will be able to quickly enter the emotional process of primary maternal preoccupation and will be able to share these feelings with her husband, thus achieving triadic unity.

MOTHER–INFANT BOND

Also of importance in this respect is the development of the mother–child bond. Clearly if these psychological processes are respected the bond will be able to develop, while if they are harmed the bonding phase will be more difficult. Marshall and Kennel (1976) describe a series of disturbances which occur when things do not go smoothly. They note the great importance of the mother being with the baby immediately after birth and having physical contact with it, talking to it, looking at it, and touching it, actions which they believe reinforce the process of bond development.

The question of what comes to life in the relationship between mother and child, seen from the viewpoint of her own self and the family romance, is also of importance. (According to Freud [1909] the paradigmatic form of the latency child's family romance is his wish to be an adoptee in order to overcome ubiquitous and inherent disappointments in the relationship with the biological parents.) There will, for instance, be a difference if the baby represents a desirable part of the mother's self or an unacceptable part; if the baby symbolizes, for her, a person she loves or hates, or if in the infant she revives parts of the family romance she had as a child which may in the end affect the relationship between mother and child. More profound psychological conflicts may hinder a woman from assuming her maternal role and reaching the stage of primary maternal preoccupation. One example of this would be the woman who identifies with a masculine model.

Reasonably good maternal behaviors also depend on the mother's genetic predisposition, in addition to the support, love, and appreciation which she receives from her husband, socioeconomic factors, and, above all, the mother's relationship with her own mother and with both her parents in more general terms. Experiences of deprivation, separation, and other family disasters and unpleasant experiences will undoubtedly affect the mother's ability to provide the environment of care and love which is so important for the normal development of the child's personality.

The image which the mother and father have of themselves will also have a significant influence on their ability to respond to their maternal and paternal roles. For example, a mother who underestimates herself and believes she is incapable of becoming a mother may have difficulties in meeting the needs of her child. Another point to be assessed is whether the parents have the essential ability and skill to understand and show empathy for the developmental needs and crises of their child as he or she grows. This means that they themselves must have overcome the psychological conflicts they underwent at the same developmental period.

In adoption, matters are quite complex, particularly when it is not possible for the child to be adopted soon after birth. In this case other intermediate problems will arise, which may affect the child's psychological development and create paranoid anxieties, which in turn may make the role of the adoptive parents much more difficult. It will be seen from the above that many of the conflicts, fears, and worries of the biological parents may be the same as those of the adoptive parents.

I should like to turn at this point to the research work of Tizard and Rees (1974, 1975) and Tizard (1977), which shows the positive result of adoption on children who had previously been resident in institutions. These projects compared the results of children in high quality institutions with those who had been adopted and brought up in families. The studies showed that adoption of itself had a positive effect on the development of the children's intelligence. In addition, children who had been adopted before the age of four years developed satisfactory relations with their (middle-class) parents and displayed improved language development. At the age of eight years, however, they continued to have some difficulties in social relations with their peer group and, generally, demanded more attention from their environment than their nonadopted peers.

ADOPTIVE PARENTS

Let us now turn to the subject of parents who wish to adopt. I shall be referring to the largest category of prospective adoptive parents, that is, those who would like to have their own children but are unable to do so. As an aside, we must remember that the reasons for this sterility may be psychological, however unlikely that may sound. We should also bear in mind that prospective adoptive parents may approach the relationship with the adopted child with a narcissistic desire to see the extension and continuation of themselves through their own child frustrated. At the same time, mothers and fathers who are to adopt children have, of necessity, to begin a relationship and develop behavior that enables them to form a bond with the child without having gone through the stages of expectation, conception, and satisfaction at having created their own child. Since adoptive mothers do not go through the process of pregnancy, they are not always able to experience primary maternal preoccupation. In short, the capacity for supplying the relationship with feedback to develop the bond is often missing. What they do bring to the relationship is the desire to adopt a child and other experiences, such as their relations with their own parents, feelings of deprivation and disappointment, and all the previous failed attempts at pregnancy.

It is necessary for adoptive parents to be helped to work through the feelings which arise from their frustrated and natural narcissistic desire to have their own children and the feelings of inadequacy and weakness which are generated within them. These feelings are different for the mother than for the father. The way in which both parents have worked through the feelings of inadequacy in their own relationship—that is, how far each of them and both together have accepted the state of affairs without mutual accusation—is of great importance.

Obviously, the less these feelings have been worked through the more likely it is that any stress both parents may suffer will be greater, with all the possible negative effects on the child. If, for example, the feelings produced by wounded narcissism have not been worked through the parents will continue to feel emotionally handicapped and experience severe anger, which may express itself in the way they rear the child.

One possible extrapolation of this situation is that the adoptive parents' disappointments and any failures they encounter may be attributed to heredity and they may fall back on the somewhat deep-rooted attitudes which our society has toward biological parents who allow their children to be adopted. These attitudes can be rejecting: the biological parents are thought of as evil, immoral, irresponsible, and genetically deficient, particularly when, as frequently happens, the adopted child is born outside marriage, which in itself carries with it a social stigma (Deutsch, 1945). Sexuality is here seen as immoral, evil, and impulsive.

The above may be particularly important in cases of childlessness that are due to conflicts each parent may harbor over his or her sexuality. A related problem is that the adoptive parents tend to attribute to heredity any problems the adopted child may manifest. A worried and anxious mother, for example, may use projection mechanisms and attribute to the adopted child unacceptable parts of her own self and say that these were inherited from the unknown mother or father. The same, of course, sometimes happens with biological parents, especially when the marital relations are not good, when one parent or the other attempts to find evidence or proof of poor heredity.

Another phenomenon that sometimes occurs in adoptive parents is that unconscious conflicts, which may have played some part in or been connected with the sterility, come to the surface. These conflicts include the fears, anxieties, and fantasies of either the mother or the father concerning his or her own sexuality. The question, therefore, in assessing whether the couple will eventually be able to undertake their parental role is how far the mother and the father have been able to overcome their own deeply rooted and fossilized emotions of inferiority, weakness, and castration and how far they have managed to put aside their grief over their inability to have children of their own (Deutsch, 1945). It needs to be said, of course, that the revival of early conflicts occurs in biological parents, too, and may disturb the relationship with the child or that between the parents, as often happens when the first child is born.

GRANDPARENTS AND EXTENDED FAMILY

Adoption involves several sets of parents: the biological parents, the adoptive parents, both sets of parents of the adoptive parents, and sometimes both sets of parents of the biological parents. The attitudes, reactions, and fantasies of the maternal and paternal grandparents in particular color the relationship between the adoptive parents and the adopted child (Blum, 1983). The real reactions and fantasies of the grandparents to the adoption also form part of the emotional climate of the family and contribute to the conflicts, fears, expectations, and hopes created or revived in the adoptive parents as a result of the adoption. It is common knowledge that all young parents need the understanding, love, and support of their own parents when a child is born. Such understanding and support is even more essential when the child is adopted. The position of the adoptive parents will be made more difficult by an absence of such help, and still more so by a negative reaction to adoption on the part of the grandparents. In such cases the adoptive parents will feel that their parents do not recognize their role or accept their identity as parents. This may reinforce their insecurity about their parenting ability, and reinforce earlier anxieties and conflicts relating to the oedipal or pre-oedipal parents and vice versa.

Naturally enough, these anxieties and fantasies are transmitted to the adopted child and will magnify the problems of identity and the search for origins which usually occur in adolescence (Sants, 1964).

If, on the other hand, the adoptive parents have the support, understanding, and love of their own parents this will help them identify with their role and overcome their own conflicts and anxiety with greater ease. And that, in turn, will facilitate the relationship with the adopted child, who, among other things, will be able to identify with the extended family and with the parents' origins and roots.

In adoption, then, childless parents have to confront, apart from the complex emotions and fantasies related to their guilt and wounded narcissism, all the issues which become involved in the continuation of the family, whose solution will be facilitated if their own parents take a positive attitude toward the adoption (Blum, 1983).

SPECIFIC PROBLEMS AND ANXIETIES AFFECTING ADOPTIVE PARENTS

The following are some of the more specific questions adoptive parents have to deal with as the child develops. These considerations also inevitably enter into the assessment of their ability to provide parental care and/or the help which they will require as adoptive parents.

Whether to Tell, How to Tell, and When to Tell the Child. Thinking on this subject causes much conflict which has to do with how the adoptive parents themselves feel about their sterility and their more general motives (conscious or unconscious) for adoption. Nor should one forget the classic conflict among adoptive parents (Seglow, Pringle, and Wedge, 1972): on the one hand, they have to make the child feel he or she is their own child, while at the same time they must tell the child the opposite. Some parents, for instance, do not tell the child because they feel that will put them at a disadvantage. Others may begin to tell the child too early, too frequently, and in a compulsive manner which seems to operate as a counterphobic mechanism and usually has much to do with intense unconscious conflicts triggered by the adoption. A third group adopts an overprotective attitude and does not tell the child because they are afraid of losing him as he seeks out his real parents in the oedipodian style.

In some cases, the adoptive parents are unable to tolerate the natural curiosity and need of the adopted children to know about their biological parents, and feel that this behavior is a sign of their own failure as parents and an indication that the adopted child does not love them and has rejected them. At a deeper level, such reactions on the part of the adoptive parents may be a projection of their initial desire to have children of their own. The fantasies of abandonment and rejection which adoptive parents have may be connected, through identification mechanisms, with the attitudes of the child's parents who abandoned their child and allowed its adoption, the attitude of the biological father to the abandoned biological mother of the extramarital child, and the threat of abandonment and divorce that existed for the childless couple. Despite all this, however, the questions which arise in relation to whether the adopted child ought to be told are considerable and even the experts themselves disagree. Berger and Hodges (1982), in a study of the issue, review the trends which exist over the question of informing the child, and identify three fundamental positions:

- that the child should be told very early in life;
- that the child should not be told prior to the period of latency;
- that the child should be told as late as possible or not at all.

Each of these positions is supported by specific arguments based on research or clinical material. It will be seen that the task of the adoptive parents really is a difficult one and becomes even harder if we take into account other factors, such as the way in which the announcement is made, the questions of whether the child is ready to accept the information, and what the family's life in general is like when the announcement is made; for example, if it coincides with the birth or adoption of another child, and the state of relations between the parents (Schechter, 1969). It should also be remembered that telling the child always involves psychic pain both for the adoptive parents and particularly for the child. The announcement brings the child face to face with the trauma created by the realization that his parents had abandoned him (Feder, 1974). The child is the more vulnerable party, and so obviously the moment selected should be a time when the child is as capable as possible of dealing with the pain such knowledge will cause.

Problems Which Arise When the Child Starts Seeking His or Her Origins. The question of the adopted child's search for his or her origins is a controversial one. We could recall the classic findings of Triseliotis (1973). His project revealed two groups, whose motives were of different kinds: (1) those who wanted to meet one or both parents; and (2) those who simply wanted information.

Triseliotis comes to the conclusion that the search for origins was an attempt on the part of the adopted children to gain a better understanding of themselves and their personal lives, and that no one should be deprived of the need to discover his roots.

Clearly, the approach to follow when dealing with this basic need of children will depend on the way in which adoptive parents handle the internal conflicts and fantasies triggered by the adoption. It will also depend on the way the children themselves express or verbalize the request to seek out their biological parents. This last point brings into relief a further difficulty facing the adoptive parents: they have to deal not only with their own emotions but at the same time assess whether the child is really avoiding asking them and whether he or she is ready to absorb the information at that specific stage of development. It is a mistake to force the child to absorb this specific piece of information about his or her biological parents, but it is equally wrong for the adoptive parents to take a rationalized position and refuse to talk to the child about the biological parents because they believe the child is not interested.

The Problems Caused When the Adopted Child Transfers the Conflicts Deriving from Earlier Deprivation onto the Adoptive Parents. In this case, it is the type of conflict created in the adoptive parents by the emotions generated within them when the adopted child transfers his or her own conflicts and fantasies onto the parent–child relationship. These may be of two kinds: those which arise from the child's own deprivations and experiences prior to the adoption, and the conflicts and fantasies mobilized within the child by the need to seek out the biological parents.

Comments such as, "He's not my father and that's why he treats me like that," or, "My real parents are better than you" may often be heard. The balance in these relationships is a very delicate one and it is easy to set up a vicious circle between the adoptive parents and the adopted child.

THE MOTIVATION OF PARENTS IN ADOPTING

From what we have already stated, it is easy to see that the conscious and unconscious motives for adoption are complex and consequently difficult to simplify or generalize.

The principal factors which should be investigated and assessed are as follows: how far each spouse has worked through the family romance; whether or not the couple is childless; if the adoption is being sought by a person living alone; if the desire for adoption is directed toward handicapped children; if the couple would like a boy or a girl. Cultural factors, which may vary from country to country, will also have their part to play.

It was necessary to state the above points because adoption agencies often attach more importance to the financial position of the family and the educational level and moral principles of the parents than to psychological factors and the emotional maturity and motivation of the prospective parents. The assessment of motives for adoption should also take into account whether the parents have other children, of their own or adopted, and whether the application is from a person living alone. It is most important that the emotional maturity of the prospective parents be assessed. The question of whether the adoption is taking place merely to satisfy the wishes of the parents or with the needs of the child in mind should also be investigated.

There are, of course, explanations for the deeper unconscious motives, such as the desire to adopt a boy rather than a girl, which may be related to the wish to preserve the family name. Preference for a girl on the part of older applicants may indicate a wish for someone to look after them. In other cases, it may be discovered that the adoption is desired as a substitute for a loved one who has died or to save a crumbling marriage. Desires to "save" the adopted child, which may be a dramatization of deeper reparative fantasies, or desires to "steal" the child from another woman, which may reflect aspects of the family romance, need to be looked into as carefully as possible. Assessment of the parents and their motives for adoption should also take into account the emotions of the professional conducting the assessment. Assessment is often affected by intense countertransference reactions on the part of the professional which is justified, interpreted, or rationalized into more general philosophical, social, or political positions.

CONCLUSION

The assessment of the personal ability of the parents to provide satisfactory care in cases of adoption should consider all the thinking that has so far been expressed. I would like to stress, however, that adoptive parents are capable of devoting themselves to the upbringing of the child just as biological parents do, though there is no doubt that for the reasons given above their relationship with the adopted child is more fragile and the handling required is much more complex. As a result, psychopathological reactions among adoptive parents are much more likely.

On the other hand, of course, it is possible that precisely because the so-called "blood bond" does not exist adoptive parents are capable of keeping their emotions under greater control in their relationship with the child, though without becoming cold or unaffectionate (Schechter, 1970).

The techniques of interviewing prospective adoptive parents and the methods of making the assessment are beyond the scope of this chapter. I would like, however, to emphasize the following two points:

1. The personality, experience, and sensitivity of the professionals who are to undertake the assessment of the applicants and their countertransference reactions should be taken into consideration. Their role is a very difficult and responsible one, and they should be a part of a group whose purpose would be not only the sharing of emotions and support but also the identifying of countertransference reactions. Also of great importance is the way the agency handling the adoption operates, the philosophy that governs it, and the emotional atmosphere within it. The endless and time-consuming bureaucratic procedures that sometimes occur stifle any expression of the needs of prospective adoptive parents and, above all, of the children. I have the impression that these bureaucratic procedures reflect more profound prejudices and attitudes on the part of society in general toward the issue of adoption and the feelings generated within the professionals.

2. The second point concerns the need for the agency to maintain, for as long as necessary, a psychodynamic intervention to support adoptive parents and their children. My clinical experience has taught me that much damage could have been avoided if this intervention had been punctual and if there had been a way of helping adoptive parents and their children. What I would like to emphasize is that there is a need for collaboration—at least in some cases—between the various adoption organizations and agencies on the one hand and psychoanalysts and psychotherapists on the other. It is also essential that adoption agencies and organizations should realize that the effort to match the adoptive parents with an adopted child is a continuing process and not a static one. Matching should take into consideration the infant or young child—at all the stages in its development—viewed against the background of the adoptive parents and their families. Adoptive parents need to be helped to gain greater understanding of their own emotional life as well as that of the adopted child in order to enable them to empathize with the child's developmental needs and conflicts. Above all, they need help in order to understand that they are the psychological parents and nothing can happen to deprive them of that role.

REFERENCES

Berger, M., & Hodges, J. (1982), Some thoughts on the question of when to tell the child he is adopted. *J. Child Psychother.*, 8:867–888.

Blum, H. (1983), Adoptive parents: Generative conflicts and generational continuity. *The Psychoanalytic Study of the Child*, 38:141–163. New Haven, CT: Yale University Press.

Bowlby, J. (1951), *Maternal Care and Mental Health*. WHO, Monograph series No. 2. New York: Schocken Books, 1966.

Deutsch, H. (1945), *The Psychology of Women*, Vol. 2. New York: Bantam Books, 1973.

Feder, L. (1974), Adoption trauma: Oedipus myth/clinical reality. *Internat. J. Psycho-Anal.*, 55:491.

Freud, A. (1965), *Normality and Pathology in Childhood: Assessments in Development*. New York: International Universities Press.

Freud, S. (1909), Family romances. *Standard Edition*, 9:237–241. London: Hogarth Press, 1964.

Mahler, M. S., Pine, F., & Bergman, A. (1975), *The Psychological Birth of the Human Infant*. New York: Basic Books.

Marshall, C., & Kennel, J. (1976), *Maternal Infant Bonding*. St. Louis, MO: Mosby.

Sants, H. J. (1964), Genealogical bewilderment in children with substitute parents. *Brit. J. Med. Psychol.*, 37:133.

Schechter, M. D. (1969), Report: Psychoanalytic theory as it relates to adoption. *J. Amer. Psychoanal. Assn.*, 15:695–708.

——— (1970), About adoptive parents. In: *Parenthood*, ed. E. J. Anthony & T. Benedek. Boston: Little, Brown.

Seglow, J., Pringle, M. L. K., & Wedge, P. (1972), *Growing Up Adopted*. London: National Foundation for Educational Research.

Spitz, R. A. (1965), *The First Year of Life*. New York: International Universities Press.

Tizard, B. (1977), *Adoption: A Second Chance*. London: Open Books.

——— Rees, J. (1974), A comparison of the effects of adoption restoration to the natural mother and continued institutionalization of the cognitive development of year old children. *Child Develop.*, 45:92–99.

——— ——— (1975), The effects of early institutional rearing on the behavioral problems and affectional relationships of year old children. *J. Child Psychol. Psychiat.*, 16:61–74.

Triseliotis, J. (1973), *Search of Origins. The Experience of Adopted People*. London & Boston: Routledge & Kegan Paul.

Winnicott, D. (1958), *Through Pediatrics to Psychoanalysis*. New York: Basic Books.

7

Assessing Adoptive Parents Using a Combined Individual and Interaction Procedure

Dorit Sharav, M.A.

In Israel, as in many developed countries, the number of couples wishing to adopt by far exceeds the number of children, especially babies, available for adoption. During the last three years, an average of 450 couples applied for a baby each year, while only ninety-five babies and eighty-five older special needs children were available for placement. A backlog of 1,200 to 1,500 prospective parents now exists, with a waiting period of about five-and-a-half years to adopt a baby and a much shorter waiting period to adopt an older or a special needs child.

Even if a sufficient number of babies were available, a selection process for placement is necessary to avoid placing a baby in a family that is psychologically ill-suited to adapt to his needs. Such a selection can be accomplished only if some reliable criteria can be found for differentiating between potentially good, or good enough, or ill-suited adoptive parents.

Some authorities, such as David Kirk (1969), criticized and even denounced the use of predictive evaluation by social workers and

73

adoption agencies who are, to his mind, inadequately equipped for this task. At the same time he demands that adoptive parents have special qualities, such as "continuous loving acceptance of differences" and "capacity for empathic listening to young children" (Kirk, 1964). Others, such as Kadushin (1970) and Brieland (1984), acknowledge the need for evaluation and have suggested a number of assessment criteria.

The attitude of the Israeli adopting services has been to sift out those couples having serious marriage problems, or who lack the necessary emotional maturity or intellectual capacity to deal with the challenge and special task of adoption (Lion, unpublished). Until 1985, the procedure for evaluation consisted of the following: filling out a questionnaire asking for objective data about a couple's socioeconomic and educational background and physical health; individual and group interviews by a caseworker; six group meetings made up of five to six couples and a caseworker during which information about adoption is given and feelings and potential problems are discussed. Based on information received in this way, caseworkers evaluated each couple, and a team decision was reached.

This procedure, while valid, created some problems. The caseworker was placed in a role conflict—he or she had to be both a critical evaluator of the couple, one who might screen them out, while at the same time acting as a supportive counselor, who encourages trust and the sharing of doubts and fears, in order to prepare the prospective parents for their future role. This double role obviously confused the applicants, who feared, sometimes with good reason, that an open sharing of difficulties and doubts would jeopardize their chances of receiving the craved-for baby. Such an attitude was especially present in those intelligent, sophisticated couples who were skillful in presenting "a good front" that would convince the caseworker. Therefore, the development of an independent psychological screening procedure, administered by a psychologist who is not part of the adoption service team, was proposed as offering an independent as well as a more objective and subtle tool.

CRITERIA FOR SELECTION

Based on knowledge available in the psychological literature on mental health, parenting, and adoption, the following criteria where used as guidelines:

INDIVIDUAL CRITERIA

Approaching the adoptive parent as an individual, we look for a person of average or above average intelligence and judgment, who has attained emotional maturity and individuation; is able to express emotions adequately, relate with sensitivity and empathy to others, and respond to children's needs; who can cope with stress, is not excessively encumbered by inner conflict and disturbance, and has made his or her peace with the inability to have offspring and with the decision to adopt. Last but not least, we look for a person who shows a healthy motivation to adopt, that is, to raise a child.

COUPLE CRITERIA

Approaching the couple as a working team we are looking for a stable and basically satisfying marriage, with mutual respect and trust, with a sense of commitment and acceptance of each other's qualities and needs—partners able to communicate openly, to give and receive affection, to cooperate in solving problems, and to support each other in situations of stress (McWhinnie, 1967; Brieland, 1984; Sharav, 1989; Lion, unpublished).

ASSESSMENT TOOLS

The research literature offers a host of assessment tools for couples and families, most of them developed in the last two decades, though only a few are currently used in clinical settings. Reviews of the literature are summarized by Cromwell, Olson, and Fournier (1976) and in Jacob's and Tennenbaum's book (1988) on family assessment. Some of the authors borrow concepts and tools from individual psychology and extrapolate from structured or projective individual tests to the prediction of partner suitability and of potential interaction between the marriage partners. Others use questionnaires or problem checklists intended to assess each partner's perception or opinion of his spouse or of the marriage. Only a few researchers use direct observation of the couple in actual interaction of a problem-solving or conflict-resolution type, thus enabling the examiner to observe how the couple communicates and negotiates in a lifelike situation.

One of these instruments that has been repeatedly mentioned in the literature is the Consensus Rorschach (Singer-Thaller, 1968), which I use and will describe in detail below. Most published material about the Consensus Rorschach has focused on the discernment of psychopathology such as is found in families of schizophrenics (Shapiro and Wild, 1976; Carter, Robertson, Ladd, and Alpert, 1987). When selecting adoptive parents, however, the emphasis should not be on pathology but rather on the diversity of interacting styles characterizing ordinary couples, including healthy and successful styles as well as the more problematic ones. This prompted me to develop a new scoring system specifically designed to evaluate the interaction between spouses (Sharav, 1985), which will be described further on.

I doubt if any single instrument, even the most sophisticated, can do justice to the evaluation of husband and wife as complex individuals, as well as to the diversity of their patterns of relating to each other. Therefore, a number of different procedures combining different aspects and points of observation were used in order to present a more comprehensive and multidimensional picture.

DESCRIPTION OF THE ASSESSMENT PROCEDURE

The Individual Stage

A clinical interview by a psychologist is held, in which information is gathered about the person's history, including present and past family relationships; how infertility has affected the individual's own life and the marriage; and motivations for adoption.

Individual Test Battery

This includes two subtests of the WAIS, one verbal (comprehension) and one performance (block design), which measure intellectual functioning (Wechsler, 1958); complete Rorschach Test (Rorschach, 1932); and the Thematic Apperception Test (Murray, 1938) using six pictures, usually numbers 13BG, 2, 3BM, 4, 7GF, and 13MF (two or three additional pictures may be added if necessary).

The Couple Stage

Since the Consensus Rorschach and Consensus TAT are unfamiliar procedures, I will describe them in some detail.

In the Consensus Rorschach, the usual ten Rorschach cards are presented to the couple, with the instructions:

"You have to look at these cards again, discuss the possible answers, and try to reach an agreement on one or more answers that seem suitable to both of you. When you reach an agreement, please write it down on this sheet of paper. If you cannot agree on any response, go on to the next card."

The couple then goes through all ten cards, writing down the agreed-upon responses. They also delineate their responses on a schema block that includes a small, black-and-white version of the Rorschach.

In the Consensus TAT, three or four pictures are presented to the couple. The instructions are: "Discuss these pictures, and try to invent for each picture a story that you both agree on. When you reach an agreement, one of you can write down the story for both of you. If there is no agreement, go on to the next picture."

The examiner is present only as an observer, without interfering in the discussion. He pays attention to patterns of interaction, such as who is chosen as the representative, or secretary, of the couple. The whole procedure is tape recorded.

SCORING AND INTERPRETATION

The material available to the examiner at the end of this procedure includes:

1. The findings from their personal interview and tests of each partner, including the two individual Rorschach psychograms.
2. The "end product" of the couple's test—the Rorschach responses and TAT stories written by the couple which the examiner uses to construct a Consensus Psychogram.
3. The recorded tape and the examiner's notes of the couple's interaction and decision making during the Consensus Rorschach, Consensus TAT, and couple interview.

ANALYZING THE CONSENSUS TESTS

In addition to scoring each Rorschach agreed-upon response in the traditional manner according to the Exner (1974) method, a special technique was developed to score the pattern of interaction.

Each agreed-upon response is evaluated according to whether it was originally given by the husband—scored D.H. (Dominance Husband)—or by the wife—scored D.W. (Dominance Wife), or if it had originally been given by both husband and wife in their individual Rorschach—scored F.A. (Former Agreement).

For example, if on card 1 the husband said "bat" and the wife "a mask" and they agree on "bat," the scoring is D.H. If on the same card both partners originally say "bat" and this is also the agreed response, it is scored F.A. If the new response contains elements of both husband's and wife's individual responses, it is scored COM (Combination). If the husband saw an airplane in the white space of card 2, and the wife saw fire in D3 of the same card, and the agreed-upon response is "a jet plane, with the backfire here," the response in COM.

New responses created during the interaction stage are scored CR.H. (Creation Husband), CR.W. (Creation Wife), or CR.Co. (Creation Couple), respectively. No agreement on a card is scored N.AG.

Another category, unusual but interesting is PS.AG. (Pseudo Agreement). It is kind of an "as if" agreement in which the couple pretends or seems to agree, but each actually keeps his or her original choice. This may indicate unresolved conflicts and a "sweeping under the carpet" style of relationship.

The consensus TAT stories are interpreted according to the same principles as the Rorschach, though no formal scoring is used. The examiner relies on a more impressionistic style of analysis, noting which partner is the leader, and if his or her leadership is absolute and rigid or shows some flexibility; what themes are highlighted by the couple and what themes are played down or even hidden in the interaction. The examiner also notes the extent and quality of cooperation between the partners, their style of communicating, the intensity of the manifest conflict present, and their typical ways of conflict resolution.

On the basis of this material the examiner writes a psychological report on each partner, as well as a report about them jointly as a functioning couple, and makes a recommendation. This report is given to the caseworker, who makes the decision about adoption. The caseworker may use this material for preparing the couple for their future role, for suggesting personal or couple therapy when this seems advisable, or for explaining to the couple the reasons for rejecting them as applicants for adoption.

CASE ILLUSTRATIONS

CASE No. 1

Ivette, thirty-five, and Omer, thirty-eight, a lower middle-class couple of Moroccan origin, had been married for nineteen years and had come to Israel fourteen years earlier.

Omer had two years of high school education and worked as a mechanic. In the individual interview, he appeared tense and a little reserved, described himself as ambitious but shy in social situations. In the test situation, his perception and thinking were flexible and adaptive, and his reality testing adequate. Intellectually, he functioned much better on verbal tasks than on tasks demanding analysis and synthesis of nonverbal material (Table 7.1). Emotionally he was somewhat restrained, and his achievement was hampered by a pessimistic attitude. On a deeper level, as revealed by the projective material, Omer viewed life as a continuous struggle, where one had to fight for everything, often without success. The hero in his TAT stories strained hard, but usually failed. This sense of failure was not only related to difficult life circumstances (immigration, for instance) but to the failure in procreation and possibly also the failure in sexual potency. As a developmental background to his depressive tendency, there were experiences of disappointment in relation to a rigid, cold mother figure. In two stories where a mother was depicted with either a son or a daughter, there was an atmosphere of tension and estrangement.

In spite of these underlying handicaps, Omer was able to relate to others in a cooperative, pleasant manner. He coped well, suppressed anger and aggression, and usually got his own way, using patience, roundabout ways, and a persuasive kind of logic.

The wife, Ivette, had only seven years of formal education and was employed as a factory worker. In the interview she appeared

TABLE 7.1
Couple No. 1

	Wife	Husband	Couple
WAIS			
Comprehension	10	14	——
Block Design	10	7	——
Rorschach Psychogram			
R	18	21	16
F%	100	57	75
F + %	40	79	82
X + %	40	83	81
P	2	7 + 1	7
	noP on card 5		
EB	0:0	2:1	2:1
H: Hd	1:0	2:0	2:0
anat %	66	5	6
FC	0	2	2
Interaction Scores			
D.H. (Dominance Husband)		13	
D.W. (Dominance Wife)		0	
CR.H. (Creation Husband)		1	
CR.W. (Creation Wife)		0	
CR.CO. (Creation Couple)		0	
F.AG. (Former Agreement)		2	
COM. (Combination)		0	
Total		16	
N.AG. (No Agreement)		0	

excited and expressive, eager to get a child, envious of every pregnant woman she saw, and fearful of being rejected by the adoption service. She described a long series of unsuccessful medical procedures and operations that she had undergone in her efforts to conceive. Her only pregnancy had ended in miscarriage. This resulted in an emotional crisis, with Ivette feeling that she caused suffering to herself and to the whole family. After the miscarriage, Ivette and her husband decided to adopt. She described the marriage as good and peaceful. They have "a similar nature" and only minor quarrels which are easily reconciled.

Ivette's tests displayed a normal intellectual capacity, in spite of little schooling and a restricted cultural background. Her general and social comprehension was adequate, and she did well on nonverbal tasks, utilizing minimal help from the examiner in dealing with momentary stress and confusion. The projective tests showed a discrepancy between a layer of superficial adjustment and a deeper layer indicating underlying problems with body and self images as a woman. The Rorschach indicated a preoccupation with the inner body that is manifested in a high percentage of "anatomy" responses, such as "X-rays of the human body," "embryos in uterus." This theme dominated her perception and ideation at the expense of emotional expression, and with little regard to the reality features of the stimulus.

It should be mentioned that anatomy responses and especially those pertaining to sexual and fertility themes, such as "uterus," "ovaries," or "embryos," are commonly found in protocols of couples with infertility problems. These responses represent their actual preoccupation with medical tests and medical procedures as well as their underlying feelings of vulnerability and damage caused by the failure to conceive and to procreate. Sometimes these responses also reflect the fantasies and hopes to become pregnant and to bear a child. With this as background, we can regard Ivette's protocol as less pathologic than it would be had she not suffered from a realistic problem of infertility. Nevertheless, in Ivette's case the domination of this theme over her inner world is unusually extreme and indicates a rigidity of defenses, probably intensified because of the test situation.

Her responses to the TAT pictures were characterized by a tendency to project the themes of illness, medical tests, and pregnancy on the characters in her stories. The only picture she enjoyed was the one depicting a mother, daughter, and baby (7GF), where she happily identified with the role of a mother teaching her daughter how to hold a baby.

COUPLE INTERACTION

When Omer and Ivette worked together, their pattern was one of cooperation, with a clear definition of roles—the husband being strongly dominant.

Ivette kept bringing up her stereotyped response "X-ray of the human body," Omer, while not rejecting or devaluing his wife, kept pointing out the vagueness of her responses, leading her slowly and patiently to see and to accept his better organized and popular responses. Ivette reacted to his response with surprise, but his manner, as well as her respect and admiration for him, made it easy for her to accept his suggestions.

Here are some examples from the interaction in the Rorschach:

C.1—H: Looks to me like a butterfly. (whole)
W: I also thought of a bat at first, and then I thought something of the human body, and X-ray. (whole)
H: Yes, but more a butterfly.
W: Yes, and also a bat.
H: We both agree it looks like a butterfly and a bat.

They write these down, with "Butterfly" scored as D.H. in the interaction, and "Bat" scored F.AG. (Former Agreement). Note that the idea of "X-ray" has disappeared.

C.3—H: What did you see?
W: Two people laundering, here a bridge over a stream.
W: I also thought people, in the belly, twins, in the womb.
H: (laughing uncomfortably) What about those on the side? (D2) Let us say two little animals hanging on something?
W: I agree on two people filling up water. I said twins at first.
H: It can be anything, it is not a clear-cut picture so as to decide for sure. But what are they doing? They are so separate.
W: What, in the belly they are stuck together? (But she gives in eventually)
W: Two people filling up water is clearer than twins.

The agreed-upon response is then a well-organized, popular response, with positive human interaction, scored D + Mo H P, and the interaction score is again DH.

The combined product (see Table 7.1) contained sixteen responses, of which fourteen were dominated by the H. and two were Former Agreement. There were no responses dominated by the W. On the whole, the combined product was well organized, included a variety of content, some expression of fantasy (2M) and of emotions (2FC), some interpersonal interest (2H), and no signs of psychopathology.

Comparing the couple and the individual psychograms we note an increase in reality testing and in common sense (F + % 82, 7P), and a drastic reduction in "anatomy" content (6%).

We can see that in this couple the husband, superior in his personality organization and ego functioning, succeeds in pulling his wife in the direction of better reality orientation and common sense. He manages to extricate her from her compulsive and morbid preoccupations with her damaged body image and her fears. She leans on him and is reassured by him. This seems to be not just an instance of traditional, patriarchal male dominance, but a case where the couple interacts in a way that compensates for each other's liabilities. The wife is supported at the cost of some stifling of her individual expression, while the husband's damaged self-esteem is bolstered by his wife's trust and admiration.

In other cases, of course, the interaction may demonstrate an influence in the opposite direction—the disturbed spouse dominating the picture and pulling the couple toward a morbid, or even psychotic, ideation, creating a pattern of "folie à deux." Such pathological patterns emerge very clearly on this interaction test.

The recommendation for this couple was to accept them as candidates and to offer supportive psychotherapy for the wife.

CASE NO. 2

Yafa, thirty-two, and Dov, thirty-seven, had been married for seven years. They had already been rejected for adoption, but have appealed against the decision. They arrived for the test after several hours of driving, and appeared tense and tired. Both were hostile and expressed criticism about their being unjustly rejected, so the examiner had first to spend time calming them down.

Dov, a large, stout man born in Eastern Europe, was a university graduate and worked in import and marketing. His tests reflected a high intellectual potential, but his functioning and judgment were impaired by tension, impulsiveness, and defensive efforts. He had difficulty in concentrating, and sometimes got stuck in trying to solve even simple problems (block design), becoming angry and confused and insisting that his (erroneous) solution was correct.

The projective tests showed a rich, but unstable personality. His reality orientation vacillated between accurate, even acute, perception on the one hand, and vague perceptions, with unwarranted generalizations, on the other. He tended to spout symbolic and philosophic ideas such as "The old opposite the new—a symbol of progress" (card 10), responses that were unfounded and loosely organized. His good social perception enabled him to adjust and to manipulate others; but he was also rebellious, conscientious, and dogmatic, and insisted on principles even when this was to his disadvantage. In stress situations he tended to become rigid, stereotypic, and even paranoid. For instance, during the Rorschach when he warned the examiner, "You will not succeed in breaking me on this subject. I was already singed because I had talked too much."

Dov tended to get into an intense emotional involvement with others, but was easily disappointed and became highly suspicious when his expectations were not met. He vacillated between self-accusations and projection of blame onto others. Diagnostically this seemed to be a borderline personality with paranoid features.

It could be predicted that as a father, Dov would be highly involved. He would dedicate himself to the child, but would impose high expectations and conflicting demands on him. He would react to the child inconsistently, driven more by his own emotions and needs than by the child's developmental needs.

Yafa, Israel born, is a university graduate teacher. She was obese and untidily dressed. Having some former knowledge about psychological tests, Yafa felt she knew how she should react, but at the same time she was anxious lest she defeat herself, so she was evasive and cautious, giving few responses. However, all these efforts were dwarfed by her main, overpowering motive—to be prominent in a provocative, rebellious manner. Although intelligent, she avoided commonsense answers owing to her need to challenge the premises behind the questions asked, thus reaching absurd solutions. Her tendency to rebel and dominate became even more conspicuous in the couple interaction, as will be seen further on.

Yafa seemed to be an insecure woman, who tried to bolster herself by demonstrating her knowledge and by dominating others. She craved for attachment and warmth, but was also afraid of intimacy, and used intellectual mechanisms to achieve control and a "safe" distance. As a mother, one could predict that she would be domineering and intrusive, would not be able to allow her child an autonomous development, and would be impervious to criticism and to the child's needs in spite of her efforts to be a good mother.

COUPLE INTERACTION

Dov and Yafa's behaviors were extremely deviant. Considering their intense desire to get a positive evaluation and to receive a child, we might have expected some attempt or at least some "show" of cooperation. However, Yafa took command of the situation, became extremely domineering and aggressive, devaluing her husband's ideas and even actively silencing him. Dov was more accommodating, accepting Yafa as an "expert" on psychological tests. But often, after trying hard to suppress his own impulsivity and accept her response, she would back off and demand that he agree on a vague, empty response. For example, on Rorschach card 1, W. suggested "Bat" (whole), H., though he originally saw three different percepts on his individual Rorschach, accepted her idea of "Bat."

Wife: "No, I do not see anything clear. Let us write 'a thing without a form.' " Only after a long, tiresome argument did they agree on "Bat," scored W.D. This futile struggle continued throughout the test, and Dov, though angry, was unable to hold his own against his wife. Yafa, though aware of the projective nature of the test and of their responses to it, was completely oblivious to the impression their behavior was bound to make on the examiner.

On TAT card 4, for instance, where a couple in some sort of conflict is depicted, she said, "This is about our relationship." A tempestuous argument ensued about the right story, and Yafa not only wrote down the story for both of them, but also dictated each detail. She childishly insisted that they not describe the woman in the story as pleading, "The time has not yet come that I will plead with you and it will never come!" She demanded that they write that the woman in the story was right and that the husband regretted his anger, and this was what was finally written down in the agreed-upon story.

As can be predicted, the final product reflected the couple's disharmony (Table 7.2). It was meager, only eight responses on the

TABLE 7.2
Couple No. 2

	Wife	Husband	Couple
WAIS			
Comprehension	9	13	——
Block Design	10	unscorable	——
Rorschach Psychogram			
R	16	28(6)	8 (at the most)
Rej	1	0	3
F%	68	58	75
F + %	68	56	50
X + %	75	64	62
P	4	5	3
EB	0:0	6:5	0:1.5
es	4:1	1:3	1:0
FC: CF: C	0:0:0	1:3:1	0:0:1
H: Hd	1:0	2:1	
(H): (Hd)	0:0	3:0	
"symbols"	0	7 (25%)	2
Interaction Scores			
D.H. (Dominance Husband)		3 (after long struggle)	
D.W. (Dominance Wife)		4	
CR.H. (Creation Husband)		0	
CR.W. (Creation Wife)		1	
F.AG. (Former Agreement)		0	
COM. (Combination)		0	
Total		8	
N.AG. (No Agreement)	3		

Rorschach, and consisted of either banal, commonplace responses or of vague ones on the verge of descriptions, such as "A red and green blot, with strange orange-colored figure" (c.9). The wife succeeded in harnessing the husband's baseless philosophizing, but at the same time stifled his creativity and replaced it with her barren defensiveness.

This is a couple living in disharmony and in a constant power struggle in which the wife usually came out the winner, and the husband remained frustrated.

The recommendation was, of course, negative. But the couple was very insistent and appealed repeatedly, mobilized other psychological opinions (based solely on clinical interviews), and finally got a child for adoption. The follow-up that happens to be available for this case is sad, but instructive. Two years later, the wife applied for a second child. A home visit revealed that the couple had separated, the wife keeping the child. The husband was found dead under mysterious circumstances a year later, and was suspected of having committed suicide.

Such mutually destructive couples are seen more often in marriage counseling clinics, where their problems are more openly acknowledged, since they come for help with their difficulties. When such a disturbed couple applies to adopt (perhaps in the hope that a child will repair the damaged relationship), it is very important to diagnose them correctly. For this purpose our procedure has been found very helpful.

In positive and harmonious couples the atmosphere of the interaction is benign and supportive. Though arguments and bargaining may occur, there is usually a process of give and take, of mutual cooperation in solving the presented problem, while allowing some personal expression to each partner.

In such couples there are several characteristics that we have come to expect in the interaction test: a relatively high number of agreements (>10); a more evenly distributed dominance pattern; some instances of F.AG. (Former Agreement), which reflect the "common ground" the couple has brought to the marriage or has developed during the years of mutual adaptation; some COM. (Combination) responses, reflecting the ability to cooperate in problem solving; some novel responses, given by either H., W., or both (CR.H., CR.W.). These reflect the process by which a supportive, mutually enhancing relationship encourages either partner to become bolder and more creative.

The above procedure has been available for the last five years, and caseworkers have reported it to be very helpful in making their difficult decisions about adoptive applicants. The material now being accumulated may serve as a basis for future follow-up studies that are necessary for validating the procedure and developing more refined criteria for selecting and predicting successful adoptions.

SUMMARY

The above discussion presents a procedure for the assessment of adoptive parents. This procedure was developed in response to the following problems:

1. The need to sift out those couples who are ill-suited to the special task of adopting a child because of personal psychopathology or serious marital problems.

2. The need to free the caseworkers from the role conflict of being both evaluators and supporters, by supplying them with an independent, more refined and objective assessment.

The procedure combines individual measures, such as a personal interview and individual personality tests, with couple measures, such as the Consensus Rorschach and the Consensus TAT.

A special scoring system was developed to assess the style of communication between the spouses, as it emerges in the interaction tests. The procedure and the scoring system have been described in detail. Several examples of couples with different interaction styles have been presented, and the implications of the findings for their evaluation as future adoptive parents have been discussed. The procedure enables us to assess the strengths and liabilities of each couple, and contributes valuable material for the caseworker in reaching the difficult, sometimes even painful, decision about accepting or rejecting a couple.

REFERENCES

Brieland, D. (1984), Selection of adoptive parents. In: *Adoption, Current Issues and Trends*, ed. P. Sachdev. Toronto, Canada: Butterworth & Co.

Carter, L., Robertson, S. R., Ladd, J., & Alpert, M. (1987), The family Rorschach with families of schizophrenics: Replication and extension. *Fam. Proc.*, 26:461–474.

Cromwell, R. E., Olson, D. H. L., & Fournier, D. G. (1976), Tools and techniques for diagnosis and evaluation in marital and family therapy. *Fam. Proc.*, 15:1–49.

Exner, J. E., Jr. (1974), *The Rorschach: A Comprehensive System*, Vol. 1. New York: John Wiley.

Jacob, T., & Tennenbaum, D. (1988), *Family Assessment, Rationale, Methods and Future Directions*. New York & London: Plenum Press.

Kadushin, A. (1970), *Adopting Older Children*. New York: Columbia University Press.

Kirk, D. H. (1964), *Shared Fate*. New York: Free Press.

————— (1969), The selection of adopters—Questions regarding authority and reasoning. In: *Exploring Adoptive Family Life—The Collected Adoption Papers of David H. Kirk*, ed. B. J. Tansey. Brentwood Bay, British Columbia: Ben Simon Publications.

Lion, A. (1986), Adoption in Israel. In: *Adoption in Worldwide Perspective*, ed. R. D. C. Hoksbergen, Swets North America Inc. Lisse: Berwyn, Swets, & Zeitlinger.

—— (unpublished), A set of criteria for selection of adoptive parents, 1976.

McWhinnie, A. M. (1967), *Adopted Children. How They Grew Up*. London: Routledge & Kegan Paul.

Murray, H. A. (1938), *Explorations in Personality*. New York: Oxford University Press.

Rorschach, H. (1932), *Psychodiagnostik*. Bern: Huber.

Shapiro, L. N., & Wild, C. M. (1976), The product of the Consensus Rorschach in families of male schizophrenics. *Fam. Proc.*, 15:211–224.

Sharav, D. (1985), Assessing couple interaction with a battery of tests. Paper presented at the Talbieh Health Center, Jerusalem, Israel.

—— (1989), Couple assessment and couple treatment in the light of the individuation level of each partner. Paper presented at Hebrew University, Jerusalem, Israel.

Singer-Thaller, M. T. (1968), The Consensus Rorschach and family transactions. *J. Project. Techniques Person. Assess.*, 32:348–351.

Wechsler, D. (1958), *The Measurement and Appraisal of Adult Intelligence*. Baltimore: Williams & Wilkins.

8

Training Professionals in Interviewing Techniques for Couple Eligibility: The Shared Fantasies

Giuliana Milana Lisa, S.W.

In teaching a group of social workers at the International Social Services, I tried to make them aware that the task of assessing adoptive parents would neither satisfy us nor give us certainty once we completed it. I emphasized that together we were going to try to acquire ever more significant elements for assessment, while being careful not to give in to the temptation of accumulating data in the search for an illusory certainty. At the same time, we were going to be valid and indispensable to the judge. But the assessments were also going to be far from certain. The aim would be to search for more significant data.

Very often, the concluding reports that the operators send to the courts are marked by an abundance of data that were obtained and presented with great care, but these reports are often surprisingly monotonous. They present an endless array of couples who, apart from differences in age and economic and cultural conditions, seem

Acknowledgments: I want to thank my colleagues who always followed me in a spirit of cordiality and creativity.

91

more or less attached to each other, even though sometimes differences in opinion exist between them. They are well integrated in their environment, with satisfying jobs, and even have some enjoyable hobbies, which the husband and wife often share. The grayest touch comes from the homemakers who admit to some moments of loneliness and give some signs of dissatisfaction. To all this we must add the good relationships these couples have with their families of origin, though with some criticism regarding their own parents' child-rearing methods, mitigated, however, by the observation that this was normal behavior for their time; obviously no racial prejudice; and excellent ideas on child rearing.

Reading various reports one after the other creates the same impression one has when reading compositions written in class by school children writing on an assigned subject. In our case, however, things are not really like this: there is no actual construction of the report. Our adoptive parents offer us an image of themselves they have created, and how could they do otherwise? The problem is that the tension present when a person or a couple seeks help from a doctor, social worker, psychologist, or other professional is absent in these interviews. In the former cases, suffering and the expectation of relief are the links that unite the patient or client to the professional, making the relationship lively and meaningful. This is the condition that allows one party to reveal itself and the other to understand. In the interviews for the declaration of eligibility not only are these elements missing, but it is unequivocally a testing situation. And we should not excuse ourselves by saying we also intend to offer the couples advice to help them decide, and that the decision will be the court's. Though our intentions are good they do not alter the fact that the interview is in fact an exam, a blind exam, where there is no course of study, and the criteria for passing or failing are not defined. It is this situation that gives the interview its meaning, and we must deduce from it what the consequences are.

One consequence is that the clinical interview or psychotherapy is not valid in this case. I want to strongly stress this point because there is often confusion between the use of psychoanalytic concepts and the use of psychoanalytic techniques. This happens because both are closely merged in the literature; and this is how they are transmitted and learned in the phase of formation. A lack of clarity on this point can make the relationship deeply mystifying; one cannot conduct an exam as if it were psychotherapy.

For example, the clinical psychologist with psychoanalytic training may have learned that it is important to let the patient take the initiative in opening the dialogue. He knows that even if this creates anxiety the theme that emerges will be highly significant because it is the first one. If this psychologist behaves with a couple or with a single would-be parent in the same way, the theme that emerges from the silence could in fact have some significance. However, the initial vacuum in which the person has been left would be incongruous in this situation, and would in reality become a confusing and intrusive element.

The relationship would begin with ambiguity, and the gap that always exists between professional and client, a gap already large in situations of this type, would grow to huge proportions.

With these premises, the elements we could obtain from this type of interview and from a situation manipulated in this manner would not offer us sufficient guarantees. From this example we can see that a technique aimed at reducing to a minimum the therapist's interference in the patient's material, which is so important in a therapeutic setting, has the opposite effect when used in a different situation.

And so to use psychotherapy correctly outside of the therapeutic setting, something both possible and to be hoped for, the theoretical concepts must be separated from those inherent to the technique.

The danger of using dynamic psychology in an incongruous manner is stronger for those professionals with more training in the psychodynamic field, and who have undergone training in psychotherapy. In fact, social workers, though trained more to help than to evaluate, often find themselves in situations in which they must make operational decisions because of the social mandate given to them. Consequently, they are more used to working with this mandate in mind.

THE COUPLE–PROFESSIONAL–GROUP RELATIONSHIP

Let us now see how we used some theoretical concepts, such as projective identification and "container–contents," in our group experience. I will present the material by means of the following two examples: a social worker presents the interviews with the Dull couple to the group (we will give them this name, because dullness appeared to be the most visible element in this case). Mr. and Mrs. Dull were of average culture, wealthy, and from a small town in the province. They were kind, industrious, and calm. To the social worker, they were nice, attentive, and punctual for appointments. They answered all the questions in the questionnaire appropriately. However, as the interviews proceeded, the social worker felt more and more depressed. The Dulls transmitted this message: we are serious and responsible persons who have thought about adoption for a long time. Now that our decision has been made, we have nothing further to add. We feel we know everything there is to know about inter-country adoptions, but since bureaucratic regulations demand that we go through these interviews, here we are.

Actually, the situation is very straightforward for the Dull couple, though slightly boring for this young social worker who is so serious and dedicated and refuses to take short-cuts. The social worker, however, tells us that she feels more and more exasperated; she will have to write one of those dull reports she has always criticized at hearings.

As a last resort, she tries using provocation. "Don't you think the child will want to return to his own country and to his own people one day?" "We would be willing to help him"; "What if he wanted to stay there where he came from once he becomes an adult?" "He has the right to choose where to live if he is of age." Finally the social worker asks the couple to imagine a difficult situation with their eventual future son, and to imagine how they would face it. Mr. Dull is a bit taken aback; the question makes him slightly indignant. He cannot understand why daydreams have been brought up in such a serious situation. However, Mrs. Dull readily answers that she thinks about a wide range of things regarding this child, even that he might encounter difficulties and obstacles, but she knows what she must do and what she will do: she will keep her child close to her. She then adds, "When children are kept close they grow up well." She continues in this vein and finally concludes that in life she has always been able to get along with everybody. However, when someone has hurt her, she has ignored that person.

On listening to this dialogue, we hear a social worker asking questions, giving the couple cues to reflect on and think about, and a

couple answering in a correct, nice, and general way. But if we change
our observation point, we see a couple going through an extremely
important and difficult interview; together they are taking an exam
in which they will pass or fail as parents. Nonetheless, they have
managed to overturn the situation from an emotional point of view;
it is not they but the social worker who is in trouble. The sense of
impotence which takes hold of a person obliged to depend on another's opinion has been completely transferred to the social worker.
Now it is not they but she who is worried and afraid she will not be
able to write a good report—in other words, not be able to pass the
test honorably. If we focus our attention on what the wife said we can
see a pattern: her imagining that her son will not have problems only
if he stays close to her is a strange fantasy! It resembles more a form
of delirium, said as it is with assurance and without any supporting
data. The key expression seems to be: "When a person hurts me, I
ignore him." In fact, in the course of the meetings with the social
worker, she systematically put aside all stimuli, all thoughts which
could have caused her fear, uncertainty, and worry.

The theoretical concept used here is projective identification; the
fantasy that develops inside the real scene does not remain confined
to the mind of the person who created it, but moves around in the
interpersonal relationship, until somehow, it reaches the listener. In
our study of the case, we displaced the magnifying glass. In general,
the focus is on the client or couple, with their history, their expectations, their social worker in the picture. However, in this case, we put
the relationship that developed between the social worker and the
client at the center.

However, this relationship was not seen from the outside the way
a witness to the interviews would have done, but from the inside,
starting with the emotions and feelings of the social worker who had
participated in the interviews. Consequently, the attention is transferred from the contents of the interviews to the dynamics of the
ongoing interviews. At the outset the contents of the interviews,
though important in certain aspects, are not very useful in others,
because they are somehow manipulated and distant, contrary to the
experience of the interview, which is immediate and direct for the
interviewer. When training interviewers, one often insists that they
should not let themselves be influenced by their own feelings when

they are working; their professional mantle must be made of attention, skill in observation, and objectivity. I agree on attention; the capacity to observe without the emotions that are within remains external, and in this manner one never manages to see the other side of the coin either. As to objectivity, it is an aspiration which can lay the most insidious traps if we are not careful. The search for objectivity often leads to obtuse and partial visions, for in our attempts to dominate observed reality, we simplify it arbitrarily.

Certainly, to structure work by starting from a professional's emotions and comparing them to other data, it is necessary for the professionals to be trained in a particular way. The group work conducted with the social worker had this aim, but it was also used in another manner: as we gave more importance to the "here and now," with respect to the content in the study of the interviews, we also gave our attention to the dynamics created in the group while the case was being presented and discussed, because these dynamics were related not only to the members of the group but also to the material we were discussing. In this way it was possible to acquire further elements to understand the would-be parents. I will illustrate this with the second example.

We will call the couple we are going to talk about now the Differents, because the immediate impression they gave us could be expressed as: "Different is beautiful."

They lived in a very unusual house in the country; a kind of industrial hangar, but with all the modern comforts. The furniture was cluttered and casual, but a large library indicated cultural interests.

Contrary to what usually happens on a home visit, it was clear that nothing had been prepared for the arrival of the social worker. Mrs. Different was wearing an apron wrong side out. Having said this, we should add that both husband and wife were visibly obese. They already had an adopted daughter who had been with them for a few years. She was a spastic girl with serious characterological problems who had lived the first years of her life in an institution. The Different couple had made a request for an inter-country adoption and had put no limits on the country of origin. They would have easily accepted, even preferred, a child with very different somatic traits, such as dark skin. As opposed to the Dull couple, both, but especially Mrs. Different, recounted interesting stories about their lives. She told of various organizations she belonged to in which, in the role of leader, she had acted to defend the rights of minorities being discriminated against.

The social worker who presented the case had been very impressed by these people, but when she presented them it seemed as if she had to defend them in our eyes and convince us that they were exceptional but different. The group reacted in a way opposite to what the social worker had hoped. One by one, with a lot of insistence, each member gave a good reason not to advise adoption. The more the negative aspects of the couple were pointed out, the more the social worker presenting the Differents found arguments in their favor. Very soon the group had polarized into two opposing camps, and the situation could have reached a standstill if I, the leader of the group, had not considered these two parts as elements of conflict which, before becoming the group's, had been the social worker's. In fact, in the course of the discussion, the social worker said that she had come out of the interview in an uncertain and confused state of mind. At the time, she, herself, had the same doubts that the group was now voicing, but subsequently, she put these doubts aside so as not to seem a conformist and almost a bit racist. She felt it was unfair to evaluate this couple with the same criteria used for all the others. Her initial hesitations disappeared in the group when she decided to side firmly with the Differents.

After this meeting, the social worker was able to focus on the problems of an eventual inter-country adoption. Mrs. Different first became angry, but then was able to consider the arguments presented to her by the social worker. She admitted that she was having great problems with her daughter and had hoped that a new child was going to make her task easier. One cannot say that she had completely changed her mind, but her attitude was different now: she was less sure of herself and more perplexed.

On the basis of other information which we acquired later, we were able to reconstruct the dynamics of the couple–professional–group. Mrs. Different, who was the dominant figure in the family, had gone through a period of deep depression during her adolescence because of her obesity, and had emerged from this state by changing her sense of depression into a sense of triumph. From that time on, apart from a few recurrent episodes of depression, supported by her new attitude, Mrs. Different had started a kind of war against the mediocre and normal, waving the banner of diversity.

The ideas behind her social battles were certainly of the type one can share, but I believe it was not so much these ideas that had impressed the social worker, but rather the fantasy of war and challenge which, though unspoken, had insinuated itself into the relationship. Because of this fantasy, the social worker had felt forced to make a certain choice, as if Mrs. Different had told her: "You are either with me, or against me." The conflict between giving in to intimidation and continuing to exercise her own judgment had not been experienced on a conscious level by the social worker. However, it was transferred to the group and acted out there.

After we had observed and understood what was happening in the group, a movement in the opposite direction began: the reunion of the two parts. Previously, they were divided—one side being taken by the group and the other by the presenter of the case. Now the group no longer remained paralyzed by the fantasy of struggle and opposition. Consequently, the social worker who participated both in the group and in the relationship with Mrs. Different now transferred a different level of consciousness into the relationship. This, in turn, enabled the woman to reach a new stream of thoughts and feelings.

The theoretical frame of reference for my work with the group are the theories of Bion (1961) on group dynamics. These theories have been developed by the author into the concept of "container–contents."

Various studies have followed this line of conceptualization. It has been reported by many the fact that a particular type of patient is able to project his or her problems onto the professional's activity.

It is difficult, but also of importance, both in pinpointing the cause of the individual's underlying anxiety and finding and containing the interviewer's underlying anxiety; and this for two reasons: first, the type of fantasy which appears with the anxiety in the interviewer can give us some idea of the type of anxieties and defenses present in the individuals; and second, the interviewer's mental and emotional makeup is the instrument that reveals data and processes it. There is no substitute for it and it must, therefore, be carefully considered.

In the group work with the social workers of the International Social Service, Italian Branch, I tried to respond to these needs, and

I promised myself I would do a work of containment with them. I do not know how well I have succeeded. However, the dominant feeling was one of curiosity and the desire and pleasure of gradually understanding what was happening in front of me. There were some tedious moments, during which it felt as if the work was becoming blurred; but both in the stimulating moments and in the tedious ones, I always felt supported by the group, which made my task easier in facing the challenges.

REFERENCE

Bion, W. R. (1961), *Experiences in Groups*. London: Tavistock.

Part IV

Preparation of Special Needs Children

9

Preparing Older Children for Adoption

Vera I. Fahlberg, M.D.

In this chapter I will elaborate on the tasks involved in preparing an older child psychologically for adoption. Each task involves sharing information with the youngster and providing opportunities for the child to express his feelings. First, children need information about their biological beginnings (Thoburn, 1988). They need to know about their birth parents and to understand why they no longer live with them. Feelings about this kind of information are usually strong and painful and need considerable time and support for adequate resolution. Second, when older children are being prepared for adoption they should be given a clear understanding of their history while they are still in the foster care system. It is important for them to know if the plan is to remain with their current family or if the adoption will involve another move. Information about the differences between biological, foster, and adoptive parent roles needs to be shared in ways geared to the child's ability to understand and constitutes the third task in the preparation process (Dromey, 1985).

The final two tasks involve dealing with separation and with feelings about succeeding in the future. Children need a chance to say actual or symbolic goodbyes to important past caretakers and to say hellos to future caregivers. They need an opportunity to sense that

103

important parent figures of the past wish them well and hope that they will be happy, successful, loved, loving, and safe in a permanent family setting. All of these tasks must be approached and carried out in a way that allows the worker to promote and strengthen the child's self-esteem.

HELPING CHILDREN UNDERSTAND THEMSELVES AND THEIR HISTORIES

Ideally, each child in any form of out-of-home placement would have a record which contains everything of importance in his or her life. A child's past is a part of his personality, and his feelings about what has happened in his life color the way in which he views the world. Links with the past—stories about things they did as young children; pictures of themselves with parent figures, pets, friends; trips to visit places they used to love—all help give children a sense of their own history and identity.

For those who have been in a series of foster homes, memories are sometimes painful and are often of events they did not fully understand. Especially for children who have been placed in a series of foster homes, many links with their culture and their past may have become dim and obscure. An important part of preparing a child for adoption is helping to unravel and understand what did happen and giving permission to express feelings about these events. As a child begins to understand and accept past events, he can begin to turn attention toward the present and the future. In that way, both the child and the caseworker gain: the caseworker gains a better understanding of the child and the child gains important knowledge of himself.

THE LIFE BOOK

A Life Book (Ryan and Walker, 1985) is one of the most helpful tools that the caseworker has available in getting to know a child and in helping him to understand birth family issues and foster family issues. In the process of constructing a Life Book the caseworker and child will likely form a stronger alliance, and at the same time it will help the child understand his history and will provide tangible links, such as pictures or letters, to the past. By providing a record of the child's growth and development, self-esteem may be enhanced, and in the future the child will be able to use the Life Book as a vehicle for sharing his or her past with others. It will also contribute to the adoptive family's understanding of the child's past and his uniqueness (Fahlberg, 1979a).

> *Example*: Janet, age six, was noted to have marked behavioral problems whenever she accompanied her foster mother to the grocery store. The foster mother described Janet as "like a different girl" then. She seemed preoccupied and would wander off during these outings. In the course of completing her Life Book, Janet and her caseworker learned that due to a very unusual set of circumstances, when Janet was age three, the birth mother had handed her over to the authorities at the parking lot of a grocery store of the same chain as the one the foster mother frequented. Once everyone understood that Janet's feelings about the parental separation were being resurfaced by trips to the grocery store, acknowledgment of her fears and appropriate emotional support could be provided.

HELPING THE CHILD COPE WITH FEELINGS ABOUT THE PAST

Many adults have a tendency to try to reassure children when they are feeling pain, sadness, or anger, but it is important not only to hear the child's pain but also to be accepting of the depth of that pain. The worker's task is to help children cope with their strong feelings, not to protect them from the feelings or minimize them by reassurance; to accept the intensity of the feelings while at the same time helping the child express them in appropriate and nonharmful ways (Jewett, 1982).

There are a variety of reasons why workers may have difficulty helping children process their feelings. If, for example, the worker was responsible for the decision to move the child, there is often the temptation to "sell" this decision to the child so that the worker does not have to feel responsible for the strong feelings stirred up by the separation. Workers themselves may have unresolved grief reactions;

they may have past life experiences that make them feel uncomfortable with strong expressions of anger or sadness. They may be fearful that the intensity of feelings will somehow damage the child, causing him or her to lose grip on reality or lose self-control in a dangerous way.

Anger, sadness, and despair are normal, appropriate responses to the grief process (Kübler-Ross, 1975). Children frequently cry or are angry. When children are allowed, even helped, to express their feelings instead of storing them up, the feelings somehow seem less overwhelming and will gradually assume more manageable proportions on a day-to-day basis.

> *Example*: Andrew, age four, had recently joined his adoptive family. They noted that at the end of any outing—a movie, a trip to the park, a doctor appointment—whether pleasurable or not, Andrew would scream and cry. Initially he would sound angry but gradually the crying would sound more like inconsolable grief. Their therapist helped the parents understand that going from one activity to another caused Andrew's feelings of separation and loss to resurface. By providing physical closeness and being supportive of his emotions at these times, the past separations were gradually resolved and the crying behaviors ceased.

If the messages that "everything is going to be all right" or "don't cry" or "don't be angry" or "stop, you are making me uncomfortable" are given, the expression of emotions is blocked, and the child's behaviors will likely worsen as the feelings are expressed through behavioral acting out (Fahlberg, 1981). In addition, children may feel that there is something wrong with them that causes them to feel the way they do, and they may grow to doubt the validity of their own feelings. This not only has a profound negative impact upon their self-esteem but interferes with their developing the ability to interpret feeling responses in themselves and others.

It is not unusual to work with children who have received strong messages that it is not acceptable to have negative feelings toward adults. Sometimes this is an outgrowth of past expressions of emotions in ways that were misunderstood, not recognized, or unacceptable. When children misbehave and are told, "don't do that," without the underlying feeling being recognized and accepted as separate from the unacceptable behavior, they frequently interpret the message to be, "don't have that feeling." In this case, children often resort to avoidance, and it is not surprising for the foster parent to report that the child does not seem to cry over things that cause most children of the same age to cry or that the child does not become angry in situations that would cause anger in most children. Or, often there may be a report that the youngster lacks awareness of or empathy toward the feelings of others.

EXPLAINING ADOPTION

Adoption is a way of providing a permanent parent–child relationship including full legal rights and responsibilities. Although many children have heard the terms *foster care* and *adoption* frequently, they do not understand what each of the terms means and the differences between the two. The caseworker should have a realistic understanding of the advantages of adoption to both the child and the family as compared to long-term foster care. In addition, these differences, with all the advantages and disadvantages of each, should be shared with the child.

IDENTIFYING THE PARENTAL ROLES

One way of explaining adoption to children is by dividing the parenting roles into three groupings—the birth parent, the legal parent, and the parenting parent (Spencer, unpublished).

Everyone has birth parents. Each child has one birth mother and one birth father (see Figure 9.1). No one can ever do anything to change the identity of these two individuals. In most countries children have someone who is identified as having legal custody of them. The legal parent makes the major decisions in a child's life and is accountable for seeing that the child's needs are met. The parenting parent role represents the adults who, on a day-to-day basis, meet the child's needs for nurturance and discipline. For many children one set of parents fill all three roles. The definition of adoption, however, is that the parenting parents are also the legal parents but not the birth parents (Fahlberg, 1979b).

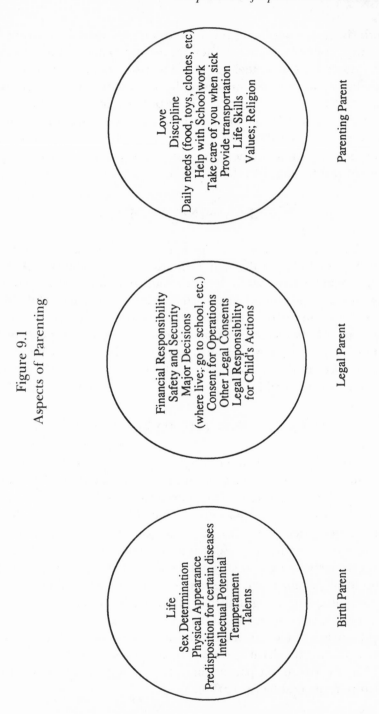

Figure 9.1
Aspects of Parenting

Birth Parent

Life
Sex Determination
Physical Appearance
Predisposition for certain diseases
Intellectual Potential
Temperament
Talents

Legal Parent

Financial Responsibility
Safety and Security
Major Decisions
(where live; go to school, etc.)
Consent for Operations
Other Legal Consents
Legal Responsibility
for Child's Actions

Parenting Parent

Love
Discipline
Daily needs (food, toys, clothes, etc.)
Help with Schoolwork
Take care of you when sick
Provide transportation
Life Skills
Values; Religion

Example: Adoption is being explained to Ron, age thirteen, who recently became legally free for adoption. His caseworker is explaining the difference between adoption and foster care. She explains that if Ron remains in foster care with his current parent substitutes the relationship will not be legally protected. For example, if Ron's foster dad has a job transfer to another state, the foster parents and Ron do not get to make the decision as to whether or not the latter accompanies the family. That decision will be up to the representative of the agency that holds legal custody of Ron. On the other hand, if Ron is adopted, then decision-making power will be held totally by the adoptive family.

MOVING TO ADOPTION

Preplacement visits with the adoptive parents provide the child with opportunities to address fears and worries about the unknown and to start building commitments for the future. During this same period there are opportunities for transferring attachment and initiating the grieving process. Sometimes no matter how well the caseworker expresses anticipation about a proposed adoptive move, the child only believes it when a family actually materializes.

At times of stress one's psychological defenses are not efficient. Feelings about past separations or losses are likely to resurface. This means that for some children feelings about leaving their birth parents or about moving from one foster home to another, feelings which have been buried, may begin to resurface. These feelings become "available," and children have another opportunity to work toward resolving them.

It is not uncommon for children who have successfully avoided meaningful conversation about birth parents to spontaneously start talking about them with the approach of placement in an adoptive home. The feelings stimulated by the move revive memories associated with previous ones. It becomes a time for again clarifying and exploring perceptions about the emotions related to previous losses.

Unfortunately, many times adults shy away from the opportunities for such resolution as they feel that the time of a move to an adoptive home is not a good time to focus on past issues. On the contrary, the time may be opportune for helping children explore long-ignored feelings so that they can resolve or say "goodbye" to some of the past and turn their attention to the present and future. Sharing the strong feelings involved in the resolution or healing process with the adoptive family may also facilitate beginning attachments with the adoptive family.

The importance of previous parents giving the child permission to become attached to adoptive parents cannot be overemphasized. Letters or audiotapes from previous parental figures, whether they be birth or foster parents, can aid the caseworker in helping the child resolve his feelings about separation. Communications that give messages such as: "We care about you. We no longer will be caring for you on a day-to-day basis, but we want things to go well for you in the future," are the most helpful types of communication. These messages can be listened to again or reread as the child attains new developmental levels and reinterprets past life events. Acceptance of the feelings increases the child's self-esteem and takes the primary focus off the negative behaviors which tend to lower self-esteem.

If foster parents meet the adoptive parents they can say to the child in believable, reassuring ways: "These are good people. They want you to be their child. We think things can work out well for all of you. We will be glad when you can feel close to them. We will always remember you and be happy for you." In this way foster parents clearly give their blessings to both child and new parents.

Another opportunity for positive transitioning occurs during the preplacement visiting period when the child's Life Book is openly shared with the adoptive parents. Children need to know that their adoptive parents want to share as much information as possible since they are going to be sharing a life together. While the caseworker and child share the Life Book with the adoptive parents, the caseworker can model acceptance of the child's strong feelings. During this period the child may be relieved to know that the caseworker has shared "the worst of the worst" of the child's behaviors with the prospective parents. Frequently children do not believe that anyone would really want them if they knew all of their past behaviors. The opportunity to see and hear that the adoptive parents are accepting in spite of negative behaviors in the past can help the child learn new behaviors. Adoptive parents' acceptance may prevent children from having to act their worst to see if the adoptive family will keep them "no matter what."

Example: Steven, age eight, was being placed for adoption. At age four, Steven, on the day of a move to the Green foster home, stood at the head of a flight of stairs laughing after tripping Mrs. G. down them. The latter, understanding that Steven could not learn to trust her if she could not care for herself, did not verbally confront him about this action but said, "In this home, we do not laugh when someone is hurt."

Steven demonstrated a variety of other severe behavioral problems while living in the Green home. After much work on the part of the foster family, the caseworker, and Steven, most of the inappropriate behavior had subsided prior to the selection of an adoptive family. However, Mrs. G. had overheard Steven relating the stairs episode to another foster child the week before the move.

On the day of the move to the adoptive family, with both foster and adoptive parents present, the caseworker initiated talk of the tripping episode. Steven was understandably apprehensive and anxious. However, when he found out that the adoptive family not only knew of this event, but still wanted to adopt him, he became more relaxed. The caseworker then went on to discuss with Steven and his various parent figures more appropriate ways for him to check out their ability to care for him.

As the child visits back and forth with the adoptive parents he prepares for saying a permanent and final goodbye to one living situation and a committed hello to another. Opportunities must be created for saying goodbye and hello to people, house, school, and neighborhood. At the time of the final move, the child needs to know that this time he will be staying in the new home. A formal, ritualized goodbye with the foster family helps make this evident to all. There also needs to be a formal, ritualized hello from the adoptive family (Jewett, 1978). A party for the new child and his family might be one way to mark this special occasion as something lastingly important. Some families involve their church or synagogue by asking that their family enlargement be announced in the newsletter or during a service.

SUMMARY

During the preparation process we try to help the child focus on expectations, hopes, fears, and worries about the past and the future. We work hard at helping children see that our alliance with them is to their benefit, that we are working together for a common goal. We support the child's right to a permanent family, while also having knowledge and feelings about past life events. We work to help raise self-esteem.

Areas of work the older child needs to complete in order to be prepared for a move into an adoptive family include understanding the past, understanding what adoption means, and positive transitioning. However, in some cases, regardless of how skilled the worker or how much time is invested, the child will not have completed all aspects of the preparation process. One or more tasks may be left incomplete, but often the child will find a way to complete the unfinished work once he joins the new family. Caseworkers can help adoptive families understand and predict difficulties by identifying the areas that need to be addressed. After placement, the adoptive parents can then help the healing process with a minimum amount of irritation and a maximum amount of understanding.

REFERENCES

Dromey, S. (1985), *Workbook: Preparation and Work with Children.* London: Fostering and Adoption Section, London Borough of Brent.

Fahlberg, V. I. (1979a), *Putting the Pieces Together: Helping Children When They Must Move.* National Resource Center for Special Needs Adoption.*

———— (1979b), *Putting the Pieces Together: Common Behavioral Problems of the Child in Placement.* National Resource Center for Special Needs Adoption.*

———— (1981), *Putting the Pieces Together: Child Development.* National Resource Center for Special Needs Adoption.*

Jewett, C. L. (1978), *Adoption for the Older Child.* Boston: Harvard Common Press.

*These three workbooks plus another have been combined in a single volume entitled *Putting the Pieces Together* published in London in 1988 by the British Association of Adoption and Fostering.

——— (1982), *Helping Children Cope with Separation and Loss.* Boston: Harvard Common Press.

Kübler-Ross, E. (1975), *Death: The Final Stage of Growth.* Englewood Cliffs, NJ: Prentice-Hall.

Ryan, R., & Walker, R. (1985), *Making Life Story Books.* London: British Agencies for Adoption and Fostering.

Spencer, M. (unpublished), Paper presented at an advisory board meeting at the Welfare League of America, 1978.

Thoburn, J. (1988), *Child Placement: Principles and Practice.* London: Wildwood.

10

Placing Children with Special Needs for Adoption

Gerry O'Hara, C.Q.S.W., Dipl.S.W.

Major changes have occurred in the last ten years in the way in which local authorities in the United Kingdom responsible for services to children and young people who come into care plan and look after such children. Strategies and policies designed to prevent many children coming into care lead to the discharge of those who do come into care as quickly as possible and use, instead, family care in the community as a direct alternative to a residential care one.

Children's homes have been closed and the resources were allocated to meet the needs of children and young people who come into care, the vast majority of whom stay for a short period only. In this chapter, I will outline, examine, comment on, and evaluate some of the policies and practices underpinning a particular aspect of these strategies, namely, the drive to place children who cannot grow up in their own families in adoptive families, or in permanent foster homes. There will be a brief overview of the historical background to the placement of children with special needs for adoption; an outline of the understanding and principles and planning for children in care; and a description of recruitment, preparation, and assessment methods. Finally, the need for supporting adoptive placements will be discussed.

HISTORICAL BACKGROUND

The plight of children growing up in residential care was high-lighted by Rowe and Lambert (1973), who revealed that large numbers of these children were growing up without meaningful links to a natural family. The study also indicated that the chance of children remaining in care beyond a few months was very high! The more recent Dartington Cohort study (Rowe, 1987) suggests that if children remain in care beyond five weeks, their chances of still being in care two years later increase significantly. The Rowe and Lambert study encouraged local authorities to examine the way they planned for children, particularly those who had no realistic chance of returning home. The Children's Act (1975) encouraged agencies to achieve permanence by means of either adoption or fostering for children who could not return to their own families. The shortage of babies for placement in the late 1960s, and the pioneering work of agencies in the United States and also in the United Kingdom, from the mid-1970s onwards combined to encourage the placement of older children for adoption in new families. Very rapidly the belief that any child could be placed in family care grew to the point where today the vast majority of all children and young people in care are in family care, usually some form of foster care, but for the small number who will never be able to return to their own families, adoptive homes are usually found. Residential care now is seen only as an option for a minority of teenagers, and usually not at all for children under twelve.

PLANNING FOR CHILDREN IN CARE

Permanency planning has been described by Maluccio, Fein, Hamilton, Kilier, and Ward (1980), Maluccio, Fein, and Olmstead (1986) among others, in the United States, and by MacKay (1980) in the United Kingdom. This approach to providing child care services and formulating clear plans stresses the following:

1. An emphasis on preventing children coming into care by maintaining family contact where possible.
2. If a child must come into care, restoration to his or her natural family should be the major focus of intervention.

3. If restoration to the natural family proves impossible within a time scale relevant to the needs of the child, then a permanent substitute family should be found.

This approach, which my own agency and others in the United Kingdom have embraced, stresses that time scales and planning for children in care should take into account the needs young children have for meaningful attachments and sources of nurturing. It acknowledges the dangers of children drifting into care, and accepts some of the known possibilities, but also the limitations, of social workers and other professionals in affecting change in extremely poorly functioning families. The need for clarity of purpose is emphasized, along with the explicit articulation of mutual rights and expectations of both the care agency and parents of the children. In other words, the biological families need to understand that the goal is to work toward returning their child to them, and that inaction may lead to the placing of their child with another family. Foster care has been reorganized to take account of these new directions. That is, it offers temporary family care to children who need this service until plans for their long-term future are sorted out. For the majority of children this involves very short stays of no more than a few months, but for others uncertainty about their future can mean that temporary foster care can last for two years or longer.

It is important to draw a distinction between teenagers and young children when planning. If a young child is unable to return to his own family and permanent placement is needed, then adoption is favored for most children under twelve. For teenagers, long-term fostering is preferred, with a clear expectation that the teenager should remain with the foster family for the rest of his childhood. However, it has been extremely difficult to find suitable and successful placements for teenagers and, therefore, something different was needed. A professional fostering service with high levels of training and support has been developed throughout the United Kingdom, and teenagers previously considered too difficult or too disturbed to be placed in families have found homes. Usually this fostering service meets the needs of young people who are still in touch with their own families and communities and who may well return there later.

Both Parker (1985) and Triseliotis (1986) have described changes in the population coming into care and pointed out that the majority are now teenagers and likely to have closer links with their parents. This is in contrast to the population of teenagers who were in care when our specialist fostering scheme was begun in the late 1970s to meet the needs of young people who were growing up within the care system. Parker (1985) points out that during the last twenty-five years the percent of children coming into care who are under five has fallen from 55 to 31 percent. Sixteen- and seventeen-year-olds now make up a quarter of the total population in care. The number of children in residential care has been dropping, but more significantly there has been a dramatic drop in those eleven and under.

One consequence of these developments is that social workers are now left to deal with an expanding number of older children who may or may not require new families. An increasing number of children and young people who come into care do not want permanent new families, especially not adoption, nor have their parents asked to give up the children permanently. Yet the problems of caring for twelve- to seventeen-year-olds who cannot return to their families are different from those posed by young children.

However, let us return to permanency planning for young children. Although an intensive examination of the permanency planning model is not realistic, we can look briefly at one or two ideas of Maluccio et al. (1986) which demonstrate something of the complexity underlying permanency planning: "Permanency planning is a systematic process of carrying out within a brief time period, a set of goal-directed activities designed to help children live in families that offer continuity of relationships with nurturing parents or caretakers and the opportunity to establish lifetime relationships" (p. 5). This involves the following:

- Protecting and promoting the welfare of all children, including handicapped, homeless, dependent, or neglected children.
- Preventing or assisting in the solution of problems which may result in the neglect, abuse, exploitation, or delinquency of children.
- Preventing the unnecessary separation of children from their families by identifying family problems, assisting families in resolving their problems, and preventing the break-up of the family where keeping the child in his family is both desirable and possible.
- Restoring to their families children who have been removed by providing services to the child and the family.

- Placing children in suitable adoptive homes in cases where restoration to the biological family is not possible or appropriate.
- Assuring adequate care for children away from their homes in cases where the children cannot be returned home or cannot be placed for adoption.

Whatever the arguments for or against a permanency planning model, agencies who have taken this approach have done so in order to have a more clearly articulated framework within which decisions can be made.

Let us now look at the various aspects of an adoption and permanent fostering program geared to recruiting, preparing, and assessing families to permanently care for children with special needs and to support those placements. Children with special needs are usually defined as those aged five to thirteen or fourteen, or part of a sibling group, or with a severe physical and/or mental handicap. However, most children aged two, three, or four who have lived with their own families for some time can also be described as having special needs.

PLACEMENT OUTCOMES

Jane Rowe (1987) has pointed out how complex assessing placement outcomes and interpreting breakdown rates can be. She also reminded us that foster care is underresearched, although the Berridge and Cleaver (1987) study in the United Kingdom is a major contribution in this area. Placement outcome in special needs adoption and permanent fostering is also underresearched in the United Kingdom but will be considerably helped by Rowe's recent study in six localities, Thoburn, Murdoch, and O'Brien (1986), and Thoburn and Rowe's (1988) outcome study of over 1,100 placements made by voluntary agencies in the United Kingdom. There are also useful contributions from different agencies such as Parents for Children (Reich and Lewis, 1986), Bernardos (Kerrane, Hunter, and Lane, 1980), Triseliotis and Russell's (1984) study of adoption and residential care outcome, and the Adoption Resource Exchange placements study (Wolkind and Kozaruk, 1980).

However, most of the permanent placement outcome studies are American, and a good deal of evaluation in the United Kingdom needs to be done if we are to continue with confidence what has amounted to a permanent family placement revolution. Our own study assessed the outcome of permanent placements by means of adoption or fostering, for children age two and older, made by the agency from September 1982 to September 1987. The children placed were a small proportion of the total number received into care (i.e., less than 5 percent) but included children who may well be described as among the most disturbed in the community. A recent survey of fifteen children placed by one adoption panel indicated that all but one had been subjected to some form of physical or sexual abuse. In contrast to the past, children placed permanently in the 1980s were much more likely to have spent less time in care; experienced repeated failed rehabilitation efforts; been abused, either physically or sexually; come from stormy and turbulent backgrounds; been part of a sibling group who will need to be placed with them; been less than ten years old; and received therapy of some kind.

Additionally there are a small number of severely or profoundly mentally handicapped children who require permanent care, which may or may not also involve contact with their family of origin. A number of agencies in the United States have set up permanency projects that work with children either in their own homes, away from their own homes but with a view to returning, or in permanent new families; and the evidence suggests that children can do very well in these permanent new families (Barth and Berry, 1987).

We decided to identify every breakdown from the placements made between September 1982 and September 1987. Breakdowns are defined as any placement which ceased before the child reached the age of sixteen, regardless of the circumstances. Other than in four cases where children returned to their birth family on a planned basis after short stays in new families, we have highlighted those placements made:

1. Directly for adoption
2. Placed on a fostering basis with the intention of permanency
3. Adopted after a period of fostering

We have excluded placements of babies or children under two. Every placement was formally made by one of the agency's five adoption panels (Table 10.1).

TABLE 10.1
Permanent Placements of Children Aged Two or Older,
by the Agency
September 1982–September 1987

	No. of Children	Percent
Total Placed for Adoption or Permament Fostering	335	
Disrupted Placements	39	11.3
Disruptions of Those 10/Older at Placement	—	21.7
Disruptions of Those 9/Younger at Placement	—	4.6
Total in Permanent Adoptions	290	86.0
Total in Permanent Fostering	45	14.0
New Adoptive Placements	262	90.4
Claims by Existing Caretakers	28	9.6
Approved Adoptional Allowances Paid	85	29.0
Total with Severe/Profound Mental Disabilities	39	—
Total Disruption in the Mental Disabilities Group	3	7.7
Total Disrupted Placements	39	11.3
Placed in Teenage Fostering Scheme	18	—
Replaced in Permanent Placements	11	—
In Temporary Foster Care	6	—
In Residential Care	3	—
In Supported Accommodation	1	—

PREPARING CHILDREN

Much has been said and written about the importance of working actively with children in care regardless of the plans for their future. The inspirational and imaginative work of American practitioners such as Fahlberg (1982) and Jewett (1978) particularly spring to mind. We have come a long way from the notion that protecting children means telling them as little as possible so as "not to worry them unduly." We know that fantasy is usually worse than reality, irrespective of how unpalatable that can often be. However, we must be realistic about our aims and must not fool ourselves into thinking we can cure deep-rooted emotional damage. If we accept that it can take a lifetime to overcome parental rejection, neglect, and abuse, then the practitioner's aspirations have to be as realistic as they are limited. What can we really do for these children?

• We can ensure that their temporary care needs are met and actively plan for their future.
• We can ensure that their point of view is heard and decisions are taken in their best interests.
• We can be honest with them about what had happened to them and their family.
• We can explore and acknowledge the range of feelings they have for their birth family.
• We can assess, acknowledge, and plan in a way that takes into account their significant attachments.
• We can explore their feelings/fantasies and aspirations about new families.

PREPARATION, TRAINING, AND ASSESSMENT

The dilemma for those working with prospective adopters or foster parents is how to find out what their needs and expectations are, and what they really feel and understand about the children available for placement and the often intractable problems these children bring with them. We are asking families who want to make a permanent commitment to a child with special needs to have respect for what the child is now and to value him enough to allow his individuality to impact on and make changes in the rest of the family, which will never be quite the same again. Most applicants, when faced with this challenge, might agree in principle but in reality will not be able to understand the hard work involved without a lot of help from the agency.

Therefore, part of the preparation and assessment process must be the acceptance by both the family and the agency worker of their shared responsibility for finding out together how the family really operates, where their areas of strength and vulnerability are, including the quality of nurturing and stimulation, the sources available for support and understanding, and their values and outlook. For example, are their values seen as immutable truths, or do these values change and develop with new experiences? They need to learn, with the agency's help, that their family is an operational system that will be very much changed by accepting a child with special needs. The assessment and preparation process should not be focused on looking at individual strengths and weaknesses, but should be looking in a nonjudgmental manner at the way the members of the family function together as a unit. The families can then begin to look at the ways the placement of a new child will initially upset the balance and ultimately and irrevocably alter the family structure. The major theoretical influences underpinning this approach to parent preparation were described by Hartman (1979). She defines the assessment process as a shared responsibility between social worker and family. As far as possible the worker's role is to help members of the family gain more information and understanding about their family as an operational system and to give them as much information as possible about adoption and fostering in general and about the particular child to be considered. On the basis of a deeper understanding of their family and of the demands of the task, the worker helps the family make a decision, and if they decide to adopt or foster, the worker helps them prepare. This model has been influenced by Satir's (1967, 1978) work and from the work of Berne (1964), but also, much closer to home, one of our own Scottish transactional analyst experts, Jean Morrison (1981).

Families need to understand that accepting a child with special needs in their family will provoke a crisis that needs to be met as a challenge and a chance to begin to understand themselves in a new way. This model promotes mutual responsibility for decision making but rejects self-selection. The placement agency has the enormous responsibility to make certain that families chosen have the potential to meet the needs of these children who have already been rejected and damaged. We have learned much from failed placements, both about children who should not have been placed and families who should not have been approved.

It is also important to stress that the agency will need not only to work with the families, but will be setting the tone for ongoing postplacement support work. It is now widely accepted that such support is necessary, even if it is only occasional. The children cannot simply be slotted into new families and left there without follow-up care. A former colleague described the "slotting in" theory as follows. "There may be a lot of trials, tribulations, testings and general traumas on all sides, but when all that is finally over the child should know that he is wanted and loved and will be able to become a full-fledged member of his new family" (personal communication).

The danger, of course, is that a child who is not grateful and who does not slot into his allotted place in his family may be rejected. Families need to have their expectations questioned, and workers may need to reexamine what it is families can be expected to give to children who have been damaged as a result of separation from their biological families.

We need to resist ideas which implicitly seek solutions and happy endings. What is required is a realistic and gritty approach to the challenge which will inform more relevant preparation and ongoing support of these placements, and we must acknowledge the agency's responsibility and its authority to accept or reject any applicant.

To summarize, the assessment and preparation process can be divided into three distinct stages:

1. The initial recruitment stage which involves giving information about children who need families and can be done at meetings with a number of families or individual family sessions.
2. The preparation training and self-assessment stage, which is done in small-group settings, usually lasting six sessions, and led by social workers and experienced adopters.
3. The home study and final decision-making stage described earlier.

THE NEED FOR SUPPORT

The remainder of this paper will concentrate on the sometimes harrowing experiences of families trying to meet the needs of children who have experienced early separation or loss and the range of services that are required to support families. The children placed will have difficulties in adjusting to their new families and will have a range of behaviors symptomatic of early experiences of separation and loss. Usually, the symptoms manifest themselves as behavioral problems, such as lying and stealing, which are the most commonly reported problems and persist several years after the adoption order. Children who have been adopted at school age often underachieve at school, frequently have problems in making and sustaining peer relationships, and can be seen as not trusting their adoptive parents.

This accepted "practice wisdom" view has been borne out by a study in my own agency (Yates, 1985). Although overall the children were seen as "improved from the time they were in care with general progress and happiness noted," adoptive parents worried about deep-rooted problems concerning security and trust. Spaulding for Children (Donley, 1975) expected the families would have difficulty in raising their adopted children throughout childhood and possibly into adult life.

Other authors considered postplacement support to be essential for the successful continuation of many placements. They emphasized the partnership between social worker and family as being vital, that there was a need for strong ongoing support by the adoption agency to be available (Donley, 1975; Jewett 1978; MacCaskill, 1985; Thoburn, Murdoch, and O'Brien, 1985).

If one can accept Germain's (1979) description of the task facing children who are placed in permanent new families, then the need for support is obvious. He says, "The child who must be placed in substitute care at any age, and regardless of the reason, is torn from the biological and symbolic context of his identity. No matter how nurturing the substitute care, the child's ongoing task will always be to reweave the jagged tear in the fabric of his identity to make himself whole again" (p. 82). Much has been written in the last few years about working with children to explain their past and to help them begin to understand and come to terms with it.

A lot of hard work has been done with substitute families to help them develop the insights vital to sustaining placements. However, if we accept that it is a lifetime task to overcome parental rejection and/ or abuse, and to work out an identity in such circumstances, then both families and children require a great deal of help. As one adopter recently said:

> When the adoption agency takes us on we have pride in being coping adults, in coping families, and we are ready for the challenge of living with the damaged child. The reality can be frightening. Our marriage relationships become strained as we blame each other when we are personally overstretched. We see our existing children display anxiety as they watch our coping levels fall. All very confidence lessening. What distresses us most of all is to be regarded suddenly as a noncoping family instead of a family under stress, which, if you think about it, had been very predictable. We need help where we are, on the basis that something was bound to happen when a hurt child joined our family. In fact, if the family is working, this ought to be showing. We like to know that the workers who help us, respect us. The more we learn to love our children, the more it seems to us that we cannot cure emotional handicap. When more and more is demanded of us by our children at a deep level, we have higher expectations of our helpers. We seem to meet two crises times in our placements. Around two years when we begin to sense the depth of the hurt to our children and again around four years when we are undermined by fear of the future, and by fatigue. At these points our workers should know that we will need to turn to them. We need quality help to work through our panic and to look at ways of alleviating the tiredness and stress.

Catherine MacCaskill (1985) in her research found the two-year mark again to be a significant stage in the life of an adoption placement when children thrive. However, beyond two years the reality of some of the problems begin to be seen. Families seem then to have to make an enormous adjustment in terms of their expectations. The child is not going to be anything like the child they dreamed they would have, and time may be running out.

What then are families saying they need and what supports can be developed? Perhaps the greatest service to families will be to acknowledge that in the main they are well-functioning units who, when they adopt a child with special needs, will from time to time function poorly because of the problems these children bring to placement. It is very easy when families present difficulties to blame them for the problems and to vent our disappointment on them for their failure to achieve a miracle cure.

The small but growing body of research emerging in this field suggests that children can do remarkably well in new families, but the cost is high and not all expectations will be met.

Adoptive parents should be mobilized to develop relevant services to make these placements work. It might be best to finish with another quote from an adoptive parent: "We can remember years back when failure was a crime, when all the people who were with us in success would vent their guilty anger on us in failure." Social workers really ought to know better because that is what society does to them so unfairly when they fail to work miracles. Perhaps the biggest achievement that has gone into adoption from both sides of the partnership is the recognition that adoption is not in itself an end. "We are on a journey and it will not always be appropriate for us to be with them all the way. If we have begun to address the issue of responsibility and have introduced the concept of choice, then this may have been good enough." Most adopters struggle to find and accept that base line, but once reached the children may at last have the conditions which allow them to be people in their own right.

REFERENCES

Barth, R. P., & Berry, M. (1987), Outcomes of child welfare services under permanency planning. *Soc. Serv. Rev.*, 61:entire issue.

Berne, E. (1964), *The Games People Play*. New York: Grove Press.

Berridge, D., & Cleaver, H. (1987), *Foster Home Breakdown*. London: Basil Blackwell.

Children's Act, The (1975), London: Her Majesty's Stationery Office.

Donley, K. S. (1975), *Opening New Doors*. London: BAAF.

Fahlberg, V. I. (1982), *Helping Children When They Must Move*. London: BAAF.

Germain, C. B. (1979), *Ecology and Social Work Practice: People and Environments*. New York: Columbia University Press.

Hartman, A. (1979), *Finding Families*. London: Sage Publications.
Jewett, C. L. (1978), *Adopting the Older Child*. Boston: Harvard Common Press.
Kerrane, A., Hunter, A., & Lane, M. (1980), *Adopting Older and Handicapped Children: A Consumer's View of the Preparation, Assessment, Placement, and Post Placement Support Services*. Social Work Paper 14. London: Barnardo.
MacCaskill, C. (1985), Parents' perceptions of post-placement services. Paper presented at Conference, March 15, 1983. Post-Placement Support Services. London: BAAF.
MacKay, M. (1980), Planning for permanent placement. *Adopt. & Foster.*, 4:19–24.
Maluccio, A. N., Fein, E., Hamilton, V. J., Kilier, J., & Ward, D. (1980), *Beyond Permanency Planning*. London: Tavistock.
——— ——— Olmstead, K. A. (1986), *Permanency Planning for Children*. London: Tavistock.
Morrison, J. C. (1981), *A Tool for Christians*. Edinburgh: Church of Scotland.
Parker, R. (1985), *Child Care in the Melting Pot: Child Care in Perspective*. Edinburgh: SCAFA.
Reich, D., & Lewis, J. (1986), Placements by parents for children. In: *Finding Families for "Hard to Place" Children*, ed. P. Wedge & J. Thoburn. London: BAAF.
Rowe, J. (1987), Fostering outcomes—Interpreting breakdown rates. *Adopt. & Foster.*, 11:43–48.
——— Lambert, L. (1973), *Children Who Wait*. London: ABAFA.
Satir, V. (1967), *Finding Families*. London: Sage Publications.
——— (1978), *People Making*. London: Souvenir Press.
Thoburn, J., Murdoch, A., & O'Brien, A. (1985), Routes to permanence, CWAH evaluation. *Adopt. & Foster.*, 9:50–55.
——— ——— ——— (1986), *Permanence in Child Care*. London: Basil Blackwell.
——— Rowe, J. (1988), Outcome in permanent placements. *Adopt. & Foster.*, 12:29–34.
Triseliotis, J. (1986), Older children in care. In: *Finding Families for "Hard to Place" Children*, ed. P. Wedge & J. Thoburn. London: BAAF.
——— Russell, J. (1984), *Hard to Place: The Outcome of Adoption and Residential Care*. London: Heinemann.
Wolkind, S., & Kozaruk, A. (1980), "Hard to place" children with medical and developmental problems. In: *Finding Families for "Hard to Place" Children*, ed. P. Wedge & J. Thoburn. London: BAAF.
Yates, P. (1985), *Post-Placement Support for Adoptive Families of Hard to Place Children*. Unpublished M.S.C. Thesis, University of Edinburgh, Scotland.

Part V

Independent Adoption

11

Independent Adoptions and the "Baby Market"

William Pierce, Ph.D., Robert J. Vitillo, A.C.S.W.

Given the imbalance between the number of healthy infants who are available for adoption today and the number of couples and singles, married or otherwise, who are seeking to adopt, it is not surprising that some people are attempting to address that imbalance by means of a "baby market" or other alternative means to locate adoptable children.

The imbalance between available infants and people wanting to adopt is not a recent phenomenon, nor is it limited to the United States and other Western nations. Newspaper and other media files in the United States clearly demonstrate that infertility was sufficiently widespread even fifty years ago to lead to a number of incidents involving "baby buying." Both at that time and today, some people resort to this market because they are frustrated at being unable to adopt through voluntary or governmental agencies. Others resort to

Authors' Note: The comments contained in this paper may not necessarily represent the views of the National Committee For Adoption, its Board of Directors, its member agencies, or its individual members.

private or nonregulated adoptions, however, because they would be rejected by adoption agencies due to problems such as alcoholism, insufficient length or stability in their marriages, and physical or emotional illness and age.

Age of the adoptive parents is an important factor and Kadushin (1980), in his list of the factors that agencies should take in consideration in selecting among adoptive applicants, points out that "the age of the parents in relation to the age of the child's is the number one factor" (p. 565). The adoptive dyad/triad should "not depart too much from the model of the biological parent–child relationship . . . a common sense practice of a rough limit of 40 years difference between the age of the person to be adopted and the adopter should be observed" (van Loon, 1990, p. 104).

EVOLUTION OF INDEPENDENT ADOPTIONS

Let us now examine how independent adoptions actually evolved in the United States. For many decades preceding the enactment of comprehensive adoption laws, the usual way to arrange adoptions was through independent or "direct" means, since there were no statutes governing the placement of infants by agencies or individuals. Adoption was seen as a relatively simple matter—a person with legal custody of a child would transfer that custody to another person or couple, with or without the assistance of an outside party. Many adoptions were carried out following the same procedures governing the transfer of real property, and children were deeded to others as chattels.

As time went on, some sensitivity was developed to the needs of the adoptable children themselves. They were no longer seen as mere commodities, or pieces of property, to satisfy the wants of infertile couples for extra "hands" to manage their land holdings or for legal heirs to preserve the family's material possessions. Thus, in 1851, the State of Massachusetts passed a law to regulate the adoption of unrelated infants. Until that time, because adoption was not known in English common law, children were transferred by other means, such as deed, or were informally made a part of the family. In subsequent years, especially during the decade of the 1920s, each state enacted similar legislation to govern adoptions.

For the most part, however, these regulations did not exclude the involvement of independent practitioners from the adoption process. Since lawyers generally drew up contracts for property transfer, they were asked to handle the legal technicalities of the transfer of children in adoptions, even after adoption legislation was developed and agencies began to attend to the social work aspects of such service. As late as 1951, 53 percent of the adoptions of unrelated children were handled by those in the "independent" sector, comprised largely of attorneys, physicians, and members of the clergy (*Adoption Factbook*, 121, 1985).

When the field of adoption became more professionalized and when social work emerged as the leading profession to provide problem pregnancy counseling and adoptive placement services, the percentage of children placed by public and other agencies increased. By 1971, at the peak of this latter trend, about 21 percent of adoptions were arranged by the independent sector. At that time, public agencies accounted for 36 percent of adoptive placements, and voluntary agencies accounted for 43 percent of these placements.

At this point in the history of adoptions, a critical change took place. Abortions were becoming legalized in many large states, and fewer babies were available for adoption. In 1970, the peak number of adoptive placements was reached at 89,200. By 1971, the number of adoptions fell by nearly 10 percent, to 82,800; by 1972, the number fell by 20 percent, to 65,335. We have evidence of this decreasing trend until 1975, when an estimated 47,400 adoptive placements were made. After that year, the United States government terminated its collection of statistics on adoptions.

During this same period, a variety of changes began to occur in the agencies offering pregnancy counseling and adoption services. First, a substantial number of agencies were staffed by professionals who decided that, since abortion was now legal, it should be offered as an option equal or in preference to adoption. Many social workers rationalized: "Given the option of legalized abortion, why would anyone carry a pregnancy to term, unless she consciously or unconsciously wished to raise the child?" Second, in an attempt to do some contingency planning, many agency directors decided to close down their maternity residences and adoption programs in anticipation of the decreased demand for their services because of the widespread use of methods of contraception and the legalization of abortion. Thus the staff, buildings, and other resources of many adoption agencies were committed to alternative programs.

Also, during this time a number of factors contributed to the increasing rate of infertility in the United States. These factors include the side effects of some contraceptive measures (e.g., the pelvic inflammatory disease caused by intrauterine devices), an increase in sexually transmitted diseases as a result of promiscuity, delayed marriage, and various environmental factors.

Thus we note that, while the number of adoptable babies and agencies providing adoption services were declining, the number of couples experiencing infertility (and seeking to form a family by means of adoption) was increasing. Frustrated at not being able to adopt from traditional agency sources, many infertile couples turned to the only option available—lawyers who had long been involved in adoptions in most states and who were willing to find adoptable babies for a fee.

Lawyers were able to help couples who wished to adopt a child in part because they did not experience the same professional constraints as did social service agencies, which are bound by the ethic of the "best interests" of the child. In 1967, the Child Welfare League finalized its *Standards for Adoption Services* (1968), which stated: "The main purpose of an adoption service should not be to find children for families." Most agencies still adhere to this ethic, which certainly has the full support of the National Committee For Adoption.

Nonagency, independent practitioners, however, can legally contract with families to find them a child. They can accept fees to represent the interests of their clients alone (the adopting parents) to the exclusion of, or in preference over, the interests of the other parties (i.e., the biological parents and/or the child). The task of these independent practitioners is quite simple: find a child and, preferably through legal means, transfer the child into the custody of the adopting person(s).

CALIFORNIA ADOPTION LAW

As an example, let us review some events that occurred in California. This state's adoption law specified that only agencies could legally arrange adoption, unless the parties to the adoption already knew each other, in which case an attorney could be involved in the adoption to ensure that the necessary legal steps had been taken to protect the rights of the child. The theory behind this provision in the law was that should a pregnant woman know a couple who would, in her judgment, be able to provide a good home for her child, she ought to be able to place that child with the couple without any interference from a state agency or other outside group. Thus, it was presumed that this type of adoption would take place only among close friends in the community—contacts from work, school, and religious institutions—and there would be relatively few. But, a loophole in the law was found. Attorneys could be involved in adoptions as long as the parties "knew each other." Thus, it was reasoned, attorneys could provide adoption services as long as they arranged for their clients to meet, talk, or otherwise "know" each other. In this manner, the confidentiality which had been assured and expected in agency adoptions was degraded and rejected by the independent practitioners.

In the United States, and most especially in California, where being "open" is a virtue, while being "closed" or "closed-minded" about anything is unfashionable, the lawyers have capitalized on the situation which has just been presented. They promote the only kind of adoptions they are legally allowed to perform as being "better" since they conform to the American tradition of being "open." They claim to offer their clients an added advantage—in "open" adoptions, the adoptive parents could know a great deal about, and possibly even meet, the biological mother of the child. Thus, the independent practitioners could give their clients, particularly the more sophisticated and wealthy among them, the chance to examine not merely the baby, but also the baby's mother, before they would be expected to commit themselves or their money.

RIGHTS OF THE UNWED FATHER

Other advantages were also found to promoting independent adoptive placements of children. The 1972 U.S. Supreme Court decision *Stanley v. Illinois* declared that certain unwed fathers were entitled to notice of custody and adoption proceedings relating to their children. Agencies in particular felt constrained to follow the dictates of the Supreme Court, and, in many cases, went beyond the Supreme Court's instructions to seek contact with biological fathers. Many young women feared or refused to name the fathers of their babies and thus were discouraged from seeking agency services. Some of these women felt compelled to resort to abortions or sought help from independent adoption placement agents—clergy, physicians, or lawyers. Once again, independent practitioners were able to use the fine points of the law to their own benefit and to help pregnant women who wished to avoid naming the biological fathers.

Many pro-life groups, whose primary concern was to deter women from abortions, set up their own child placement services and promised their clients absolute confidentiality without pressure to name the biological father. Most of these pro-life groups are not licensed as professional adoption agencies nor do they conform to most licensure standards. The Supreme Court decision, therefore, had the unintended effect of bringing a substantial portion of women in problem pregnancy situations into contact with individuals or groups who promised absolute confidentiality—physicians, clergy, pro-life groups, and attorneys.

REDUCTION IN FINANCIAL SUPPORT OF MATERNITY HOMES

Another important factor that assisted independent practitioners after abortion was legalized was a reduction in financial support for maternity home services. While abortion was illegal, there was little alternative except to pay for maternity home costs of pregnant women, especially those who were adolescents, even though the costs were substantial. When the less expensive option of abortion became available, funding for residential maternity services was terminated or shifted to other services. Many agencies exhausted their reserve funds and then became incapable of absorbing the costs of residential maternity services. It is important to note here that adoptive parents were not allowed to pay for the prenatal costs incurred at maternity homes. On this point, the Child Welfare League in *Standards for Adoption Services* (1968) declared: "the cost of services rendered prior to the decision that adoption is a suitable plan should not be included in computing the cost of adoption" (1968, p. 66). Consequently, agencies encouraged their pregnant clients to turn to public welfare benefits. The resulting mix of services provided was more limited, of poorer quality, and often placed the client in a degrading situation before the public welfare system. Not surprisingly, many clients opted out of agency services and turned to the independent sector, where they would be treated like any other pregnant women and would receive equitable services.

ADVANTAGES ENJOYED BY INDEPENDENT PRACTITIONERS

When we compare independent practitioners with agencies in the fields of maternity services and adoptions, we note that the former have clearly enjoyed three major advantages. First, the "independents," especially lawyers, could aggressively seek out children for clients, and often use newspaper advertising to do so. Second, independent practitioners could promise a pregnant woman that she would not have to name the father of the child. Third, a pregnant woman could be assured a wider range of private medical and other services—all paid for by the adopting couple. For these reasons, independent placements have far outpaced agency-related placements during the 1980s. This is not surprising if we consider the classic marketing rule—unregulated industries always drive out regulated industries.

What is so unfair about the competition offered to agencies by the independent practitioners? First, the lack of regulation often leads to an overall lack of accountability. Clients, both biological and adopting parents, can easily become the "victims" of these independent practitioners. Second, these practitioners may be trained in one profession—law, medicine, or religion—but, for the most part, they have not been trained to respond to the intricate psychological and social needs which emerge in all members of the adoption circle. Finally, the "independents" are not bound by a specific code of ethics which focuses on the interests of all members of the adoption circle but is most especially concerned with the "best interests" of the child.

One might expect the regulated portion of the adoption field, the agencies—especially through their board members and other lay and professional leaders—to resist such an invasion of their field of practice. By and large, they have not done so. Until the advent of the National Committee For Adoption and its promulgation of a more modern and practical set of standards, very few agencies sought to advertise the high quality of their services. There were also very few efforts to redress the imbalance between the rights of biological mothers and those of the biological fathers. In fact, lawyers pressed their advantage by writing into a Model Adoption Act, endorsed by the Family Law Section of the American Bar Association, a number of provisions that would make it even easier for nonagency placing agents to deal with fathers' rights and more difficult for agencies to do so. Finally, many agencies that have survived must limit themselves to funding from the public welfare benefits that are received by individual clients. Only a minority of agencies, especially those affiliated with the National Committee For Adoption, endorse the use of adoptive parents' fees for prenatal and other prerelinquishment costs.

There is no question that most independently arranged adoptions turn out well. The issue here is which system addresses better the needs of the people involved in the adoption process. Kadushin (1980) reports that ". . . the success rates of such [independent] placements were generally high, *although not as advantageous as agency placements* . . ." (p. 515), about 25 percent of those adoptions were found to be "definitely unsatisfactory" (p. 519), and 13 percent "legally questionable" (p. 513).

Kadushin lists five main advantages of agency adoptions:

1. A professional staff with special knowledge of adoption problems.
2. A pool of adoptive homes from which to select the one that meets the needs of a particular child.
3. Consultants—psychiatrists, psychologists, geneticists, pediatricians—who aid agency staff in dealing with special problems.
4. Uniform records of all transactions in line with the agency's accountability to the community.
5. Alternative resources—foster homes, institutions and so on—that are available to care for the child while he is awaiting adoption, if placement fails, or if the child proves to be unplaceable [p. 515].

INTERNATIONAL ADOPTIONS

In other countries, similar competition between agencies and independent practitioners is taking place. An international market has developed, with cooperation across national boundaries, between attorneys and others who seek to meet the demands of prospective adopters, often without regard for ethical or legal requirements. "Prices may vary between $10,000 and $15,000 but can sometimes be substantially higher. The profiteers are generally neither the biological parents nor the adopters but the intermediaries . . ." (van Loon, 1990, p. 90).

In many countries where nonagency adoptions are legal, the lawyers operate in a manner similar to that of their counterparts in the United States. It has been reported by many that payments are made to biological mothers and to ensure that a child is turned over to the adoptive parents. Fraud and duress are accomplished, van Loon explains, in this manner: "A convincing intermediary (often a female scouting about children) may persuade a pregnant young woman or young mother that a great life awaits her child in a rich country, will reassure the mother and help dispel any feelings of guilt and . . . get her to accept money so as to eliminate any suspicion of kidnapping" (p. 86).

One book, entitled *Beating the Adoption Game* (Martin, 1980), has been published in the United States to offer advice to those who want to adopt from Latin America. It has this to say about payments made to judges and to biological mothers in Mexico:

> [T]he Mexican contact woman was able to prepare them and inform them how things were done in Mexico. The lawyer whom they had met was prepared to handle the case in court. He was also the one who was to give some extra money to the judge to make certain the adoption was expedited. This same lawyer also had the birthmother sign the relinquishment papers. At the last minute, the birthmother said she wanted something in exchange for relinquishing the baby. This was expected. The lawyer and the birthmother agreed that a sewing machine would be a gain exchange. . . . The payments made to all these people are highly irregular to our way of thinking . . . it makes the adoption look like an illegal or black market adoption. Yet in Mexico there was nothing irregular at all [p. 169].

The practices we have been reviewing with regard to domestic adoptions in the United States and international adoptions, though highly questionable, would probably be considered technically legal. "Gray market" adoptions might be judged "legal" but definitely include unethical elements. In this category, we would put those adoptive placements which involve the pirating of clients. It is not unusual, for example, for independent practitioners to contact a resident client in a maternity home or a pregnant student in a college dormitory in order to lure her away from services provided by a social service agency and into an independent placement arrangement. Then there are "black market" adoptions, which use methods clearly proscribed by law. In some of these black market adoptions, the biological mother might be furnished with an automobile or a college scholarship, or the placing agent may receive a fee that far exceeds the efforts expended in making adoption arrangements. Many independent adoptions by U.S. couples are known to cost $20,000 or more.

Adoption professionals, governments, and the community at large are pressing for preventive steps against such exploitation of pregnant women, the adoptable children, and the adopting parents. Biological mothers, moreover, should be entitled only to reimbursement of appropriate and reasonable expenses. All unethical agencies and individuals in the adoption field should be barred from making further placements. Those who violate adoption statutes must be prosecuted to the fullest extent allowed by each nation's laws. Governments should undertake an extensive review of existing adoption laws and should develop new laws to meet the current challenges faced in this complex field.

We might note here that many of the above-mentioned principles are contained in an important document, approved by the United Nations General Assembly on February 4, 1987, and entitled *Declaration on Social and Legal Principles Relating to the Protection and Welfare of Children, with Special Reference to Foster Placement and Adoption Nationally and Internationally*. At a June 1987 meeting in Vienna, adoption professionals from various parts of the world subscribed to these principles and recommended that they be used by all governments and social welfare organizations alike in a timely review of adoption laws, policies, and practices. Such a review is now under way by The Hague conference and the paper by van Loon (1990) was prepared for the sixty countries expected to participate in a three-year effort to draft workable norms and procedures, coupled with an effort to draft a convention to which the various states can prescribe. A major goal of those who will be participating is to examine the role of independent adoption vis à vis agency adoption. As van Loon observes, "There is a growing tendency in many countries to discourage independent adoptions (also referred to as 'direct,' 'private' or 'parent-initiated' adoptions) and to promote the intermediary services of adoption agencies" (p. 38).

Eventually, adoptions in all countries should be under the auspices of properly regulated and monitored social service agencies employing trained, professional staff. While many of those engaged in independent adoptions are honest and well-meaning persons, better services can be provided to all involved if these individuals—whether lawyers, physicians, clergy, or others—would work as a team within the framework of an ethical agency. We would not want delicate surgery to be performed by amateur, freelance medics outside hospital settings. We would not want court cases to be tried by any two attorneys or advocates who could find any judge to sit and hear them. We must insist that children, pregnant women, and families who are members of the adoption circle receive appropriately monitored, high quality services from licensed, professional social welfare institutions.

To be fair, we must comment here on the fact that many of the more questionable practices of some independent adoption intermediaries are now being utilized by licenced agencies, including some not-for-profit, voluntary agencies. The temptation to take "short-cuts" of all sorts is not limited to independent adoptions practitioners alone. No exclusive claim to virtue can be made by agencies. Indeed some of the more interesting case histories cited by Baker (1978) involved agencies that were organized as nonprofit charities. Baker writes: "One of the most convoluted adoption agency–foundation–corporation chains in the world may be the one run by Chicago attorney and adoption entrepreneur Seymour Kurtz. The forty-seven year old Kurtz heads—and in some cases is the sole staff for—five agencies, foundations, and corporations in Illinois, Delaware, Mexico, and the Netherlands" (pp. 80–81).

The situation today, sadly, is that questionable agencies as well as questionable independent adoption practitioners have, in an increasingly deregulated atmosphere, grown in numbers, influence, and affluence. Agencies that found themselves facing tough and sometimes unfair competition decided to fight "fire with fire" and now it is frequently difficult to tell the two competitive marketing approaches apart. Indeed, increasingly lawyers are incorporating as agencies and agencies are linking up with lawyers.

SUMMARY

The desperation of those who want to adopt and the willingness of some individuals to profit from that desperation comprise a formula for disaster in the adoption field. The serious lack of accountability in many independent adoptions (and increasingly in agencies as well) can easily lead to additional "baby selling and brokering," which has plagued many nations for too long. Such brokering claims many victims. It corrupts judges and public officials. It makes adoptive couples susceptible to extortion and blackmail. It demeans biological mothers. It insults national pride to suggest that a country's ethics may be waived for the right price. It can even force governments to consider banning all adoptions, especially those arranged on an international level, even those which have been pursued in full compliance with ethical and legal norms.

Only carefully detailed regulations and laws can begin to address the rampant abuses in the adoption field—a field which has been rendered more susceptible to abuse because of its present strong reliance on independent practitioners. These regulations are required both on the national and international levels and must apply to agency and independent adoptions alike. It is our firm belief that social service professionals, most especially those working in licensed agency settings, must stand ready to advocate for and then assume their rightful role as the leading agents in adoptions and as the guarantors of the rights and interests of all members of the adoption circle, with particular attention to the needs of the children.

REFERENCES

Baker, N. C. (1978), *Baby Selling: The Scandal of Black-Market Adoption*. New York: Vanguard.

Child Welfare League of America (1968), *Standards for Adoption Services*. New York: Child Welfare League of America.

Kadushin, A. (1980), *Child Welfare*, New York: Macmillan.

Martin, C. B. (1980), *Beating the Adoption Game*. La Jolla,CA: OakTree Publications.

National Committee For Adoption (1985), *Adoption Factbook*. Washington, DC: National Committee For Adoption.

van Loon, J. H. A. (1990), *Report on Intercountry Adoption*, presented at The Hague Conference on Private International Law, The Hague, Netherlands, April. Unpublished report.

12

Private and Independent Adoptions in Greece Through the Agency of Social Welfare

Elpetha Panera, S.W.

In Greece, there are two types of agencies through which one can adopt a child:

1. There are the welfare agencies, which are under the supervision of the Ministry of Health and Social Welfare. The Metera Babies Center (see chapter 14) and the Public Institution of the Social Welfare Association (known in Greece as PIKPA) belong in this category. These agencies provide a comprehensive and holistic approach to the adoption process. Social workers conduct the initial meetings and interviews with the biological and prospective adoptive parents. At the same time, since these agencies also operate as baby centers, they have an updated file on the baby's medical and family history that facilitates the placement and matching of the child with an adoptive family. Professionals from these agencies keep close contact with the biological mother, pre- and postnatally, and help her during the pre- and postadoption adjustment period until adoption is finally legalized through the court.

2. There are the social welfare agencies, which are branches of the Ministry of Health and Social Welfare, and which address only

private or independent adoptions. In this chapter I will discuss adoption through the social welfare agencies, which in addition to offering adoption services are also involved in other intervention programs, such as aiding families in crisis, marital problems, abused women and children, child protective services, aid for handicapped people, services for the elderly, and psychiatric problems including interviewing, consulting, and processing the administrative work for hospitalization.

ADOPTION THROUGH THE SOCIAL WELFARE AGENCIES

The process of adoption through social welfare agencies follows a standard procedure: the prospective parents find a newborn baby through a private clinic, a hospital, the biological parents themselves, or through friends. Then, they approach the agency to assist them with the legal procedures. The social workers create a file with the necessary documents for the court hearing since, according to Greek law, adoption can only be legalized by the court and through a social welfare agency. This procedure requires a minimum involvement on the part of the agency; that is, only a home study and some other administrative work. There is no consultation or evaluation of the two sets of parents to determine the readiness either of the prospective parents' ability to assume the parental role, or the biological parents' feelings about giving away their baby. In addition, by the time they start the adoption procedure, they may already have had the baby in their home for several months, and sometimes it is too late to intervene and help solve maladaptive situations.

In this type of adoption we may encounter one or more of the following negative consequences: adoption may not be the right thing or a couple may not be ready to become parents, or may not be suitable parents for that particular baby. They may have never had the opportunity to explore the motives that prompted them to adopt a baby, their fears of becoming parents and raising a child, or their expectations about themselves and the child.

The biological parents or the unmarried mother do not have the opportunity to talk with a professional at a time when the psychological conflict is at its peak about whether adoption is the best solution for their baby. They are not helped to prepare for the separation if they opt to give up the baby for adoption.

In independent adoptions, there is great pressure on both sets of parents to act quickly. The biological parents must give up the baby immediately after birth, for if the mother is unmarried she may well be afraid that she will be rejected by her family, friends, or the community in general. She may also not have a steady job or a place to live with her baby. For married people who place their children for adoption, most are couples who have separated or are living apart and the woman has a lover. The latter may not be interested in having a child and, to preserve the relationship with her lover and to avoid legal problems with her estranged husband, the woman may give the baby away as soon as possible after birth. Or a married woman with older children may feel ashamed of having a newborn baby, so she spreads the rumor that her baby was born dead and gives it up for adoption. We also encounter low income families with many children who feel they are unable to raise another child and, therefore, place the baby for adoption.

The pressure prospective adoptive parents undergo is great, because in addition to the inquiries of the social workers and court, they have to accept the baby right away, otherwise the next couple on the waiting list will get the child. This fact may adversely affect those prospective parents who may not be quite ready to assume the parental role and/or may be fearful of the responsibility. They must take the newborn baby immediately from the clinic, since there are no facilities to keep babies longer than three or four days after birth. Thus, prospective parents know very little about a child's health and history and may not be prepared to face mental retardation or a developmental impairment that the child may present in the months or years to follow.

Before or during the court procedure, the biological parents may have second thoughts and want the baby back or may deny having given their consent. There have been cases where the biological parent demanded money from the adoptive parents prior to their consent. An example of the latter is that of a thirty-two-year-old divorced woman, mother of two boys, who became involved with a drug dealer and who had been incarcerated several times. The woman gave birth to a baby boy who was given up for adoption. At the hearings (and there were several) she asked to have her baby back and refused to consent to the adoption. After every hearing she would ask for money from the adoptive couple with the promise that she would give her consent at the next hearing. In this case, although social workers guessed what was going on, they found themselves at an impasse because they had to prove to the judge that blackmailing was taking place. This was difficult because of the secrecy of both sets of parents. It is illegal to pay money to obtain a child, and both the adoptive and the birth couple were afraid they would be prosecuted. In this particular case the judge was able to understand what was going on and the adoption was completed.

However, adoptive parents often refuse to consider all these difficulties and complications because their wish to have a baby immediately is so great, especially since so few children are available for adoption. Thus, prospective adoptive parents prefer independent adoptions because: (1) It is much easier to get a baby through independent channels. (2) They may have been rejected by adoption agencies because they were found to be too immature to raise a child, were too old, or because their reasons for wanting to adopt were found to be self-serving (i.e., they wanted to save their crumbling marriage through the acquisition of a child), or for reasons of inheritance (they do not want their siblings or other relatives to possess their estate after their death), or because they want someone to care for them in old age. (3) Adoption laws do not discourage a woman from giving up her child for adoption, nor is there a special requirement for preparation of both biological and prospective parents prior to independent adoptions. The law only requires parents to conduct the adoption process through a welfare agency, even if the social workers consider the match to be unsuitable.

For an independent adoption to be successful at least one of the following conditions must be present: (1) the adoptive parents are emotionally ready to adopt and adjust themselves quickly to parenting a child; (2) the adoptive parents are able to seek help when they are faced with problems; and (3) sheer good luck.

In 1986, in the city of Salonica, Greece, 103 independent adoptions were legalized, and all were processed through our welfare agency. A review of the records indicated the following:

The age of the children at the time of the request to begin the adoption procedure ranged from three months to one year. Only fifteen children were more than a year old (ranging in age from 1 to

16 years). All these children were biological children of one parent who were now being adopted by the new spouse of that parent. Five adoptions were among relatives, where a sibling adopted a niece or nephew. We found that this type of adoption usually creates problems between relatives. In one case in which a sister had given her child for adoption to her brother's family, there was great animosity and feelings of possession between the two families. It was as though no one agreed on whose child it was. The biological mother was always in her brother's house in order to be with the child. The biological mother and her brother took the child together to the doctor or for walks. When the baby cried the biological mother ran to take care of the baby ignoring her sister-in-law (the adoptive mother). The latter felt rejected in her role as mother not only by her sister-in-law but also by her husband. The biological father also felt abandoned by his wife who spent most of the time with her brother raising the child.

The socioeconomic status of the adoptive parents of the 1986 adoptive group were of middle to upper middle class. All had at least a high school education and in addition, ten were university graduates, and fourteen had some other postsecondary education, such as accounting or an Associates of Arts degree. Only five of the adoptive parents were under thirty, and most were beyond their forties.

ADOPTION OF GYPSY CHILDREN

Since 1985 it has been noticed that many gypsy children were placed for adoption through private or independent channels. In 1985, twenty-five gypsy children were processed for adoption through our agency in Salonica. The children were placed with the adoptive families immediately after birth but were four to seven months old when the adoptive parents approached our agency to begin the legalization of the adoption. In 1987, thirty-eight such adoptions were processed through our agency, and sixty were processed in 1988. There are no available outcome studies on the adoption of gypsy children, since this is a recent phenomenon. However, social workers involved with these cases usually report that the biological parents' motives are money oriented; they are selling their children rather than wanting to secure a better life for them. The Greek press very often reports that "the police caught a gypsy mother in the act of selling her baby" and intervene when a baby black market is involved. However, since gypsy families are isolated and rarely use the social services, it is difficult to draw conclusions as to how gypsy mothers feel.

From the point of view of the adoptive parents, we found that because of their strong desire to have a child and the scarcity of available babies for adoption, they have become nondiscriminating and could accept any baby. Therefore, they rush into adoption without examining their feelings, possible prejudices they may have, and their ability to help their adopted child understand his roots and form his own identity. They adopt a gypsy baby while at the same time feeling ashamed of the baby's background and trying to keep his ethnicity a secret. However, should the child later display behaviors which they do not approve of, they may blame it on the child's heredity.

We encountered cases where a wife has hidden from her husband the origin of the child, because she was afraid that the husband would not approve or accept a gypsy baby. One example is that of an adoptive mother who came to our agency to begin procedures to adopt a newborn gypsy baby that they found by themselves. The mother knew the child's background and begged the social worker not to reveal this to her husband because he would not agree to the adoption and, in addition, might divorce her. The social worker assigned to the couple felt very responsible and afraid of being the cause for breaking up the marriage. After several in-house team consultations, it was decided to keep the woman's secret.

However, one evening the adoptive couple was watching television when it was announced on the news that a gypsy, with the same surname as the one of their adoptive child, was arrested for trying to sell her baby. The wife pretended to be very upset and disapproving and called the social worker at home, while her husband listened on a second phone, to "verify" that their baby had no relation to "that gypsy." In reality there was no relationship, but the social worker found herself again entangled in a lie and in the wife's theatrical behavior. The question then arises, what type of parenting will this child receive? How is this marriage going to work in order for the child to grow in a stable and secure environment? Had this woman gone through legal channels for adoption would she have ever been given a child? In some cases, the matchmaker involved in obtaining a child for the adoptive parents hides the gypsy origin of the baby from both husband and wife. When they discover the truth, they don't know how to deal with it since they have not been prepared to accept a gypsy child.

Adopted gypsy children might be at risk when they grow up: (1) because they are intercultural adoptions and they are not treated as such. There is no planning for follow-up and education of the parents as to how to work with the child when he grows up and notices his features are different from those of the parents and asks questions about his origins; (2) because of the way independent adoptions operate, with no preparation of both sets of parents. Thus, the adoptive family is left to its fate, and must count on good luck if the adoption is to work. Of course, if there are problems in the child's life later, they might ask for professional help.

Surely, the number of gypsy children placed for adoption would be fewer if they were made to go through adoption agencies like Metera or PIKPA. Gypsy biological parents avoid such agencies because this will mean that they will not be allowed to receive a remuneration, which they view as the main point of the transaction. The adoption of gypsy children would be more successful if the matching of adoptive parents and children were more demanding and if there were no concealment from the parents of the child's ethnic origin.

CONCLUSION

Changes are needed in the adoption law, accompanied by a new policy to change the structure and profile of the social welfare agencies so that they can offer more comprehensive services to adoptive and biological parents. Consultation services, foster families for babies, homes for unmarried mothers where they can stay during pregnancy, better trained and more experienced social workers, and collaboration with other specialists are needed. Lately the Ministry of Health and Social Welfare has recognized these needs and has moved toward meeting them by presenting a proposal to the Ministry of Justice that adoption should take place only through a state-recognized agency. Also it is proposed that the state agency should be notified immediately by a private clinic or hospital as soon as they know of a newborn baby that the parents plan to place for adoption. In response, the Ministry of Justice has created some working groups comprised of law professors in order to clarify some areas of the law and propose some legal changes and new laws.

Part VI

Adoption Programs

13

A Child's Needs in the Care System

John Fitzgerald, C.Q.S.W.

In this chapter, I would like to explore how adoption can be used as an alternative to public care for children, from the following perspectives: children's needs, family resources, and organizational resources. To begin, I will give the operational definitions of some of the terms I will use:

1. Public care: care by Local Authority Social Services Departments, funded by central and local governments.
2. Residential or institutional care: care in hospitals, children's homes, or small family group homes where children are placed for varying lengths of time.
3. Voluntary agency: a private adoption agency.
4. Home study: the process of evaluating a prospective adopter's capacity.

CHILDREN'S NEEDS

I believe children cannot flourish or reach their full emotional potential if they live in long-term public care. All children, in my view, need to be parented by people who can provide continuity of care and with whom children can be emotionally and legally secure. In attempting to consider the needs of children, it is important to remember that most children in our society live with their own families and have never lived in public care and never will. In Great Britain, for example, most children with physical or mental handicaps live with their own families, for most families can and do cope without resorting to placing their handicapped children in public care.

Despite all the changes that have occurred in society's attitudes toward family life, it is still expected that children should be cared for by a family. The definition of the term *family*, however, has changed; for example, it is now acceptable for children to be cared for by single parents. Paradoxically, while society apparently continues to support the notion that children should be cared for by their families, when those arrangements break down, there is an expectation (in Great Britain, at least) that the children involved should be placed in public care, specifically, in institutional care. Half of the children in public care in Great Britain live in institutions. So what is it about family life that enables most children to grow up happy and secure, and how does family life compare with life in an institution?

At a seminar some time ago, participants identified a number of characteristics of family life from a child's point of view:

1. Uniqueness: In the eyes of his family, the child is unique, special; through the eyes of the child the family is unique and special.
2. Commitment: A desire to care for the child throughout his childhood, which means continuity of care.
3. Love: The giving and receiving of affection, which, within a healthy family is two-way—between parent and child.
4. Time: To listen, to care, to have fun, to disagree.
5. Sense of belonging: The feeling of belonging with adults who can be trusted, who will be there when needed—in other words, home.

There is something rather interesting about this list; it does not describe the biological ties but rather the psychological parenting of a child—the way in which a child should be cared for by a permanent parental figure.

Let us now examine how and by whom a child is parented in public care. Figure 13.1 depicts a model showing the range of people who either have or think they have a responsibility for part of the parenting role for the child in public care. During a child's life in public care, most, if not all, of these people shown in Figure 13.1 will want to intervene in making the decisions concerning a child's future.

Figure 13.1

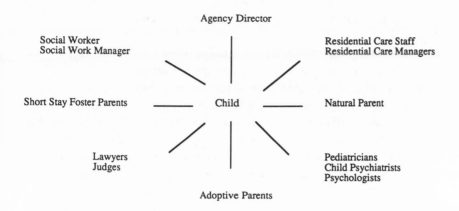

In some cases, the intervention will be an appropriate part of their role; in other cases, individuals will intervene because they feel they have a right or duty. The list in Figure 13.1 is not exhaustive, and the reader will no doubt be able to add others; for example, staff replacements or members of an auxiliary staff who will be on the periphery of the child's life.

Remembering what was said earlier about characteristics of family life, it is worth trying to answer these questions for the child in public care:

1. Where is the child's uniqueness?
2. Where is the permanent commitment and continuity of care?
3. Who is loving the child throughout his childhood?
4. Who has time to listen, to care, to have fun, or to disagree?
5. From where does the child derive a sense of belonging?

One child who grew up in public care had this to say about his experience: "They plan your life for you, but they don't let you come to your reviews, and then all of a sudden they say goodbye."

Another child, a teenage girl, who had grown up in public care told me that she would never marry, would have nothing to do with men, and would never have children. When I asked her why, she said, "No one has ever loved me, and I do not know how to love."

The capacity of a child to mature emotionally is based on family love, security, and continuity of care. Children in public care, however, may have suffered considerable emotional damage. If the child is to return to his home, the agency will need to work with both parents and the child to repair the damaged relationship. If the child has to be placed for adoption, work will be required to repair the emotional damage caused by separation from and loss of his parents.

The agency will also need to recognize that in a small percentage of cases, the interests of child and parent may conflict. In these cases, if the child is to be placed for adoption, the agency will need to seek legal means to dispense with parental agreement. If we accept that children in public care need permanent, secure family lives, then we need to face the fact that in a small number of cases the natural parents may not agree with us, and we will have to choose between the best interest of the child and the natural parents.

FAMILY RESOURCES

In order for children in public care who are unable to return home to be placed for adoption, we need to be clear about the range of substitute family resources that will be required. I indicated earlier the way in which the definition of "a family" has broadened. If children with special needs are to be successfully placed, then to keep pace with changes in society, adoption services have to broaden their criteria of what constitutes an acceptable adoptive family. The traditional criteria against which prospective adoptive parents are assessed have little relevance when considering the needs of children living in public care. The families needed for these children must come from a wide variety of backgrounds and life-styles, for the traditional criteria no longer fit.

To illustrate what I mean, I will describe some of the adoptive families we have recently used in Britain:

1. Ms. A., a single woman in her thirties, who sees no likelihood of marriage, but would like to parent a child, has now adopted a four-year-old boy with Down's Syndrome.
2. Mr. and Mrs. B., aged seventy-two and sixty-two respectively, who have four adopted children and three biological children, have adopted a fourteen-year-old child.

3. Mr. and Mrs. C., a childless couple in their thirties who applied to adopt a baby, have in fact adopted a sibling group of four children, ages seven to thirteen.
4. Mr. and Mrs. D., a miner and his wife with six children, one of whom has Down's Syndrome, have adopted a six-year-old boy with Down's Syndrome and have applied for another child with the same medical condition.
5. Mr. and Mrs. E., whose own two children are grown-up and living on their own, leaving Mrs. E. with an emotional gap in her life and feeling that she needs someone to be dependent upon her, have adopted a mentally handicapped child who will, of course, always be dependent upon his family. Thus the needs of both the family and the child are being met.
6. Mr. and Mrs. F., a couple made up of a husband who is blind but feels his physical problem is more than compensated for by his understanding of his handicap and a wife who feels blindness holds no fears for her, have adopted a blind boy.

One could argue that these are exceptional people, but in fact they are like many other people who live in our society. What is unusual about them is that they do not fit the stereotype of typical, perfect adopters.

Clearly, if we are to enable such a wide range of people to take over the full legal responsibility for meeting the needs of children in public care, the traditional methods of assessing prospective adopters are not going to be the most fruitful. When home study is discussed, many social workers continue to talk about their "obstacle course" approach. One told me that on her first contact with a family she tried to dissuade them from adopting by relating as many problems as possible concerning available children. If the couple asked for a second interview, another series of obstacles was presented. "I really lay it on the line about the process and the checking up I will be doing," she said. She described the process as "counseling out." How many suitable families do we lose that way?

What is required is a much more open, dynamic process, like that which Kay Donley, an American director of a specialist adoption agency, describes in her book *Opening New Doors*, published in 1974 by the Association of British Adoption Agencies, as educative rather than investigative. Our more progressive agencies now make far greater use of assessment and preparation groups and visual material when working with families, so that the families are able to fully explore their own capabilities and, with help, make realistic decisions about parenting abilities. Families also need to be properly prepared for caring for a particular child, not just children in general.

Using other adoptive parents in the process of assessment and preparation is a great aid to social workers and applicants alike, for adoptive parents can discuss their adoptive experience first hand. This again emphasizes the need to open up the whole adoptive process, to let other people and fresh ideas influence the methods used.

To make the most of the family resources available in the community, it is vital that assessment and preparation processes are focused upon the needs of the children who are waiting to be adopted. This means, however, taking risks. The placement of children with special needs is always a risk; there are no guarantees of success. The number of placements that do not work is relatively small, but nevertheless occasional disruptions occur, and it is important to be honest with families from the outset if we are to help them should things go wrong. These are risks, but the risks for the child remaining in an emotional limbo in public care are far greater.

ORGANIZATIONAL RESOURCES

To pursue a more dynamic approach, it helps enormously if the agency (whether public or private) has developed a progressive policy toward family placement. There are, however, problems to overcome. In particular, even if an agency can be persuaded to pursue a more radical approach toward finding adopters, its members are liable to assume that the needs of all the children waiting for families can be met through that agency's effort alone. This may be true eventually, but it could be years before a family can be found that meets the needs of a particular child, while another agency may be able to provide a family immediately. There is no justification for making a child wait a year or two for a family in order to satisfy parochial pride. Our experience in Britain, which mirrors that of the United States and Canada, is that once an agency becomes committed to permanent placement for children with special needs, more and more children are identified as needing an adoptive family. It then becomes obvious that outside help will be required to find adoptive families for them all.

Another problem to overcome is what has been called the need to "reinvent the wheel." For some extraordinary reason some agencies insist on degrading the innovations of others. Some time ago a manager from a voluntary agency came to see me to discuss his plans for setting up a specialist family-finding agency that would be devoted solely to the placement of children with special needs. He was seeking my advice, and I suggested that he visit a number of other agencies that were highly successful in placing similar children. Obviously, this was not welcome advice because the man very indignantly told me that he did not want his project to be like the others. He wanted his to be different. I never did find out how his project was different, but to be fair he ultimately visited the agencies I suggested, and he learned a number of valuable lessons which helped him. However, I was horrified that a senior, experienced manager had initially dismissed as irrelevant the lessons learned by agencies that had pioneered in this very area and had to struggle with his type of problems at a time when other help was not available to them.

These issues have created concerns in the United States, Canada, and Great Britain as adoptive services have been developed, and it is against this background that the remainder of my comments are presented. I want to concentrate now on the developments in Britain which have increased our ability to place children with special needs; developments which, in many ways, have followed those taking place in the United States and Canada.

In Britain we have an organization called the British Agencies for Adoption and Fostering (BAAF), which acts as an umbrella organization for all adoption agencies. The BAAF provides four basic activities:

1. Training and consultancy to help the development of agency skills.
2. Policy development, which pursues institutes to strengthen the legislative framework.
3. Production of publications reflecting current research and practices.
4. An adoption exchange service for children with special needs.

It is the fourth activity, the BAAF, that I will now focus on.

BAAF EXCHANGE

The BAAF Exchange is the means by which adoption placements for children with special needs are arranged. Local authorities send BAAF regional coordinators or London-based staff details on children for whom they are having difficulty in finding an adoptive family. At the same time member agencies send details on adoptive families who are able to offer a family life to a child with special needs. The information on families is stored on a computer system. Regardless of where they are located, coordinators searching for a family for a specific child can track through the computer to learn if a suitable family is waiting either within the same region or elsewhere in Great Britain. When a suitable family is located, the family's agency is put in touch with the child's agency and together they effect the placement.

Does the system work? To date, over 2,000 children with special needs have found families. A summary of the BAAF Exchange placement statistics since 1979 and 1980 is provided in Table 13.1.

Following the example of adoption agencies in the United States, the BAAF Exchange was also the first organization in Britain to feature a child with special needs on television. This has led to many children finding adoptive families, who otherwise had little hope of experiencing family life.

As the range of disabilities of children needing families increased, so the need of other recruitment initiatives also increased. In 1980 the Exchange introduced another American method, a photolisting service now called "Be My Parent." "Be My Parent" is a folder containing photographs and written details of children who are waiting for adoptive families. Four hundred copies of "Be My Parent" are distributed throughout Great Britain by local authorities, voluntary adoption societies, and coordinators for a national adoptive parents' organization. People inquiring about adoption are shown the book. If there is a child in the book they feel might fit into their family, the "Be My Parent" organizer puts them in touch with the child's social worker who then deals with their formal application to adopt. Since the service's inception, more than 300 children, including many with Down's Syndrome, have found new families. A bonus resulting from this program is the enormous interest shown by the media. The project is high on human interest and consequently national television news programs, magazines, radio, and the national and local press

TABLE 13.1
Exchange Placements

Category	1979/80	1980/81	1981/82	1982/83	1983/84	1984/85	1985/86
Total Number Placed	100	167	171	236	174	155	141
Age of Children at Placement:							
5 months or less	8	26	18	7	10	9	9
6 months to 2 years	22	37	40	20	35	40	39
3 years to 5 years	22	29	30	11	9	7	11
6 years to 9 years	32	48	48	32	22	20	18
10 years and over	16	27	35	30	24	24	23
Siblings: Groups of 2	8	16	18	33	13	6	8
Groups of 3	4	4	4	4	0	1	5
Groups of 4	0	1	0	0	0	0	0
Down's Syndrome	1	14	21	24	38	43	29
Children with Serious Educational Difficulties	11	15	18	18	24	30	13
Placement Disruptions	7	11	12	23	17	23	22
Agencies Provding Families:							
local authorities	35	53	54	54	51	67	60
voluntary agencies	48	90	90	97	90	81	63

have provided free coverage at various times, resulting in publicity about the needs of these children reaching a much wider public.

One of the major benefits of the development of the BAAF Exchange has been that local authorities and voluntary adoption societies now work together and have developed their own expertise and confidence gained through inter-agency work.

The experience in Britain is comparable with that in the United States and Canada, but no country has a perfect system; operating such organizations is never without its management problems. BAAF, however, has not had a monopoly on family recruitment ideas; others have also developed exciting ideas. A number of specialist home-finding voluntary agencies have been established specifically to find families for children with special needs. The first, Parents for Children, is highly successful. This agency was modeled after the work of Spaulding for Children in Michigan and New York. Parents for Children and the agencies that have followed its example have pioneered not only innovative recruitment methods, but also a dynamic approach to home studies, resulting in an extraordinary range of families being accepted as adoptive parents.

A joint project organized by a local authority and a voluntary agency is called New Black Families, and is staffed by black workers who have the task of recruiting black families for black children. They very quickly demonstrated, for example, that families from Afro-Caribbean communities that do not have an adoption tradition within their own culture can be recruited for Afro-Caribbean children, something many white social workers doubted could happen.

These recruitment schemes have one thing in common which no amount of organizational structure or resource can replace. Each project, each organization, has one or more people totally committed to finding adoptive families for the most difficult children to place.

We can theorize about whether or not one scheme is more effective than another; we can argue about the appropriateness of one set of organizational structures versus another; and we can complain about the inadequacies of the legal framework (and workers in most countries do), but in themselves these problems are not important. Of course placing children with special needs would be easier if there was a blueprint for successful recruitment schemes, or all organizational structures were perfect, or the legal framework was uniform. However, the difference between success and failure is simple. There needs to be at least one person, preferably more than one, who believes that children with special needs can be placed and who has the personal commitment to want to find families for these children.

Perhaps another way of putting it is to quote from George Bernard Shaw:

"You see things; and you say, 'Why?' But I dream things that never were; and I say, 'Why not?' "

REFERENCE

Donley, K. (1974), *Opening New Doors*. London: Association of British Adoption Agencies.

14

Adoption and the Metera Babies Center

Tassoula Koussidou, M.S.W.,
Billy Maganiotou, B.A.

ADOPTION DEVELOPMENTS IN GREECE

During the past four decades, adoption in Greece has followed similar changes and developments as in the countries of Western Europe and North America, though the pace of change has been slower.

In the 1950s and 1960s, those interested in adopting were significantly fewer in number than the healthy babies available for adoption and the older or special needs children had no chance of finding a home. Greek society was ambivalent toward adoption, prejudiced against unmarried parenthood, and fearful of "bad blood" and heredity. When childless couples decided to adopt, they preferred children of close relatives or legitimate children from large, poor families. Most of those who adopted children born out of wedlock were from the lower socioeconomic class, which was thought of as having less concerns about matters of origin.

In addition to the children adopted from the local babies' institutions, which operated at that time, many adoptions were the result of private agreements between adopters and the biological parents or a

167

third party. These babies were usually placed for adoption directly from maternity clinics and it was not rare to find illegal registration of the baby as the natural child of the adopters.

The small number of adopters led many unwanted or orphaned children to grow up in institutions, such as orphanages, or often, in low-quality, unstable foster placements.

Moreover, many children were adopted abroad, mostly in Europe and North America, something which was of concern to the Greek government at that time (Mastroyannis, 1962).

Those adopting nonrelated children preferred healthy baby girls with normal psychomotor development and "normal" family history, free of any hereditary deficiencies or "social" problems (Paraskevopoulos, 1971; Maganiotou and Koussidou, 1988). The preference for girls over boys, at a two to one ratio, seemed to be related to fears that boys may exhibit more problematic behaviors and may be more difficult to raise than girls. There was a belief that girls are more loving and are able to develop stronger bonds with the adoptive family, could take care of the parents when they get older, and generally, are more dependent and stay closer to the family, so that the risk of their leaving the parents is very small. Also very young age children were preferred because it was believed that adoption at early age could guarantee the development of strong attachment to the parents, would be free of early traumatic experiences, and would offer the adoptive mother an opportunity to "experience motherhood" with a baby. The above authors point out that, in most cases, the parents' motives and their preferences for the child were self-serving and in almost no case had there been concern for the best interest of the child.

Kaloutsi-Tavlaridou (1970), in her study of fifty adoptions in Greece, stated that the Greek community did not favor adoption. Adoption, as a solution to the biological and social "disadvantage" of childlessness, was considered a heavy handicap which had to be kept secret, at any cost. The adopted child could not be considered equal to the biological child. Thus, Greek adoptive parents were discouraged from admitting their status, and in order to be accepted presented themselves as the biological parents of the child.

These social attitudes, among others, were a strong factor that led many adoptive parents to keep adoption secret from their children, friends, and relatives. Even in those cases where an adoption was known in their community, the adoptive parents had strong reservations about revealing the adoption to the child. In a study by Paraskevopoulos (1971) of school-age children, only in six out of sixty-two cases (10%) had the parents made some reference to the adoption. Kaloutsi-Tavlaridou (1970) mentions that in only one out of forty-six adoptions had the child been told about his adoptive status, while Maganiotou and Koussidou (1988), in their study of children adopted from the Metera between 1955 and 1970, found that in 19.36% of the cases the parents had told their children before they reached the age of ten years that they were adopted. Most parents in these studies had heard about the importance of telling the child and perhaps some of them intended to do so, but somehow they did not follow through their intention.

Beginning in 1970, there has been a gradual increase in the interest of Greek couples to adopt. This change of attitude, however, has been followed, as has happened in Western countries, by a gradual decrease of available babies for adoption. In 1969, the total number of adoptions of minors (up to 18 years old) in the country was 1,201—445 children out of wedlock and 756 born to married parents, while in 1988, it was reduced to 535—245 children out of wedlock and 290 born to married parents (Greek Ministry of Health, Welfare and Social Security, 1969–1988). It is worth mentioning that usually the out-of-wedlock children were adopted in infancy, while many of the legitimate children were adopted at an older age and mostly by a relative. What seems to contribute to the decrease of children available for adoption are better living standards; the scarcity of multimembered dependent families; the low percentage of babies born out of wedlock, which is about 2 percent of the total number of births per years (National Statistical Service, 1988) while in Western countries it ranges from 5 to 35 percent; more single parents keeping their babies as a result of better services to single mothers; and, a diminution in the social stigma traditionally attached to parenthood out of wedlock.

At the same time, however, adoption agencies are faced with the challenge of finding families for children who come from broken or disadvantaged homes, who are older and with special needs, who are abused and/or neglected, or who come in sibling groups. For the adoption of these children, quite often social agencies need to ask the courts to terminate parental rights. Because these cases might provoke ambivalence, dilemmas, and tension in social workers, only the Metera and the Program for Child Abuse and Neglect of the Institute of Child Health, in Athens, have undertaken such placements because a system exists where group decision making, team work, supervision, and support are integral parts of their working methods.

The increasing interest of Greeks in adoption stems from changes in the social attitudes, which, particularly during the last decade, seem to be much more positive toward adoptive parents and adoptees, and more accepting of their respective adoptive roles, though there are still some prejudices, anxieties, and fears. Adoptive parents feel much more secure in their role, seem to recognize the value of helping a homeless child, and are more open to accepting children with special needs.

The more "open" attitude toward adoption is partly evidenced by the increase in those parents who tell their children about their adoptive status. According to a new, unpublished study by Koussidou and Maganioutou, the percentage of children who were informed about their adoption by the age of eight years and who were adopted from the Metera between 1974 and 1977 was about 62 percent. Though this percentage cannot be considered satisfactory, especially because it refers to adoptions through an adoption agency and not to independent ones where the number is estimated to be lower, it is indicative of changes in attitude. There is valid evidence that the percentage of children adopted through the Metera after 1980, who are told of their adoption, is much higher.

Overall, adoption (and fostering) have offered families to many children. However, these practices have not been used adequately by state and voluntary agencies, such as child protection services, to secure permanent home placement for a substantial number of children (including babies and infants) who continue to be cared for in various types of institutions. At the end of 1988, 3,300 children (300 of them being from birth to five years of age) grew up in institutions (Ministry of Health, Welfare, and Social Security, 1989). Several hundreds of these children could be adopted, if there was a plan for each child, according to his needs, reviewed on a regular basis by a professional team and less bureaucratic procedures.

In conclusion, while there are more people interested in adoption in Greece today, there are fewer children available. The independent or third party adoption, where selection and preparation of the future adopters is virtually impossible under present procedures and legal provisions (Panera, chapter 12) and the subsequent "baby market" have been of great concern to social agencies and professionals, but this matter is not a priority to the officials. Legal measures have to be taken as soon as possible to restrict these independent placements.

THE GOALS AND SERVICES OF THE METERA BABIES' CENTER

As early as 1953, a group of enlightened professionals led by the memorable social scientist Litsa Alexandraki and professor of pediatrics Spyros Doxiadis, decided to apply Bowlby's (1951) ideas on child care practices, which considered the baby's early bonding to a single mother figure as the cornerstone for the development of a healthy personality. A babies' center which, in contrast to traditional institutions with the well-known negative effects, would put these new ideas into practice with homeless infants, seemed the most appropriate. As a consequence, the Metera Babies' Center was founded in 1955, in Athens.

The Metera is a nonprofit organization, financed and supervised by the Ministry of Health, Welfare, and Social Security. It offers specialized and individualized services to parents and children in difficult or potentially high-risk psychosocial situations. It serves a population comprised of single parents, babies, and infants deprived of a family environment, abused and neglected children, foster and adoptive parents, and adoptees seeking their roots.

The Babies' Center maintains that the best family welfare is rooted in good family welfare and that all children have the right to enjoy a normal family environment. It also believes that the first priority for a child is to be cared for by the biological parents and that in cases where the biological family is unavailable or unable to provide for the basic needs of the child, a substitute family care (foster or adoptive) should be considered.

Based on the above policy, the Center has defined its goals as follows:

1. Protection of children, especially infants and toddlers, who are deprived of a normal family environment.
2. Assistance to single parents—particularly unmarried mothers—and in general parents who have difficulty with childrearing.

3. Education and research in the fields of child health and development and of the psychosocial problems of parents and children.
4. Communication of attitudes, principles, and work methods which relate to physical and social welfare of children.
5. Promotion of legislation in areas concerned with child welfare.

To implement its goals, the Center has developed a variety of services, including:

1. Residential care for 100 children, newborns to four-year-olds, in small homelike nurseries of twelve children each, staffed with professional nurses and nurses aides.
2. Accommodations for eighteen single women for the pregnancy and postpartum period. Besides room and board, the women are given close medical attention and receive individual and group counseling with social workers and, if needed, with psychologists and psychiatrists. Occupational, educational, and recreational programs are also available. Occasionally, mothers with babies may be admitted for short periods of time.
3. Counseling and financial support is available during pregnancy and the postpartum period for single women who live in the community.
4. Special service departments for abused and neglected children and their parents.
5. Foster home placements for children, regardless of age, until the child can be restored to a permanent family environment or until the child becomes socially and financially independent.
6. Adoption placement, with emphasis on the adoption of children with special needs.
7. Counseling services and financial support to parents and children in potentially difficult psychosocial situations, such as single parents who have kept their children, adoptive and foster families, adoptees seeking their biological parents, and so on.

SERVICES TO SINGLE PARENTS

The Metera was the first social agency in Greece to offer protection to unmarried mothers, at a time when a social stigma was strongly attached to out-of-wedlock motherhood and many unwed mothers-to-be were driven away from their homes, left without shelter and food, and in some cases were battered or killed by fathers and brothers because of the stigma they had inflicted on the family. In other cases desperate girls, under overwhelming social pressure, were pushed to infanticide, while the phenomenon of abandoning the newborn baby outdoors was quite common.

The Metera brought about a dramatic change by establishing the first residential unit for unmarried pregnant women, offering besides room and board, medical care, counseling, support, and confidentiality.

Today, most pregnant single women prefer to stay in the community, close to their relatives and friends and the Metera's Mothers Home, which has remained the only one in the country, is more often used by women who, in addition to the pregnancy, have other handicapping conditions, such as mental health problems or physical impairments, or are in early adolescence, requiring a protective environment. Additionally, mothers with babies and young children, going through a personal or family crisis and needing to leave their homes, may be admitted in an effort to keep mothers and children together until the crisis is over.

While the need for residential care has been restricted to fewer cases, the Metera has expanded its services to include single parents, not necessarily unmarried, and families in crisis, with the basic goal of helping them during a difficult time in their lives with the hope that they will keep and care for their children or decide for other alternatives, such as fostering or adoption. Counseling, short-term psychotherapeutic treatment, financial support, training and job facilitating services, legal advice and help, linkage with other resources in the community are offered by a multidisciplinary group of social workers, psychologists, psychiatrists, midwives, nurses, pediatricians, and lawyers.

To secure an early bond attachment between mother and child and avoid the baby's admission to Metera's residential unit, the professionals of Metera are trying their best, by offering counseling and material help, to encourage mothers who have decided to keep their children to take their newborn babies with them directly from the maternity hospital. However, many single mothers feel they are unable to cope right away with the demands of the baby, for whom they were quite unprepared emotionally and in practical terms, and prefer to have the baby admitted to the residential unit for some time, until they feel they can cope with the situation. This early separation, in addition to possible negative effects on the child's development, may increase the mother's ambivalence toward the baby and, in many cases, works against her original decision to keep the baby. For this reason, daily and hour-long visits of mothers to the babies are strongly encouraged, while every effort is being made by the nurses to complement the mothering or provide substitute mothering if necessary. Social workers are helping the mother so that the baby will stay in residential care for the shortest possible period of time.

As a result of the above efforts the percentage of the mothers who keep their babies has doubled in the last ten years, rising to 40 percent (*Year Books,* Social Service, Metera Babies Center, Athens, 1978 through 1988). Though this is not indicative of the percentage throughout the country, which is estimated to be much higher, it is quite satisfactory, if one takes into consideration that the mothers who contact Metera are the ones with severe or long-time psychosocial problems, which makes it more difficult for them to undertake responsibility for their children.

FOSTER CARE PROGRAM

The Metera has always had a small foster care program. The children who are placed in foster homes are usually (1) severely handicapped, unwanted by their parents, or children for whom no adoptive family could be found and (2) children who will eventually return to their parents. Also, during the last ten years, we have placed in foster homes older, abused and neglected children, and children whose families are in crisis.

The difficulty in finding good-quality foster families (for reasons that are not within the scope of this article to discuss) has resulted to the necessary operation of the Metera's Residential Unit for Babies and Infants, to cover usually urgent admissions. Thus, most babies are placed with biological, foster, or adoptive parents after a period of stay in the Unit. In the future Metera plans to replace residential care with fostering for babies and infants.

Foster parents are carefully selected and prepared and are in close collaboration with Metera's professional team. They can share with the staff member the difficulties and problems they encounter and receive support and guidance in their handling of the child. Most foster placements are medium- and long-term. Foster parents are paid a monthly allowance for room and board for each child, which amounts to about half of the unskilled worker's salary. In addition, Metera covers all other expenses for the child (including medical care, clothing, entertainment, etc.). For children whose special needs require extra care and attention, a higher allowance is paid. There are no professional foster parents in Greece.

In conclusion, fostering in the country has not yet been adequately developed and Metera still has to promote this type of child care service. It is worth mentioning also that there are no relevant legal provisions covering foster care.

THE ADOPTION PROGRAM

From its inception Metera made a systematic effort to educate the public on adoption in order to secure families for children and, at the same time, to encourage people to adopt through social agencies and not through private channels, in order to guarantee a proper preparation of all parties involved.

It also developed an inter-country adoption program, in cooperation with officials of foreign countries, so that children adopted abroad could be placed and followed up by authorized social agencies of the receiving countries.

The following data are indicative of Metera's activities: from 1956 until the end of 1988, 3,350 children were placed in adoptive homes by Metera. The first fifteen years (1956–1970) from a total of 1,820 adopted children, 63.57 percent were adopted abroad (12.37 percent of them by families of Greek origin). In the decade that followed (1971–1980) the increased interest of Greek couples in adopting resulted in only 189 (19.68 percent) children being adopted abroad (7.29 percent by families of Greek origin). Children who are adopted abroad are mostly special needs children for whom no families could be available in Greece. During the next eight years (1981–1988) there was a further decrease in the number of children placed with foreign families (only 7.55 percent of all adoptions), and these are now exclusively children with severe handicaps (*Metera Year Books*, 1955 through 1988).

Over the years, Metera has developed a quite efficient adoption program for infants and older children including preparatory work with the child and his or her biological parents; preparation and selection of adoptive applicants mainly through individual home studies and partly in groups; follow-up of the child's placement; legal advice, and postadoptive counseling and support services. A multidisciplinary group of social workers, nurses, psychologists, pediatricians, psychiatrists, and others collaborate to ensure the best possible results.

The Metera was the first adoption agency in Greece to use the diagnostic method for selecting adoptive parents and emphasize preparation for adoptive parenthood, especially such issues as informing the child about his adoption and of his possible need to seek his roots. Also, in cases where the individual home study suggests concerns about the applicants' mental health status or behavior difficulties, a psychologist's or psychiatrist's opinion is requested.

Support and counseling have always been offered to adoptive parents and adoptees. However, in 1984, the Metera organized a special department with a multidisciplinary team to offer supportive services to adoptive families and to help adoptees who are seeking their roots. Concerning the latter, Metera, respecting the adoptee's right to know about his origins and meet with the biological family, works with the adoptee on a counseling basis, offering information on file, examining his motives and expectations, and preparing him for possible frustrations. Because of the lack of relevant specific legal provisions, Metera does not initially give the adoptee information about the identity of his biological parents (although he or she could find it through other ways) but it contacts the biological mother to examine her attitude and feelings and whether she opposes meeting with her biological child. In this way, social and family problems are avoided, since it has been evidenced in many cases that the biological mothers' husbands and other children are not always aware of the existence of the adopted child.

It is interesting to note that from the children adopted abroad in the years 1955 to 1965, all of whom have been informed about their adoption, and who were over eighteen years old in 1984 when the special department started, only about 5 percent contacted Metera wanting to know about or meet their biological mother in the period between 1984 to 1987. Although this percentage is rather low compared to relevant research data from other countries, one has to consider the fact that these adoptees do not live in Greece and may have more practical difficulties in starting their search.

ADOPTION OF CHILDREN WITH SPECIAL NEEDS

In Ancient Sparta handicapped babies were thrown down to the Kajad to secure a society free of physically impaired people.

In modern Greece, quite often, social agencies and social workers have to find solutions for families who reject and do not wish to keep their handicapped newborn babies. Greek society is still reluctant and fearful to accept and protect the handicapped. Many of these children are born to married, fairly well-organized couples who could otherwise have kept them.

The Metera Babies' Center, responding to current needs, oriented its efforts early on toward this very sensitive and challenging aspect of child care, in a two-goal service: (1) to work with the biological family (and the community) to keep their child, and (2) to find and prepare adoptive (or foster) families for these children.

Feelings of fear, shame, and guilt overwhelm the biological parents, more so if it is their first child, and lead to their rejection of the child and even to their refusal to see him or her. In many cases, particularly if the parents live in small rural communities, relatives, friends, and even the local authorities may be unsupportive and encourage the parents to give up the child. We have come across many families, where the father takes on the responsibility and the emotional burden of rejecting the child at birth, by concealing from his wife the child's true condition and telling her that the baby was born dead.

Even in cases where the parents seem to be definite in their decision to give up the child, our work to bring them into contact with the child, to inform them fully about the medical diagnosis and prognosis, and get them both involved in the final plan, has been fruitful. In several cases parents have changed their minds and kept their babies. It is worth pointing out that the sooner after the birth of the baby our service gets involved in working with the parents and the community, the more likely it is that the family will decide to keep the child. Later on, the rejection mechanisms have been established for good, several false stories have been told, and it is more difficult to break through the "protective" wall around the parents.

It was only after 1975 that Greek applicants, in view of the shortage of babies available for adoption, began to discuss the possibility of adopting special needs children. During the last ten years, the percentage of special needs and high-risk children for whom Metera secures adoptive families has ranged between 30 and 50 percent of the total number of children placed for adoption through the Center. Still, the children who are more easily accepted are those with slight to moderate problems, such as serious perinatal conditions, seizures during infancy, orthopedic problems, strabismus, heart murmur, or with genetic vulnerabilities, such as mental illness or mental retardation. The externally "intact" child appeals better to the Greek parents-to-be. The "tangible" handicap, which cannot be fully repaired, provokes feelings of fear and pity, and the parents are emotionally unable to cope with the situation, despite their good will, in some cases, to help the child. Of course, there have been some families who have pleasantly surprised us with the acceptance, on a reality basis, of children with serious handicaps.

STUDIES' OUTCOME

A number of scientific studies have been completed or are in progress at the Metera Babies' Center on subjects concerning child health care and development and in the area of psychosocial problems of parents and children.

In the area of adoption, we will present, indicatively, the findings of two studies referring to two different periods of Metera's operation. These findings have pinpointed our weaknesses and the areas where we ought to put more emphasis in working with adoptees and biological parents.

Maganiotou and Koussidou (1988) assessed the adoptive parents' experience of adoption in a random sample of 176 adoptive couples who had adopted 186 children from Metera during the period of 1956 to 1970. The adoptees' age ranged from six to twenty-one years, at the time of the survey.

According to the parents' views, 159 (85.5%) of the adoptions unfolded in a satisfactory way. Parents were generally pleased, expressing positive feelings and thoughts about their children, who seemed to be fairly well adjusted. The percentage of boys and girls was about the same. Even the parents who reported problems, in almost half of the children, felt content and considered those problems as typical of the problems observed in many families, especially when the children reach adolescence. For the age group six to twelve, in forty-one (48.2%) cases the parents were concerned about the poor performance at school and unacceptable behavior, such as rudeness, irresponsibility, aggressivity, irritability, obstinance, lack of concentration, and naughtiness in their children. For the age group thirteen to twenty-one, in fifty-four cases (46.53%) the parents reported problems of poor performance at school and of dropping out of school, and behavior problems, such as disobedience, irritability, aggression, keeping bad company, and feelings of insecurity and anxiety.

The parents of only twenty-seven children (14.51%), twenty girls and seven boys, expressed discontent, frustration, negative views about their children, and worry for their problems, which they did not seem able to handle. Of those children, twenty-two were adolescents. In some of these cases, serious problems, such as stealing and drug use, were reported.

Of course, given that 80 of the 159 children were still between six and twelve years old, while another 55 were going through adolescence, and that 108 (67.92%) children had not been informed about their adoption, one must have some reservations about the future development of these adoptions. Finally, the authors point out that many of the parents who reported problems with their children had oppressive, authoritarian, and overprotective attitudes toward the youngsters, elements encountered in many Greek families, especially those with only one child.

Tsitsikas, Coulacoglou, Mitsotakis, and Driva (1988) studied seventy-two children, adopted through Metera between 1974 and 1977, in order to (1) compare the neurodevelopmental status of the adopted children and that of normal controls; (2) to measure adopted children's temperaments and to correlate them to school adjustment; and (3) to investigate the characteristics of early school adjustment of adopted children and to find out whether these differ from those of the control groups.

The children were 5.6 to 6.6 years old at the time of the study and were just starting school. The adopted children and their unmarried biological mothers were matched and compared to a control group of married mothers and their children. It was found that the adopted group was at high risk, because they had seven or more risk factors (according to a scoring scale based on Prechtl's system, 1968) which was a higher percentage (45.4%) than in the control group (10%).

Most of the children were adopted before the age of one year by families who had a considerably higher than average socioeconomic status, and who showed marital stability but were quite insecure about telling the child about his adoption.

When starting school, physical growth and health of adopted children did not differ from that of the controls. The adopted children, however, had behavior problems and problems of school adjustment more often than the controls. Behavior problems ranged from nail-biting to enuresis and hyperactivity. Adopted children were less able to adjust and less ready to go to school. They also had lower scores in motor proficiency, practical reasoning, and in writing and drawing.

Because most of these children were adopted in infancy and, prior to their adoption, they were cared for in Metera Babies' Center, which offered high-quality care and a stimulating environment, the authors suggest that other factors, such as prenatal and perinatal care, the mother's psychological history, and the situation in the home of the adoptive family, were important in these children's development and adaptation. They proposed early detection of the unmarried pregnant woman and appropriate instruction and prenatal care for her. Furthermore, they called for more attention to the appropriate selection of adoptive parents, as well as to the provision of postadoptive child guidance and supportive services to them. The latter is suggested, too, by Maganiotou and Koussidou (1988), particularly in issues of telling the child about his adoption.

CONCLUSION

The contribution of the Metera Babies' Center in child care and welfare has been, undoubtedly, significant in breaking through old-fashioned views about single parenthood and the needs of babies and infants, as well as in promoting current theory and practice in child care, in Greece. After thirty-five years, Metera remains the leading social agency offering an integrated child care program, in organizing national and international seminars and conferences in the field, and in proposing and lobbying for legislative changes.

REFERENCES

Bowlby, J. (1951), *Maternal Care and Mental Health*. Geneva: WHO.

Kaloutsi-Tavlaridou, A. (1970), *Contribution to an Understanding of Adoption Problems. Identity Disturbance in Adoption*. Doctoral dissertation. Athens: University of Salonica.

Maganiotou, B., & Koussidou, T. (1988), A general assessment of adoptive parents' experience of adoption. In: *Children and Families: Studies in Prevention and Intervention*, ed. E. D. Hibbs. Madison, CT: International Universities Press, pp. 385–397.

Mastroyannis, I. (1962), *Adoption as a Social Institution*. Athens: Estia.

Ministry of Health, Welfare and Social Security (1969–1989), *Adoption Statistics*. Athens: Child Care Department.

National Statistical Service (1988), *Bulletin of Population Changes*. Athens.

Paraskevopoulos, I. (1971), *Experiences and Views of Adoptive Parents about the Institution of Adoption*. Salonica: P. Pournara.

Prechtl, H. F. R. (1968), Neurological findings in newborn infants after pre- and perinatal complications. In: *Aspects of Prematurity and Dysmaturity*, ed. J. H. Jonxis. Proceedings of Nutricia Symposium. Leiden: Stenfers Kroese.

Tsitsikas, H., Coulacoglou, C., Mitsotakis, P., & Driva, A. (1988), A follow-up study of adopted children. In: *Children and Families: Studies in Prevention and Intervention*, ed. E. D. Hibbs. Madison, CT: International Universities Press, pp. 399–414.

——— Koussidou, T. (1989), *Social Work in Adoption and Fostering*. Athens: Metera Babies Center.

Year Books, Social Service (1955–1988), Athens: Metera Babies Center.

15

Rising to the Challenge: Building Effective Postlegal Adoption Services

Linda M. Claxton-Brynjulfson, M.S.W., A.C.S.W.

With our growing understanding regarding the needs of the adoption triad (adoptive parents, birth parents, adopted persons), the challenge to design and provide timely and relevant postlegal adoption services emerges. Postadoption services do not reflect a static service concept but rather one continually evolving and changing as the needs and issues of the triad itself change, as indeed does society's response to adoption-related issues. Adoption is a complex social, psychological, and legal arrangement, one frequently not fully understood. One of the primary aims of postadoption services is to strengthen the adoption family tie by assisting clients with understanding the complexities of adoption and their implications, which have lifelong effects on all three members of the adoption triad.

In this paper, a comprehensive postlegal adoption services model is presented. We will examine the philosophical base upon which postadoption services are built, the clients who are served, the issues clients face, the services they receive, how postadoption services may be financed, and what may be the most functional administrative structure. The model proposed here is based on the postadoption service delivery provided by the Children's Home Society of Minnesota's Postlegal Adoption Services Department, which was the first postadoption department in the United States. It incorporates the experience and learning which have accumulated over the past twenty-two years of serving over 50,000 clients. Table 15.1 gives an overview of this comprehensive postadoption service model.

It is important to think about adoption within a societal, historical, and cultural context, for all three perspectives impact and influence adoption practices and the provision of postadoption services. For example, in the United States, there is now the understanding that adoption has lifelong implications for all three members of the adoption triad. There was a period of time in the past when adoption was surrounded with an air of secrecy. The societal structure reflected this with its sealed records, its nonaccess to genetic information, and its unwillingness to grant permission to discuss adoption-related concerns. In time, various members of the adoption triad began to speak out with the result that national organizations such as ALMA (Adoptee Liberty Movement Association), CUB (Concerned United Birthparents), and NACAC (North American Council on Adoptable Children) were formed and made an impact on society's perspective and understanding of adoption-related issues.

Words are a powerful carrier and transmitter of the cultural, historical, and societal contexts within which adoption occurs. As a result, serious thought needs to be given to the words that are used to talk about adoption. The words used to speak about adoption-related matters are frequently negative and not supportive of the adoption family tie. They fail to generate a feeling of positive regard for the members of the triad. Instead, they tend to create a sense of competition and, indeed, may contribute to a negative sense of self. A culture is often not equipped to provide appropriate words concerning adoption. Positive language needs to be created to constructively support the adoption family tie.

POSTLEGAL ADOPTION SERVICES: PHILOSOPHICAL PREMISES

Adoption exists to meet the needs of children who do not have families, adults who desire to parent and (perhaps) cannot themselves conceive a child, and persons who are not in a position to assume the rights and responsibilities of parenthood. The provision of postadoption services is rooted in the philosophical view that when one creates

TABLE 15.1: A Comprehensive Postlegal Adoption Service Model: An Overview

Cultural Perspective

Issues			Client Groups					
			Adopted Person	**Adoptive Parents**	**Other Family Members of the Ad/Par;, Ad/Per.**	**Birth Parents**	**Other Family Members of the Birthparents**	**Community Support System**
Other	Counseling: Individual; Couple; Family; Group		Same Ethnic Desent	Adoptive Mother	Other Children	Birth Mother	Other Children	Freinds of Family
	Genetic Background History Information		Transracial		Grandparents		Grandparents	Neighbors
Parenting	Intermediary Services		International	Adoptive Father	Aunts/Uncles	Birth Father	Aunts/Uncles	Teachers
	Group Service: Discussion, Problem solving, Support, Therapy		Older		Nieces/Nephews		Nieces/Nephews	Religious Leaders
Adoption	Consultation		Sibling Group		Cousins		Cousins	Medical Persons
	Workshops		Special Needs		Godparents		Godparents	Other
Developmental	Public Education							
	Advocacy							

Triad-focused Services

Financial Base	Administrative Structure

Postlegal Adoption Services Philosophical Premises

Social Perspective

Historical Perspective

a family by adoption, there are differences and complexities which must be understood and addressed. In addition, the implications of the adoption decision for *each* of the adoption triad members must also be understood and addressed. It is vital, when providing such services, that one believes in adoption as a valid and authentic way to create a family. If this conviction is not held, then one is not in a position to serve as an advocate for adoption and the needs of the adoption triad members.

POSTLEGAL ADOPTION SERVICES: CLIENT GROUPS SERVED

The primary client group includes adopted persons, adoptive parents, and birthparents. The client group we have called "adopted persons" is the one that has experienced the most changes over the years. Because of a marked decrease in the number of Caucasian infants in need of adoptive families, there has been a substantial increase in interracial and international adoptions. Furthermore, children who have special needs, and previously were considered unadoptable, are now successfully joining adoptive families.

Although special needs adoption is receiving much current attention, this subgroup of clients ought not to be singled out at the expense of serving other adopted persons or triad members. It is vital not to fragment services within or across client groups but rather to serve all whose lives are affected by adoption under the auspices of a postlegal adoption services department.

The adoption triad does not exist in isolation from its familial and social context. There is a need to educate and inform extended family members, the community, and society in general because the views and opinions which exist in society regarding adoption have a marked impact on all members of the triad, as in fact do the views and opinions of extended family members.

POSTLEGAL ADOPTION SERVICES: ISSUES ADDRESSED

There are four categories of issues which postlegal adoption services address. The first is a solid understanding of human development, which incorporates a birth-to-death life cycle, and knowledge of what are normal developmental life stages, tasks, and events.

Upon this developmental foundation is added the second category which addresses adoption-related concerns. There are issues that all parties of the triad will need to address for themselves at various life stages. For example, clients need to work through the losses which each may experience: for birth parents, the loss of not raising the child for whom adoption was planned; for infertile adoptive parents, the sense of loss engendered by not being able to conceive a child; for adopted persons, the loss of not being raised by their birth families.

Within this second issue, it is important to separate out the influence of environment and genetics, identity questions, and the need to know about one's past and origins. Questions frequently raised by adopted persons are: "What nationality were my birth parents?" "What is my medical history?" "How tall will I be?" "Why was adoption planned for me?" and "What is the identity of my birth mother/father and could I meet her or him?" Birth parents have questions about how their child is faring and whether the decision made on the child's behalf was a "good one." Adoptive parents experience the need for more genetic background information in order better to understand and incorporate their child into their family.

Additional adoption-related concerns are role questions and definitions. What role will each have in the lives of the others? How can adoptive parents be assisted to feel secure in their parental role? What are appropriate expectations for adopted persons and birth parents who have met one another?

The third category involves parenting concerns. Adoptive parents may need assistance in assuming the role of educators in explaining adoption not only to their child, but also to their relatives, friends, and the community of which they are a part. Helping parents to define realistic expectations from their children, supporting the parents through stressful times, and helping to incorporate fully the child into the family will enable them better to understand and accept the child. John Triseliotis (1974) states that one of the main tasks of adoptive parents is to come to feel and experience the child as their own, to integrate the child into their family, and develop in him or her a sense of trust and belonging. For, indeed, once the adoption has been finalized, the child is their own.

The fourth category is "other," which might include questions about enculturation, dealing with ethnic differences, marital problems, and sexuality. Because postadoption services are not static and unchanging, the category of "other" also provides a safety net for the inclusion of new areas that may arise.

An important component of the "other" category is legislative activity, advocacy, and public education. The postadoption service experience in the State of Minnesota shows that when adoption triad client groups and agencies work together in a spirit of cooperation, constructive legislative changes are possible. Advocacy efforts do have an impact and can improve the image of adoption.

POSTLEGAL ADOPTION SERVICES: SERVICES OFFERED

Eight different areas comprise postadoption services at the Children's Home Society of Minnesota. All members of the adoption triad are eligible to receive these, although not all clients request every service. Certain services, such as counseling, background histories, and intermediary services, comprise the majority of postadoption services.

Because the services are triad based, the needs and desires of all its members are represented and held in balance. Some of the services provided are backed by legislation in the State of Minnesota which mandates their provision, and was the result of the expressed needs of the triad members.

INDIVIDUAL AND FAMILY COUNSELING

The counseling is supportive and educative. It is eclectic in that it draws on many disciplines, including anthropology, sociology, political science, medicine, history, genetics, psychology, and education versus the psychoanalytic, Freudian-based counseling mode, or one that is strictly a family-systems approach. Although long-term therapy is sometimes indicated and therefore offered to the clients, counseling is frequently short term and focuses on increasing knowledge and understanding around adoption-related issues. This is due to the fact that the majority of the clients served are normal, well-functioning individuals needing additional clarity, perspective, and problem-solving skills. It has been our experience that most counselors and helping professionals in the community are not trained to address the needs of the adoption triad members. One needs to have an understanding of the legal, social, and emotional bonds that adoption creates and the implications it holds for each of the triad members. If clients are approached with a preconceived mind-set regarding adoption, problems frequently are not resolved. Clients report feelings of increased frustration and an intensification of their problems. It is important to provide support for how the family was created, and not have parents feel they need to justify their decision to adopt or be told by their counselor to "Bring the child back." Because community service providers do not have information from the record to utilize as part of the counseling process, returning to the placing agency for service or assistance is vital.

NONIDENTIFYING GENETIC BACKGROUND HISTORY INFORMATION

Because the need to know has been documented, the question becomes, how do we meet this need? Is the background history information even being collected? Is there an understanding of the kinds of information that need to be collected and why? Is the information being relayed to the adoptive parents and the adopted person? It is vital in the identity quest of the adopted person and in the parenting process that well-collected genetic information is available. When it is not collected or not shared, the need to know remains and sometimes is met through the creation of fantasies, usually of a more negative nature. When one adopts, one needs to embrace not only the child but also the child's genetic history. The genetic ancestry information must be made available to adoptive parents and adopted persons. It is important that this service includes a counseling component so that parents and adopted persons learn how to accept and incorporate this information.

INTERMEDIARY SERVICE

Minnesota has legislation that allows the adoption triad members to make requests for updated nonidentifying information, which includes medical and social information, face-to-face meetings, and

identifying information, which includes names, addresses, and telephone numbers, if the parties choose to waive their right to confidentiality. These requests are made through an intermediary, who is a
professional staff person working for the agency that arranged the
adoption. The intermediary serves as a bridge between the requestor
and the requestee to facilitate the exchange of information. Since the
passage of Minnesota's intermediary services laws in 1977, 1982, and
1987, over 1,500 clients have requested intermediary services from
the Children's Home Society of Minnesota alone. Preparation is vital
for those who decide to request contact with their birth relatives, as
is counseling afterwards, since there are no well-defined rules and
answers to questions such as: "What should I call my birth mother if
I meet her?" "What type of relationship should we have?" "What if I
don't like her?" Intermediary services assist clients in both the pre-
and post-outreach situations.

GROUPS

The various groups which have been created over the many years
of providing postadoption services have been an outgrowth of client
expressed need. As the needs of clients have changed over time, the
groups have changed accordingly. A group may have as its primary
focus discussion, problem solving, support, therapy, or a combination
of these characteristics. Group offerings have included a support
group for adopted persons who have requested intermediary services;
birth mother support groups for women who made adoption decisions anywhere from five to fifty years ago. Issues addressed in the
birth mother groups include the following: (1) the impact of the unplanned pregnancy in their lives; (2) grief, loss, and shame issues; and
(3) what currently is happening in their lives regarding the decision to
meet with the adopted adult. Korean preteen and teen groups help
young persons of Korean heritage better understand adoption and
to define their own identities. A support group for families under
severe stress is attended primarily by adoptive parents dealing with
the stresses of raising adolescents. Another group offering was a mid-
dle-childhood therapy group for children who have experienced
physical, sexual, and emotional abuse prior to joining an adoptive
family.

CONSULTATION

Consultation is available to clients working with other helping professionals and to other helping professionals per se. Because the demand for postadoption service is so great all existing needs cannot be fully met within the agency. It is imperative that other community services become better equipped to help respond to the service needs of the adoption triad. Consultation is one means by which the sharing of expertise can take place and clients can be assisted.

POSTADOPTION WORKSHOPS

The foci of postadoption workshops include understanding adoption as a family-building method, communicating positively about adoption, changes on the modern adoption scene, raising a child born in and adopted from another country, and dealing with children's developmental stages. One of these stages is adolescence, a time of tremendous change not only for young persons but also for parents who may need assistance in better understanding the dynamics of this age group and how to parent accordingly. The two primary workshop audiences are triad members or helping professionals. The workshop offerings are determined by client- or professional-expressed needs and frequently involve resource persons.

PUBLIC EDUCATION

Offerings are geared toward helping the community and its members to better understand adoption as a social institution in our society. This is achieved by writing articles, conducting public forums, being interviewed on radio and television, and speaking at churches, schools, and special interest groups. In the role of advocate on behalf of the adoption triad, these offerings help create a deeper understanding of adoption-related issues within the community.

ADVOCACY

The postadoption services worker is an advocate for all three members of the adoption triad. Advocating on behalf of one's clients may be within the legislative and political arena, the community, or one's service agency. The compilation and thoughtful interpretation of service data help to provide the basis for these advocacy efforts and good service practices. An example of advocacy within one's agency is utilizing the experiences gained at the postadoption level to rethink and redefine the service components that are offered to birth parents requesting pregnancy counseling and to prospective adoptive parents preparing for adoption.

These eight service areas reflect the extensive nature of postadoption issues and client needs.

POSTLEGAL ADOPTION SERVICES: FINANCIAL BASES

The clients served are charged fees for services. Children's Home Society of Minnesota is a nonprofit, nonsectarian, voluntary organization. Fees are based on a sliding fee scale and differ with the service being requested. Legislative support was given to the charging of fees for services such as background history information and intermediary service. Other monies are received from purchase of service contracts, health maintenance organizations, third-party vendors, foundation grants, United Way, and the general agency operating budget. It has been our service experience that once postadoption services are understood by funding sources, monies for the provision of these services have, at times, been granted.

POSTLEGAL ADOPTION SERVICES: ADMINISTRATIVE STRUCTURE

The postadoption department is a separate administrative entity within the agency. The word *legal* serves as a delineating factor for when a client begins to receive services under its auspices. It is past the point of finalization of the legal adoption that clients receive service, when requested, from the department. By having a separate department, adoptive families who may be hesitant to come back to their adoption worker to seek help and birth parents who may feel uncomfortable seeking service from the counselor who helped them with their unplanned pregnancy, experience a "fresh start" with a new worker who is assigned to respond to their needs. The workers provide *only* postadoption services and do not mix their caseloads with adoptive family preparation or unplanned pregnancy counseling services. When a worker carries a mixed service caseload, postadoption services frequently are last in service priority. Mixed caseloads also prevent the development of an extensive and comprehensive postadoption knowledge base. By working with all members of the adoption triad rather than referring birth parents back to unplanned pregnancy counseling services or adoptive families back to adoption services, one is able to develop the triad perspective and be an advocate for all three client groups, thereby avoiding conflicting relationships.

SUMMARY

The need for postadoption services has been documented. It is no longer a question of "Is there a need?" but "How do we respond to the need?" Agencies offering adoption services must provide their clients with access to postadoption services, even if they are not in a position themselves to directly provide these services on an ongoing basis. This can be accomplished by advocating on behalf of clients to other agencies or helping professionals, or by forming an agency consortium of service delivery. There must be an ongoing commitment of families created by adoption and the needs of all the adoption triad members. This philosophical support needs to be actualized in terms of tangible administrative and financial support. In providing postadoption services, one must remain open and ready to respond creatively to the clients' changing needs. For as adoption continues to change, postadoption services must be fashioned to continue to meet the new and current challenges.

REFERENCE

Triseliotis, J. (1974), Identity and adoption. In: *Child Adoption: A Selection of Articles on Adoption Theory and Practice*. The Association of British Adoption and Fostering Agencies, Surrey, UK: Unwin Brothers, pp. 113–121.

Note: For more information regarding Minnesota postadoption service laws, contact: Adoption Unit, Department of Human Services, 444 Lafayette, St. Paul, MN (U.S.A.) 55155-3831.

16

Preadoption Parent Education

Maria Berkowska, Ph.D., Jadwiga Migaszewska-Majewicz, Ph.D.

According to Polish law, every adult citizen is eligible to adopt a child of up to eighteen years of age, except those who have had children legally removed from their families. The latest census figures indicate that 3,481 children were adopted in Poland in 1987, and 3,343 in 1988.

The majority of people who apply to the court for adoption are men or women whose spouses already had a child or children from a previous relationship. This is of course the ideal way to rebuild a broken family. However, about 25 percent of all adoptions involve children who are not related to the adults seeking to adopt them. A small number of them are unwanted children left in maternity wards by single mothers. Some are children living in welfare institutions because they had been neglected by parents who were not able to provide for their security, health, and development. A few of the parents requested that their children be placed in institutions, but more often the children were placed there by court decree.

Adoption is a legal process, and adoption agencies are involved in selecting the parent for a given child. Children up to the age of three are cared for in institutions called Children's Homes, which are part of the health service system. The older children reside in homes administered by the Ministry of National Education. For this reason, there are two kinds of adoption agencies in Poland: one places infants and toddlers and the other children age three and older.

The main task of the adoption agencies is to place children as quickly as legally possible in families able to undertake the parenting tasks of meeting the children's physical, intellectual, emotional, and social needs. Selecting the parents for a child is a difficult process. For a long time it has been felt that placing a child with a family who met all formal criteria, such as financial security and education, was not enough, and that parents were in need of some preparation for their new role. Parenting styles differ and are dependent on such things as the personal childhood experiences of both parents and the quality of the relationship between them; their personalities, values, and beliefs; and their ability to cope with stress.

For couples who are able to conceive, the months of pregnancy and prenatal care give the prospective parents an opportunity to prepare for the arrival of a new family member. Adoptive families do not have this opportunity. Although it may take many months and years to reach the final decision to adopt a child, once the decision is made and the process begins, adoptive parents are more involved with the legal aspects of adoption than in preparing emotionally for parenthood. In order to fill this gap, a preadoption parent education program was established as a local initiative of the adoption agency handling young children in the city of Poznan.

Because of the legal requirement for documentation concerning adoption, home studies are done by agency social workers, followed by individual interviews of the applicants. This gives us the opportunity to assess some of the general characteristics that seem to be common to most couples seeking to adopt. Most are childless and, on average, older than natural parents, and they come from all social classes. However, to be considered as a candidate to adopt, they must demonstrate that their economic and life conditions are stable, and they must produce a medical certificate of good physical and mental health. Very often these prospective parents have had a long and traumatic experience of infertility treatment, but when all treatment has failed they are eager to adopt a child as soon as possible. The majority of the couples come from large families and in addition to their eagerness to quickly form a nuclear family they have quite specific requirements about the child they want: "We'd like to have a girl as young as possible, with fair hair. . . ." In general, they seem to feel inferior to those with biological children, and most of the women indicate a lack of confidence in their mothering ability and want to keep the adoption process a secret.

Some adoptive parents feel anxious about the kind of person the child will turn out to be. This is obvious from their questions and their need for a lot of information about the child's background. This is of course encouraged; however, should problems arise later, these parents would tend to attribute the child's misbehavior mostly to inherited characteristics rather than to experiences within the adoptive family.

Many of the above characteristics are common to the adoptive parents who apply to our agencies for a child, and although their concerns and fears are legitimate, if they are not addressed and worked through, they may lead to family maladjustment. For this reason, preparation for adoption is needed not only for the child's welfare but for that of the entire family.

PREADOPTION PARENT EDUCATION PROGRAM

In Poland, the waiting time to adopt a small child averages about two years. During this waiting period, the couples are in contact with the adoption agency. The preadoption parent education program was developed and implemented in 1984 and consists of six group sessions and as many individual consultations with a psychologist as the participant wishes or the group leader advises.

The general objectives of the preadoption program are the following:

1. To inform participants about the legal aspects and procedures for adoption.
2. To offer a basic knowledge about human development and help participants understand about the adjustments required when an older child comes to the family from an institution.
3. To create a realistic picture of adoptive family life and to show positive outcomes of adoptive families.
4. To help participants reduce feelings of low self-confidence and low self-esteem.
5. To try to decrease anxiety both toward the adoption process and following the adoption.

6. To create and maintain a supportive group where couples can share fears, emotions, attitudes, and values and where through discussion their outlook, if unrealistic, can be modified.
7. To meet individual psychological needs of prospective parents.

Couples applying to an adoption agency are informed that they are expected to follow the program and are given information about the time and place where the group will meet. They have a choice among four groups. If clients refuse to enter a group, they are invited to make an appointment with one of the agency's psychologists. Usually after individual consultations, couples seem more relaxed and join a group. Group sessions are held every two months, starting in September, and six to eight married couples belong to each group.

Each session is led by two psychologists, a group leader, and a cotherapist. Professionals from several specializations, including pediatricians, judges, social workers, and parents of adopted children, are invited to lecture and to answer group questions. Each session lasts about one and a half hours, depending on the topic and the number of questions asked, and is held in an informal, friendly, atmosphere.

TOPICS AND ACTIVITIES

1. Introduction, presentation of participants and staff, and identification of group needs and expectations. The objective of this session is mostly to create an atmosphere in which the participants will feel comfortable, and will come to understand that the persons involved are their advocates. At the same time, this session will help the staff realize the kinds of information and help the participants seek.
2. Identifying participants' expectations about the children they hope to adopt. To accomplish this, participants are first asked to answer in writing the question: "What do you think your child will be like?" After the answers are gathered the group leader analyzes the responses and points out the differences in expectations between men and women. Usually prospective fathers are more concerned with the educational level they hope the child will achieve, while mothers express expectations relating to more emotional matters. The objective of this session is to help prospective parents

clarify and at the same time pinpoint the differences in the expectations of each parent and help them to consider all the children available for adoption, instead of a child with specific physical characteristics.

3. Choosing parents for a hypothetical child. In this exercise, participants are divided into two or three small groups and are given the medical, psychological, and social documents of a child waiting for adoption and descriptions of three different couples wishing to adopt. The task of each group is to choose parents for the child and to explain their choice. The objective of this session is to get the participants to verbalize what they think an adoptive family should be like, including the most important factors needed to insure proper care for a child.

4. Meeting the judge involved in the family division of a court. This helps the couples familiarize themselves with the legal system and allows them to ask direct questions concerning the process of adoption.

5. Meeting with a pediatrician and a psychologist who have had professional experience with children deprived of a biological family and who can answer medical and psychological problems about human development.

6. Meeting parents and their adopted children and learning first hand what it is like to be an adoptive family.

The teaching methods chosen have as their aim to facilitate the active participation and the emotional involvement of the prospective adoptive parents. There are no formal lectures. The participants learn by doing the group work on prepared materials like "choosing the parents," by discussing problems, asking questions, analyzing situations, role playing, and making decisions. Group work provides the opportunity for participants to discuss problems in relation to their own life experiences. Some group sessions are organized around given tasks or problem-solving exercises, followed by presentations of the group decisions and discussion. During other sessions the participants discuss their own fears connected with child rearing and how they view the life of an adoptive family.

Between sessions the agency staff is available for individual consultation with parents. When the psychologists participating in the psychoeducational program diagnose emotional problems during the group meetings, they offer individual sessions where personal emotional problems are discussed and counseling is provided.

Evaluation of the effectiveness of the educational program for adults is a difficult task. There are no quantitative indices of the outcome, except for the number of participants (about 190 couples up to now). Thus the evaluation can only be qualitative, because this kind of education cannot end with a final examination. In addition to the information given, the program focuses on the psychological dimensions, such as self-confidence, attitudes, motivation, and behavior. The measurement of changes in these areas would be a difficult and time-consuming task. However, we have some feedback from the participants and some experts' opinions. The best evidence of progress are changes in expectations, from the very detailed— "I want my child to be 50 inches tall, have curly hair, etc."—to the more general willingness to accept a child as is. Gradually the future adoptive parents understand that having a child of a particular age, sex, or appearance is not the factor that will enhance the functioning of the family. This openness and realization was found to be a better prognosis for adjustment to adoptive family life. By the end of the program participants seem to exhibit higher self-competence and self-esteem. Because of very close contacts between the members of the group, the feelings of being different and isolated are lessened. The groups' social contacts continue between and after the sessions; friendships are formed and participants help each other in many ways. Some parents come to the agency with their adopted child to share their experiences with parents still waiting to adopt. They talk about the benefits they have had from the preadoption educational program. The feedback allows us to improve the program. During the program's five years there were no drop-outs from the group and only a few decided not to adopt. The couples who refuse to participate in the group and request individual instruction only are those who most often decide against adopting.

Some families keep in touch with the agency more than three years after adopting. These people still want to share their problems and troubles but also their successes and joys with the agency workers. Several couples come to the agency from other districts simply for the education even though they know they have no chance of adopting through this agency.

Although we feel the preadoption education program has contributed to better understanding and handling of the adoption for the parents who have participated up to now, we still think there is room for improvement. The program needs to be more flexible and be replicated in other parts of Poland. There is also a strong impetus for the staff to improve the content, methods, and organization of the education process. The program deals not only with education about the process of adoption but touches many human and developmental areas. Thus, the staff has to be well trained in order to be able to communicate with the participants concerning all life aspects. In addition they have to have training in teaching, group leading, and preparing the teaching materials. Up to now the agency has not spent additional funds for the educational program, but we are hopeful that the importance of preadoption education will be soon recognized by the government agencies and more funding will be allocated for this purpose.

Part VII

Legal Aspects of Adoption

17

Inter-Country Adoption in European Legislation

Graziella Caiani-Praturlon, S.W.

The "best interest of the minor" is a concept which appeared relatively recently in European legislation, and it affects all the decisions which must be taken regarding a minor. It is also a concept which is open to several interpretations.

From a judicial point of view, the changes that have come about in recent legislation are the consequence of a new way of considering minors in a separate category from adults in terms of their expectations and rights. For example, in Italy there are six proposed laws which deal with creating a civil defenders' office to represent minors and their interests.

From a psychosocial point of view, evaluation of a minor's best interests as seen from a dynamic point of view, anticipating the minor's future development while considering his or her past history, is a rather complex process in which objective and subjective data must be considered. This data usually derives from a highly individualized study of the minor's situation and of his or her social environment. In Europe, it is the social service organizations that are the ones most frequently asked to gather and evaluate information which is used to understand a minor's needs.

In relation to the complex problem of adoption, the concept of "best interests of the minor" appeared in Europe for the first time in

1926 in Soviet legislation in a form that was not clearly defined at that time. In it, the specific aim of the institution was to guarantee an adequate education for the minor and a suitable environment to facilitate his future development. Prior to that time the relationship between adopter and adoptee was not well defined in Soviet legislation. It considered the minor's welfare in a larger context which included the relationship between the minor and his or her family of origin.

After World War II, the concept of adoption "as placing the minor in a family unit as a substitute for the original one, and in which there are very exclusive relationships" has gained more and more acceptance in other European countries. However, the conditions thought of as the right ones for both minors and adoptive parents have gradually changed over the last fifty years, with the aim of guaranteeing the child's psychophysical development in a suitable family nucleus as nearly as possible like a natural one.

Today, simple adoption (with limited legal effects) has been superseded by full adoption in twenty-two countries. In full adoption, the relationship with the biological family is interrupted, and the child assumes the name of the adoptive parents. In ten countries both forms of adoption exist, while Turkey is the only country in which there is still only simple adoption.

It is also important to point out that twenty-seven out of thirty-two countries require a preliminary investigation and individual evaluation of a couple in order to determine their suitability for the parental role, although the concept of "potential capability for mutual harmony" is used only in some countries. The legislation in those countries stresses that it is not enough to consider an adoptive couple's qualities in an abstract manner but that a complex evaluation of interdependent factors is necessary. These factors are not necessarily the cultural standards of the adopters, or the absence of racial and religious prejudices, but rather elements, such as the capacity for a positive approach to new situations, that suggest the possibility of good integration (Italian Law n.183/84, art. 22, par. 3; Swiss Civil Code, art. 268; Turkish Code of Protection of Minors, art. 2828). It is also useful to remember that in almost all legislation the family of origin is mentioned, but it is only in a rather limited number of countries (Greece, art. 12.2, 9, 1, 2, 3; Finland, art. 10; Democratic Republic of Germany, art. 68; France, art. 348) that it is clearly stated that the family of origin should receive counseling before giving up a child for adoption.

THE CONVENTION OF STRASBURG

Signed by sixteen European countries on April 24, 1967, the Convention of Strasburg agreed to set down the conditions for adoption in the best interest of the minor. Apart from indicating objective and subjective points regarding the adoptive parents while keeping in mind the best interest of the minor, the Convention also gives guidelines for the interventions needed to evaluate the adoptive situation as a whole. The Convention is the main reference point defining the role and professional competencies in the field of inter-country adoption, and suggests means for safeguarding the minor's interest and of those who must collaborate with the magistrate to arrive at a balanced assessment. More specifically the articles of the Convention refer to:

1. The intent to give the minor a family environment similar to his original one (art. 6.1, art. 7.1, art. 8), and to protect and give preference to the minor in all phases of the adoption process.

2. The need to evaluate the situation of the family of origin (art. 9.1) and to guarantee that the mother gives her consent if she is in good psychological and physical health (art. 5.4); the need to take the minor's view into account (art. 9 f), and finally, the need for a preadoption period during which it is possible to evaluate the validity of the relationship between the minor and the adopters before the adoption is made final.

3. The characteristics and professional training of the operators who must intervene (art. 9.3, art. 19) and perform the assessment; the need for the public authorities who have the responsibility of dealing with the adoption to control the activities of the services (art. 18). And, finally, point 2 of art. 9 of the Convention gives a detailed listing of all the aspects which must be examined case by case to define the minor's interest.

OTHER EUROPEAN LEGISLATION REGARDING ADOPTION

A close examination of all the aspects mentioned in the convention shows that it does not sufficiently reflect the recommendations that came out off the Lesyn Seminar (art. 11-12) regarding the need for the adoption to be valid in both countries involved. This aspect is not only of legal importance but also has social consequences. If the minor finds himself in a situation which is not defined in all its aspects in relation to the adopting family, this can create a sense of insecurity, resentment, and a subjective feeling of exclusion which sometimes reemerges and aggravates problems of integration in the family and in the social group.

Consequently, from a legal point of view, it is necessary to have specific norms to safeguard the minor's interest, during the period which precedes the actual adoption, during the transfer, and finally to safeguard his personal and cultural identity.

Let us emphasize at this point that only Norwegian legislation (art. 30) places a condition on inter-country adoption: there must be the assurance that the "adoption is not harmful for the minor because of the interruption in his links with his country of origin." This is the only example of a law that stresses an often undervalued aspect of adoption, that affects a minor who may be traumatized by a total change in environment. Such a change often comes about after he has already experienced established family and other personal relationships. If we examine the laws in force today we see that inter-country adoptions are covered in a different way in each European country.

When there is more concern for the minor's well-being, the legislation explicitly indicates that there must be the certainty that unconditional parental consent is given and that the family of origin has been fully informed about the effects of adoption.

The norms on the validity of parental consent are given in detail in various articles in the legislation of the Federal Republic of Germany, Denmark, Greece, and Finland, and all stress a thorough assessment and need for parental consent if the mother is in good mental and physical condition.

In the Federal Republic of Germany, the foreign sentence (the foreign country's court decision, i.e., consent to adopt) becomes effective only if the consent was given according to the conditions stated by the Family Code of the Federal Republic of Germany (art. 23, p. 2); in Denmark, the norms for the validity of consent in inter-country adoptions are defined in article 5 of law 495, September 26, 1984; in Greece, the consent of the family of origin is covered by article 12, p.

2 and article 9, p. 1, 2, 3 of D.L. 610/1970; and for Finland, article 10 of law n. 153 of February 8, 1985.

THE ROLE OF SOCIAL SERVICES IN THE EUROPEAN LEGISLATION

Mention of interventions in favor of the family of origin and of the role of the social services on their behalf is for the most part missing in European legislation. In light of the existing laws and in relation to assessments which are evidently rather complex, it appears necessary to define the role and tasks that the social services assume in the whole process. It is the social services, in fact, that are most frequently indicated as the organizations which must gather all the elements to establish the adopters' eligibility and assess the state of the minor before the adoption, in addition to overseeing and evaluating the preadoption period.

It is important that the operator focuses on the psychosocial status while evaluating the relationship between the adoptive couple and their attitude toward the situation and toward the operator. This type of evaluation should be expressed not only on the basis of an exhaustive case history but above all in a clinical-type perspective.

In most countries the social services generally act as consultants to the Court, to the family of origin, to the minor, and to the adopters. It is only in some countries that the social services assume a more active role in the course of the adoption process, and the legislation indicates if more specific tasks are to be carried out.

To go from general considerations of the role given to the social services to a classification—even though approximate—of the organizations which are called upon to express an opinion on the "minor's interest," it will be helpful to put the countries in four different groups.

The first group is made up of six countries (Austria, Malta, Romania, San Marino, Hungary, and the U.S.S.R.) in which, though the need to proceed with adoption only in the interest of the minor is acknowledged, the law does not indicate by what means these interests are to be evaluated.

The second group is made up of seven countries (Albania, Bulgaria, Czechoslovakia, Ireland, Norway, Spain, and Yugoslavia) in which the law simply indicates in a generic way the need to have investigations made, but does not explain through what channels or with what means this is to be done, and the social services are not mentioned.

The third group is made up of six countries (Belgium, Iceland, Italy, Poland, Portugal, and Turkey) which include in their laws precise indications of the competence of the social services or other qualified professionals to express an opinion on the minor's interest in being adopted.

The fourth group is made up of fourteen countries (Cyprus, Denmark, Finland, France, Greece, Great Britain, Liechtenstein, Luxembourg, Monaco, Holland, The Democratic Republic of Germany, the Federal Republic of Germany, Sweden, and Switzerland) where the task of offering expert opinion on whether the decree adoption or not is given to the specialized social services and where the juridical norms also indicate the way in which the intervention should be administered and the necessary professional training and qualifications.

All the above countries recognize that it is necessary to delegate the responsibility, for the overall assessment of the minor who is to be adopted, to professionals with specialized training and to services with more specific qualifications than to social service in general. In the countries in our fourth group, the specialized social service intervenes in all phases of the adoption procedure, though with slightly differing roles, some roles being more important than others.

In all of these countries, major focus is on the assessment of the adopting parents, and the social service generally acts as consultant to the magistrates. In addition, in some countries, such as Greece, Finland, Democratic Republic of Germany, the Federal Republic of Germany, and France, more attention is paid to the family of origin and to the consent phase. Apart from acting as consultants, the social services sometimes assume direct responsibilities during the adoption process. This is common in Greece, the Democratic Republic of Germany, the Federal Republic of Germany, Holland, Denmark, Finland, France, and Luxembourg. The Greek and Swiss laws determine what professional training the operator must have and specify the contents of the requested interventions.

From the above we can see that in most European countries very precise laws have been passed regarding the interest of the minor and the social aspect of adoptions, which indicates a particular concern of the legislators regarding adoption.

Based on the experience of the social services and that of clinical psychology, it now appears necessary, in the interest of the minor, to modify the cultural attitude and the laws on adoption still further, especially in the area concering the relationship of the minor to his original home environment. Nonetheless, we can observe that as psychological attitudes change, so does the legislator's orientation both nationally and internationally. Article 17 of the 1978 United Nations "Project of Declaration on the Protection of Minors, with Particular Attention to Family Custody and National and Inter-Country Adoptions" affirms that once the adopted person has become an adult, he has the right to know his original home environment.

COORDINATION OF SERVICES IN INTER-COUNTRY ADOPTIONS

Inter-country adoptions are rather hard to manage not only because of the social and psychological implications which are inherent, but also because of the legislative differences, the differences in organizational structures, and in the levels of professional expertise and services. In addition, there is difficulty in establishing communication networks with which to guarantee that correct procedures are followed in both countries and with the necessary confidentiality. The agencies charged with coordination need to have professional personnel able to collaborate with the welfare structures of the two countries concerned. They must be able to obtain, transmit, or interpret all the information and elements of a social, psychological, and juridical nature related to minors and to adoptive parents. Consequently, they must act not only as coordinators but also as consultants to the various magistrates and services involved in the adoption procedure.

This role is indispensable, and must be covered by agencies operating under the control of the countries concerned. The agencies must be nonprofit organizations; they must not operate on the basis of ideological or religious premises, nor with personnel who are somehow emotionally involved with the issue of adoption.

In such a changing and rapidly evolving situation as adoption, the role of social services is essential and cannot be limited to interventions on an individual basis but must be extended to a larger social and cultural context. In fact, the social services are an instrument for verifying whether the norms established by the legislation are valid when applied. On the basis of their experience, the social services must ask for any necessary legal modifications to be made.

As to the validity of a comparative analysis of the roles of the social services in various European countries, we must remember that the difficulty in evaluation is not in comparing different laws but in understanding the real meaning of the interventions and of the results obtained. The following elements make it difficult to make a comparative analysis of the quality and validity of the services: (1) differences in the professional training of the social workers in the various countries; (2) differences in the structures of the public and private services and their precise role in a specific culture; and (3) the different types of relationships with the community and with individuals and the manner in which these ask for, accept, or submit to the intervention of the social services.

All these elements, though partly imponderable and yet linked to the application of a precise norm, are somewhat variable and greatly condition the results of the intervention itself. Therefore, for a more exact evaluation of the real role of the social services and of their usefulness in their fields it would be necessary to observe what happens when these laws are actually applied.

It is not by chance that in 1985 the International Non-Governmental Organizations drew up for the United Nations a document proposing and recommending a series of norms relating to the rights of the child. The document expresses the conviction that it is necessary to set up a mechanism which can assess, facilitate, and guarantee the application of the dispositions of the Convention and suggests forming a permanent committee of experts with the mandate to: (1) ask the member states for a report on the application of the dispositions of the Convention; (2) examine them; and (3) take all the necessary initiatives. As to inter-country adoption—which seems to be the form of adoption most frequently practiced today, at least in European countries—from the general outlook, we see that for the laws to be applied more efficaciously, it would be best to find more binding solutions in accord with the national legislation and welfare structures of the countries concerned.

In this direction, the most useful and feasible solution seems to be the signing of bilateral agreements which would allow any two countries to set down procedures which are compatible and integrated not only with their respective national legislation, but with the structures of the social services in each country.

This would be a means of asking for professional collaboration on an international public level; of stressing the need for sharing the decisions which are made for a minor beyond the regional borders; and of eliminating all possible suspicions of poor objectivity in the assessment of the interest of the minor.

18

Adoption in a Framework of Child Welfare Legislation

Richard A. H. White, L.B.

Awareness of a child's need for a secure environment to facilitate his development has prompted the British courts to show a greater willingness to give priority to the welfare of the child, rather than simply considering the wishes of the natural parents. Two types of situations potentially damaging to a child caused this shift in the courts' thinking: on the one hand parents who change their minds and demand the return of children they had placed for adoption, and on the other, older children who are cared for by the state for so long a period as to lose emotional ties with their parents. Making adoption orders against the wishes of the biological parents is now regularly considered by the courts in the United Kingdom. This chapter seeks to explore some of the legal problems that arise when a society decides to override the wishes of the parents in order to provide secure placements for children who cannot live with those parents.

PROCEDURAL ISSUES

Any process of vesting full and permanent parental rights in adopters obviously requires the termination of the rights of the biological parents at some point. In the United Kingdom, there are two points at which parental rights can be terminated: at the time of an order in favor of the adopters, or on the application of a (state-approved) adoption agency, which then holds temporary rights pending an order in favor of the adopters.

This creates a dilemma which may never be resolved to everyone's complete satisfaction. If termination of the biological parents' rights does not take place until the adopters obtain their order, the child may be placed with a couple whose application for the adoption may not be approved. If termination takes place on the application of the adoption agency, the relationship of a child with his natural parents may be terminated before he acquires a legal relationship with his adopters. There is a hiatus which cannot be adequately filled when a state agency must act as a legal parent (Adcock, White, and Rowlands, 1983).

In some legal systems, like that of the United Kingdom, a state agency may be empowered to decide that a child needs to be placed for adoption and may be given the authority to achieve that aim. Should these powers be vested solely in the administrative or social work systems or should they be subject to judicial or other external review? Without some objective oversight by the court, parents could effectively lose their relationship with their child without being given the opportunity to oppose such a step.

In my opinion a judicial decision is needed only when there is proof that parents are no longer capable of caring for their child, and, consequently, that there is no purpose in further assisting them to provide adequate care. If the question of the biological parents' capability is left until the adoptive parents are attempting to satisfy the court that they are suitable to become the child's legal parents, the welfare of all parties is jeopardized because of the uncertainty of whether the child is legally available for adoption. The court may disagree with the agency's view that parental rights should be terminated and conclude that the child should be returned to the biological parents. If a child has been in state care for some time, he may no longer have emotional ties to the parents and will suffer from being uprooted once again at a time when he needs a stable environment. The prospective adopters will also suffer when they must return a child with whom they have formed emotional bonds.

The emotional welfare of the child is so vital that in those cases where the agency considers that adoption is the clear plan, there should be an opportunity for all views to be challenged before an independent tribunal. The court should be asked to authorize the termination of parental rights and the permanent placement of the child, if the child's welfare so requires, or authorize restitution of the child to its biological parents.

One consequence of such a system may be that a child awaiting court proceedings will be left in an interim placement longer than is desirable, especially if a court-appointed guardian for the child has to investigate the child's situation and write a report. The only satisfactory solution is to provide resources to ensure that court proceedings are dealt with promptly. Sadly we are a long way from achieving that, even when a parent is not contesting a case. Unless additional resources are made available, we may have to accept placement by administrative decision to prevent the even worse evil of children being left in a legal limbo.

WORK WITH THE FAMILY

An essential precondition to placing a child for adoption is that reasonable attempts have been made to help his family of origin care for him. This help may be in the form of physical resources, training in parenting skills, or therapeutic work. Without the offer of this help, we may be doing a disservice to the child in separating him permanently from his family. Adoption professionals will not make a wholehearted effort to prepare children for substitute placements if they are not confident that essential work with biological families has been done.

For the law, the question is whether such "preventive" or "rehabilitative" work should be mandated as an essential prerequisite to termination of parental rights. What happens in cases where the necessary intervention has not been done? Are the child's interests and rights jeopardized? Is his welfare then placed second to the rights of the birth parent? I would have to argue no, but how then do we ensure that state agencies effectively fund and carry out the proper preliminary work?

GROUNDS FOR DISPENSING WITH PARENTAL AGREEMENT IN PLACING CHILDREN FOR ADOPTION

An essential precondition to dispensing with parental consent is that adoption is itself in the interests of the child. Should the interests of the child in itself be sufficient for the court to make an order, or should some additional factors be examined? In the United Kingdom the legislature and the courts have always taken the view that parental rights are of such importance that they should not be terminated by adoption without parental agreement, unless there are proven grounds for setting aside agreement (Adoption Act, 1976).

The wishes of the parents may be overridden when criminal neglect or ill-treatment can be proved, but otherwise the court has no clear-cut directive in which to consider whether a parent is reasonable in withholding agreement. The burden is on the adopters or the state agency to show that a parent's refusal is unreasonable. The court may, therefore, believe that the parent should agree but still be unable to decide that the child should be adopted. As we shall see below, this problem may present particular difficulties when the biological parent continues to have access to the child.

ARE THERE ALTERNATIVES TO ADOPTION?

When a child cannot live with his family of origin, adoption provides the next best option. Since adopters should now be counseled to inform a child of his adoptive status from an early age, adoption is not an attempt to hide the facts of one's birth; rather it is an attempt to accomplish the following:

1. To integrate a child fully into a new family, and give him a status which will continue after childhood.
2. To give a child and the adopters the same security against removal of the child, whether by the natural parents or by the state, as his birth parents had.
3. To vest the adopters with the authority to act as parents, and to enable them to help the child to develop an identity.

Where a child remains in state care, custodial rights and duties will be shared among various individuals who have an overriding right to apply to the court to have his status changed. In the United Kingdom, only the local authority and parents can apply to the court (foster parents cannot). There has been a recent statutory provision (Adoption Act, 1976, §33, implemented only in 1985) which enables the court to vest long-term custodial powers in substitute caretakers, such as foster parents. This removes the local authority from the scene, but for the child and his caretakers, this may present new problems. Sometimes the biological parents do not fully accept the legal caretakers as having parental authority over their child. As a consequence the caretakers are subject to frequent disruptions from forces outside their family, such as from the family of origin, social workers, and the courts, in their efforts to raise the child. This is not a normal situation for most families in our society. Adoption is the only legal arrangement which resolves this problem, and a statutory presumption in favor of adoption should be created. Careful consideration of the relationship between child care legislation and adoption is needed. Unless child care legislation is carefully examined and coordinated with adoption legislation, there cannot be a fully integrated and coherent system for promoting children's welfare.

A statutory presumption in favor of adoption would not mean that children who did not return to their parents would automatically be adopted. A range of options would remain available, but it should be necessary to show why an alternative to adoption is to be preferred. In some circumstances, there will be clear indications against adoption, such as in the case of an older child who wants or needs to maintain strong links with his family of origin. I suspect, however, that this would be true in a minority of cases, once parents and child have accepted that the substitute family is to be permanent.

ADOPTION AND ACCESS TO BIRTH FAMILY

When a baby is placed for adoption at or shortly after birth, it is unlikely that there will be any contact between the parents and the adopters or that the child will develop a relationship with the biological parent. The situation is different when an older child is being considered for long-term placement. It may well be that the child has lived with the parent for some years or has visited the parent at times while they were living apart. In either case, some relationship will have developed, beneficial or not. Consideration must therefore be given to whether the strength of the relationship between parent and child is such as to make the legal status of adoption inappropriate. Whether adoption is to follow or not, consideration must also be given to the question of future access of the parent to the child. Unfortunately, in the United Kingdom adoption law is constructed with the adoption of babies and not the adoption of older children in mind, so the issues I raise here fit ill with our legislation.

If adoption is planned for the child, in the majority of cases access to biological parents will be terminated, or at least severely reduced. The process of doing this, and whether it is necessary to do it before or after adoption, presents major problems. We have then the following questions: Should access to biological parents be terminated? Should access be phased out or reduced? If access is only reduced is adoption still appropriate? Is access desirable after adoption?

These questions raise complex problems involving the interrelated skills of social workers, pediatricians, mental health professionals, lawyers, and such diverse subject areas as social work management, child development, and legal principles. I do not want to stray too far into the expertise of other disciplines, but my experience in the legal field leads me to make the following points.

1. Access to the biological parents would need to be suspended or terminated abruptly where it is actively harmful to the child. It must also be terminated if the child is to be moved into a placement where the adopters wish their identity kept secret. Children in these two situations comprise the largest group of older children available for adoption. And we must keep in mind that many of the birth parents who are incapable of caring for the child they still consider to be theirs will abuse the right to have access to the child or the adopters' right to privacy.

With a parent who accepts the decision to give up a child for adoption, there may be a gradual reduction in visits leading to a goodbye visit before placement. If access is to be phased out with parental help, the period between the decision to seek termination of parental rights and the time of placement should be sufficient to make the necessary adjustments.

2. Different problems are presented by phasing down (i.e., reducing, but not terminating) parental access, where some continuing contact is meaningful and beneficial for the child. In my opinion, where

possible, there should still be a clear decision (open to challenge) by the state agency that adoption is in the child's best interest, since such a decision is needed for the child to begin to grow away from the birth parent.

There are cases where the nature and extent of access must be decided before placement. In such cases, whether adoption is the most suitable order for the child may be decided later. Decisions about access and adoption will be influenced by the development of the child's relationship with his long-term caretakers. This suggests a plan that will enable the child to understand that his biological parents have no authority, but he is free to reject adoption.

It will be rare for access to be phased down, as opposed to phased out, if the parent is actively contesting the adoption, since the phasing down process requires a degree of cooperation. Whether the adoption is contested or not, I would argue that once a decision has been made about long-term placement, great weight should be placed on the wishes of the prospective adopters with regard to access.

3. Perhaps one of the greatest problems is whether the law will accept that a child should be adopted where there is continuing access to his parents. In the United Kingdom the House of Lords has recently stated that if all parties agree both adoption and access are possible.

Where the parent does not agree to adoption, the legal questions are more difficult. In the United Kingdom, before an adoption order can be made without the parent's agreement, the court has to be satisfied that the parent is unreasonable in withholding the agreement. It is possible the court will think a parent is not unreasonable in refusing agreement if there is to be continuing access, or even perhaps a reasonable prospect of it.

How the courts will decide depends on circumstances, as illustrated by two recent cases of mine in which parents were withholding agreement. In both cases the judges considered that the children (both 8-year-olds) should be adopted. In one, the judge held the mother to be unreasonable because he assessed that the child would not be safe with the mother. However, in this case the adopters proposed to allow access to continue. In the other case, the judge held that the parents' desire to have the child back, and therefore to retain the hope of future access, was reasonable (though he did not contemplate returning the child to them). This was based on an assessment by a child psychiatrist who thought the parents were capable of caring for the child. The outcome was that the court could not dispense with the parents' agreement and thus not make the adoption order.

4. On the question of access after adoption, I believe we need to proceed carefully. Are we in danger of offering access to parents as an inducement for them not to contest the adoption? Are we asking adopters to undertake too much? Should the placement of older children now include the family of origin as part of the package? Is access truly in the interests of the child, or in response to pressure from the birth parents, even though it might be in the adoptive parents' best interests not to allow access?

In conclusion, I have considered some legal problems in modern adoption practice concerning older children and discussed some of the pitfalls of a complex system such as exists in the United Kingdom. The legal system must be structured to facilitate difficult placements and not become another hurdle for prospective adopters to add to their list. I would not wish to imply that there are easy answers, but I do believe that it is time we begin to recognize, learn from, and correct our mistakes.

REFERENCES

Adcock, M. F., White, R. A. H., & Rowlands, O. (1983), *The Administrative Parent*. London: British Agencies for Adoption & Fostering.

19

Opening of Adoption Records in New Zealand

Ann Corcoran, Dipl.S.W.

The Adult Adoption Information Act was passed in the New Zealand Parliament in September 1986. This Act enables adopted adults (age 20 and over) to have access to their original birth certificate unless the birth parent has placed a veto on the birth registration to stop information from being made available. The Act also gives birth parents the right to approach the Department of Social Welfare, which is responsible for the implementation of the social work aspects of the Act, with a request that they attempt to locate their child and ask whether that person is willing to have his or her name and address communicated to the applicant. The department is able to act on the request only when a veto has not been placed on the birth registration. While there is legislation worldwide allowing adult adoptees access to their original birth certificates and identifying information, a legal provision which enables birth parents to contact their child is unique to this country.

The passing of the Adult Adoption Information Act marked the end of a seven-year process initiated by adoptees and birth parents to get such legislation onto the books, debated, and finally passed into law. During that time there was much discussion about the effect such legislation would have retrospectively on the birth parents, who had been assured that their "secret" (the fact that they had placed a child for adoption) would remain a secret forever. The lengthy process enabled the community to become more aware of the issues and gave those people most deeply affected by the Act the strength to publicly state their wishes.

There was strong support for change from both adoptees and birth parents in favor of granting them the right to information about each other. In this article I will elaborate on the Act itself, the experiences of the birth parents, and the experiences of the adult adoptees.

THE ACT

The Act grants a birth parent who placed his or her child for adoption before September 1, 1986, the right to do the following:

1. Place a veto against the release of any information relating directly to him- or herself. The veto has a duration of ten years and must be renewed at that time.
2. Write to the Department of Social Welfare and ask them to locate the child who was placed for adoption, provided the adoptee is at least twenty years old.
3. Request information regarding the life history and present situation of the adoptee, provided the adoptee is agreeable.

The Act requires the Department of Social Welfare to:

1. Check that no veto on the release of identifying information has been placed by the adult adoptee.
2. Make every effort to locate the adult adoptee.
3. Make the adoptee aware of the birth mother's wishes for information or contact.

Once the Act was enacted, and prior to its implementation, social work staff met with some twelve groups of people involved in the adoption process (now referred to as Adoption Support Groups). These meetings were held to ascertain the wishes of the client group in regard to aspects of the Act. Among the questions discussed were the type of approach (through the adoptive parents or directly to the adoptee) the birth parents wanted to use.

The answer was direct and unequivocal. Biological parents wished the approach to be directly to the adoptee. They showed a lack of faith and confidence in the adoptive parents' ability to be objective in the exchange of information. Also, the adoptees who were present at these meetings stated that for too long they had been treated as children and decisions had been made for and around them. As adults now, they believed that how and when to involve their adoptive parents should be their decision.

EXPERIENCE OF BIRTH MOTHERS

From the time the Act was fully implemented in September 1986, and up to May 31, 1987, some 950 birth mothers have asked that a direct approach be made by the social work agency to their birth children. In addition to this number, some 3,000 biological mothers have asked to have recorded on file that should their son or daughter want to locate them, they were happy to be contacted. When asked why they wanted contact, birth parents stated that they wanted to offer friendship. However, understanding the difficulties contact might present, the birth parents wished to go at the adoptee's pace.

A random survey of 58 of the 950 birth parent applicants revealed these outcomes:

1. Five adoptees did not want personal contact but wanted to exchange nonidentifying information.
2. Five adoptees refused to give any information for passing on to the birth parents.
3. One adoptee was deceased.
4. The remaining 47 had exchanged identifying names, addresses, and phone numbers.

Therefore, we concluded that at least 90 percent of the contacts made on behalf of birth mothers have ended in a positive exchange of information if not in actual meetings.

EXPERIENCE OF ADULT ADOPTEES

To obtain their original birth certificates, adult adoptees must write to the Registrar General of Births giving their adopted name,

date of birth, and the adoptive parents' names. They must also nomi-
nate a counselor or an agency to provide counseling from a list available to them. Counselors are available from within the Social Welfare
Department or from a group of independent people and voluntary
agencies approved by the Minister of Social Welfare. The counselors,
both Department and independent, were selected because of their
knowledge of and/or previous experience in the adoption process.
Their training gave them the opportunity to practice telephone and
mediation counseling under supervision and made them familiar with
the searching process.

The role of the counselor is quite specific. He or she is to give
the original birth certificate to the adoptee; offer the adoptee advice
and guidance about searching and approaching; offer ongoing support, guidance, and encouragement; and provide the adoptee with
the names and addresses of local adoption support groups.

Once the adoptee has his or her original name and the name of
the birth mother at the time of the birth, it is not the role of the
counselors to do the searching but rather to act as facilitators and
reference points for the adoptee. Of the 5,000 adoptees who obtained
certificates from the Registrar-General's office in the nine months
following implementation of the Act, we believe the majority have
gone on to make direct contact with their birth parents.

The first National Adoption Conference in New Zealand was held
in May 1987 and was attended by some 200 people: birth mothers,
adoptees, adoptive parents, and social workers. There was much support for the Act and the social work practices underpinning its implementation. However, these flaws were highlighted at the conference:

1. Birth parents feel they are being treated differently from adoptees.
   They wonder why they cannot obtain a copy of the adopted child's
   birth registration.
2. No provision is made for contact by siblings, grandparents, or
   other extended family members. This becomes particularly relevant when the adoptee or birth parent is deceased.

What also became clear at that conference was the continuing
pain adoption can bring to many people. As the birth mothers have
become more vocal, they have expressed the depth of their hurt, their
continuing sense of powerlessness, and their growing determination

to ensure that their experiences are not repeated by another generation. By forming support groups, birth mothers have made our community aware of the continuing pain adoption can cause to birth parents and have promoted the worth of open adoption, which enables parents to have access to their children even though they are no longer legal guardians. Legislation has not yet been passed to make open adoption mandatory, but it is rare for social workers to approve couples for adoption if they are not willing to have some involvement with the birth parents.

The adoptive parents, in having to cope with the ongoing pain of the birth parents, feel undermined and undervalued. Their need for a family is, they believe, less clearly understood by the community at large and the birth parents in particular.

Though social workers heard some criticism of their past practices and decisions, nonetheless the conference was a powerful force for effecting change.

CONCLUSION

The Adult Adoption Information Act, granting adopted adults (age 20 and over) and birth parents of adopted adults opportunities to obtain information and access to each other, was implemented in 1986. Despite fears that such legislation would lead to discord within families and cause pain to a great number of people when adoptees found "new families," such fears were groundless. Most adoptive parents have been supportive of their adopted children's wish to discover their roots; most birth parents are sensitive to the rights of adoptive parents, and both sets of parents usually want the best situation for their children. Adoptees have made it clear that they are not looking for new parents but simply want access to the knowledge their birth parents can provide and hope that friendship ties can be forged.

Part VIII

Adoption Research

20

Does Adopted Mean Different?

Moses Leads the Way

Kathlyn S. Marquis, A.C.S.W., Richard A. Detweiler, Ph.D.

The literature on adoption continues to grow as researchers approach the subject from a wide range of perspectives, but the age-old question, "Does adopted mean different?" remains controversial. Despite the fact that the overwhelming number of adoptions appear to be successful (Mech, 1965), in a 1985 literature review, Marquis and Detweiler (1985) reported that the existing research literature on adoption suggests that adopted persons are mostly characterized by a predominance of negative attitudes and attributes. Furthermore, it is widely inferred that adoptive status is the root of these attributes. However, the results of research by Marquis and Detweiler comparing adoptive and nonadoptive youths did not support this view. In fact, we found that the adopted group was significantly more positive on a variety of measures.

Acknowledgments. We would like to thank the following for their assistance: Children's Aid and Adoption Society of New Jersey; Concerned Persons for Adoption; Adoptees Liberty Movement Association, New Jersey; Adoptees Liberty Movement Association, Minnesota; Liberal Education for Adoptive Families; Children's Home Society of Minnesota; Lutheran Social Service of Minnesota; and Bonnie Tarara of Rochester, Minnesota.

This lack of consistency with other research findings can be accounted for by a number of factors. First our study used a nonclinical population of adopted and nonadopted persons rather than the clinical populations commonly used in adoption research. Second, the research was cognitive in orientation, assessing person- and self-attributions, locus of control, and perceived parenting rather than the more typical psychodynamic or genetic measures. Third, the adopted persons in this study were young (ages 13 to 21) and preponderantly adopted within the first few months of life. Fourth, the study did not directly reference adoption, although fully informed consent of the parents was elicited.

In this chapter we will present the results of two studies and examine the similarities and differences between groups of adopted and nonadopted persons. Because the results of study 1 have appeared in the press elsewhere (Marquis and Detweiler, 1985) those results will only be summarized here.

STUDY ONE: THE YOUTH STUDY

METHODOLOGY

The cooperation of the adopted subjects was gained through a letter from an agency to a random sample of adoptive parents inviting their family to participate in this study. Data were collected on 167 subjects, of whom 46 were adopted and 121 were nonadopted persons, all between the ages of thirteen and twenty-one. All were private adoptions: 50 percent were placed within five weeks of birth, 89 percent within twelve weeks of birth, and 95 percent within a year of birth. The nonadopted subjects were volunteers recruited from a private independent day high school and a private independent college in New Jersey. These sources were used in order to closely match the upper-middle-class adopted families (Toussieng, 1971) on the basis of educational and occupational criteria. Since both adopted and nonadopted were chosen from the general population, we made no attempt to screen for psychopathology.

PROCEDURE

Each subject was given a "World View Survey" which consisted of (1) a measure of Locus of Control; (2) a Perceived Parenting Questionnaire; (3) a Personal History Form; and (4) a set of eight Attributional Stories. The survey was mailed to the adopted subjects and hand-delivered to the schools. The questionnaires were returned anonymously.

Locus of Control Scale. This scale included eighteen forced choice statements taken from Rotter's (1966) Internal–External (I-E) Locus of Control Scale (six "filler" statements and five statements with very low correlations for consistency were dropped). An adaptation of one pair of statements taken from the Multidimensional Internal External Control (IE) Scale (Gurin, Gurin, Lao, and Beattie, 1969), which is particularly relevant to the adoptive situation (changing laws) was added.

Perceived Parenting Questionnaire. This questionnaire was adapted from one used by MacDonald (1971) which was adapted from the Cornell Parenting Questionnaire (Devereux, Bronfenbrenner, and Rodgers, 1969). It contains thirteen items from MacDonald's scale that, according to his research, indexes five general parent practice variables (nurturance, predictability or standards, protectiveness, deprivation of privileges, and affective punishment), each of which was represented by at least two items in the questionnaire. All fifteen items appeared on the questionnaire in random order with no reference to the variable being measured. Because the pilot study did not show significant differences in the perceived parenting practices of the mother and the father, we collapsed the form across sex of parent and obtained data on parenting in general. Each item was followed by a set of five response alternatives ranging from 0 (never) to 4 (almost always).

Attributional task. This task reflects the attribution theory which describes the cognitive process we go through as we seek to understand ourselves and others. In general we use information about the behavior of the person (ourselves or others), and the context in which it occurred to make inferences about personal attributes (Shaver, 1975). An examination of the research literature on adoption revealed four recurring concepts used to characterize adopted persons: a feeling of lack of control ("control"), a feeling of not belonging (an outsider "status"), believing that one causes bad things to happen (negative "interpersonal outcome"), and a list of negative characteristics that are supposedly "self-descriptive." The task consisted of eight stories, each describing a unique situation. Although they appeared to be unrelated, they actually represented systematic variations of three specific dimensions: status, control, and outcome. Each story represented one of the eight possible orthogonal combinations of these three dimensions. After each story, the subjects responded to a set of fifteen questions by making attributional assessments about themselves and others on a 100 millimeter continuous scale. The questions were designed to tap attributions of (1) responsibility (if the story character or other things were seen as responsible); (2) similarity to subject (very or not at all similar to the story character); (3) self-image of story character (from very good to very poor); and (4) a series of bipolar adjectives whereby the story character was perceived as either dependent or independent, fearful or brave, tense or calm, hostile or friendly, lonely or popular, normal or abnormal, and secure or insecure as well as the self-attribution of the subject's confidence (either very confident or not at all confident).

RESULTS AND DISCUSSION

The two groups were compared on seven organismic variables, we found no significant differences for age, subject's educational level, educational level of the head of household, or occupational level of the head of household. There were significantly more males in the nonadopted sample and there were significant differences for both number of siblings and sibling position. However, when we matched a sample of thirty-four adopted subjects to thirty-four nonadopted subjects the analyses showed essentially identical results with those reported.

Analyses of variance were carried out to test for differences between the adopted and nonadopted persons on the attributional dimensions. Overall, these analyses showed that, compared to the nonadopted group, adopted youths saw themselves as more in control of their own lives; made more favorable attributions about others; rated persons who are in control and socially accepted as more similar to themselves and as more responsible, independent, brave, calm, friendly, popular, secure, and normal. They also expressed significantly more confidence in their own judgment than did the nonadopted. Finally, they rated the parenting they experienced as significantly more nurturant, comforting, predictable, and helpful.

Analyses of patterns of relationships among variables suggested that the positive parenting contributed to this overall positive attributional pattern; indeed when we combined adopted and nonadopted who had scored above the mean on positive parenting, we did not find any significant differences between the two groups demonstrating that more positive attributions were made by those with more positive parenting scores, regardless of adoptive status. Thus, the higher mean parenting score of the adoptive group accounts for the more positive attributions.

STUDY TWO: THE ADULT STUDY

The purpose of this study was to assess whether the same positive attributional pattern existed among a group of adopted adults. The majority of the subjects in this group were born prior to the 1960s—a time that brought marked changes in adoption policy in the United States, in that the early psychological needs of the infant began to be more fully recognized. Prior to this time, genetic and hereditary determinism prevailed and the adopted child, who usually came from a low socioeconomic level, was stigmatized by society in general (Kirk, Jonassohn, and Fish, 1966; Elonen and Schwartz, 1969; and Mech, 1973). The 1960s also brought marked changes in adoption policy. Bowlby's work (1951) on the harmful effects of early maternal deprivation was making inroads into the thinking of adoption professionals, who then began to make concerted efforts to bring about early infant placements whenever possible (Mech, 1973; Sorosky, Baran, and Pannor, 1978). Prior to the publication of Bowlby's work, adoption professionals had given little thought to the child's early psychological needs. We hypothesized that this older group would have enjoyed the consequences of early placement less frequently than was the case with the more recently adopted in our first study, and that it was unlikely that they would have escaped the stigma of the adoptive status. For these reasons as well as the negative reports in the literature, our hypothesis for this adult group was that they would have a more negative attitude than would their nonadopted peers.

METHOD

Data were collected on 275 subjects (176 adopted and 99 nonadopted), all between the ages of eighteen and seventy-eight with a mean age of thirty-four. The adopted subjects were obtained from a general population in a variety of ways: several adult adoption organizations enclosed a request for subjects with a newsletter mailing; another organization included a request in their newsletter, several private agencies handed out the request whenever they had contact with an adopted adult, and some adoptees, having heard about the study, asked to participate. Because of this method of selection, our sample in fact represents those who are especially motivated as a result of their adopted status. The adopted subjects represented twenty-four states and all seven geographic regions of the United States. Twenty-seven percent were placed for adoption within six weeks of birth, 50 percent were placed within twenty-three weeks of birth, 74 percent were placed within one year and 95 percent within seven years.

The nonadopted comparison group of subjects was also obtained in a variety of ways from a similar nonclinical population. Volunteers were recruited predominantly from a private independent school with a continuing education program, in order to match the age range of the adopted subjects; however, to more closely match the wide geographic distribution of the adopted subjects, other volunteers were recruited from various states. They represent six states and four geographic regions of the United States.

PROCEDURE

The procedure was essentially the same as for the youth study. Each subject was given a "World View Survey," which was either hand-delivered or mailed. It consisted of (1) a measure of Locus of Control; (2) a Perceived Parenting Questionnaire; (3) a Personal History Form; and (4) a set of eight Attributional Stories. The surveys were returned anonymously.

RESULTS

The two groups were compared on ten organismic variables. No significant differences were found for subjects' educational level, occupational level, marital status, number of children, family income, sex, or parents' educational level. There was an age difference in that the nonadopted are slightly older than the adopted as well as a difference in the number of siblings and sibling position where the adopted had fewer siblings and therefore occupied an earlier position.

ATTRIBUTIONAL ANALYSES

Analyses of stimulus stories were carried out using four-way mixed design analyses of variance with one between factor (adopted/nonadopted subject) and three repeated measures factors: the actor in the stimulus story was socially accepted (insider) versus unaccepted (outsider); the story actor was in control versus not in control; and the story outcome was positive versus negative. The results reported here have to do with differences between the adopted and non-adopted persons.

Attributions About Others. Responses to these questions ranged from 0 to 99 with a high score denoting a more negative attitude. In the case of Group there was a marginal main effect where adopted subjects made more positive attributions than did the nonadopted subjects.

In addition there was a Group by Outcome interaction in which adopted subjects clearly made more positive attributions in the positive-outcome situation than did the nonadopted subjects; but in the negative-outcome situation the adopted made attributions more similar to the nonadopted subjects (see Table 20.1). Internal comparisons using Tukey's HSD procedure (also called Tukey W; see Kirk, 1968, p. 89) indicated a significant change in these attributions among the adopted subjects.

Responsibility Attribution. Responses to this question ranged from 0 to 99 with a high score indicating that the events in the story were seen as happening outside the control of the story character. Results of the analyses of variance on the responsibility attribution showed a significant main effect for Group in which nonadopted adults attributed more responsibility to story characters than did the adopted subjects.

There was also a Control by Outcome interaction. Internal analysis indicated that story characters in the control-positive outcome situation were seen as more responsible than were those in the control-negative outcome situation, whereas in the no-control condition both positive and negative outcome situations were seen as representing

TABLE 20.1
Means of Descriptive Attributions for
Adult Group by Outcome Interaction

| | Outcome | |
Group	Positive	Negative
Adopted	26.40	32.82
Nonadopted	30.13	33.26

(HSC = 4.80; $p < .05$)
(Low score is more positive)

less responsibility for the actor. An examination of the nonsignificant three-way interaction (Group by Control by Outcome) made it apparent that the two-way interaction was to a large degree the result of the adopted in the no-control situation who ascribed less responsibility in the positive-outcome situation.

Similarity Attribution. Responses to this question ranged from 0 to 99 with a high score indicating that the story character was seen as similar to the subject. There was a marginal main effect for Group in which adopted subjects viewed story characters as more similar to themselves than did the nonadopted subjects.

In addition there was a Group by Control interaction in which adopted subjects viewed story characters in the no-control situation as much more similar to themselves than did the nonadopted in the no-control situation, whereas in the control situation, adopted and nonadopted viewed story characters as almost equally similar. Internal analysis indicated that there was a significant difference among the nonadopted in the control/no-control situations; this difference was not significant among the adopted.

There was also a Group by Status by Control by Outcome interaction in which there was a distinct difference for Control between adopted and nonadopted subjects in the insider/positive outcome situation; the adopted saw themselves as less similar to the story characters than did the nonadopted in the control situation and more similar than did the nonadopted in the no-control situation (see Table 20.2). In addition, there was a difference for Control between the adopted and nonadopted subjects in the outsider/negative outcome situation

TABLE 20.2
Means of Similarity Attribution for Group by Status by Control by Outcome Interaction

	Adopted							Nonadopted						
	Control		No-Control					Control		No-Control			
	Positive	Negative	Positive	Negative				Positive	Negative	Positive	Negative		
Insider	54.91	49.57	50.69	47.65				57.88	48.83	43.63	43.37		
Outsider	59.65	46.24	50.19	40.83				51.15	50.62	45.48	33.15		

HSD = 13.17

where the adopted saw themselves as less similar than did the non-adopted in the no-control condition.

Locus of Control Scale

No significant differences were demonstrated between the adopted and the nonadopted subjects on locus of control.

Perceived Parenting Questionnaire

Differences between groups were found for most parenting variables. The results are presented in Table 20.3, which shows that the adult adopted subjects rated their parenting as less nurturant, comforting, helpful, and more controlling, with use of nagging and yelling, deprivation of friends and things, acting cold or hurt, instilling guilt, being restrictive and interfering, than did their nonadopted peers. Only in the categories of predictable discipline and predictive behavior were there no significant differences, and only in the case of being protectively concerned was there a significantly more positive rating by the adoptees.

Using median splits all subjects were divided by their age with the adopted again being divided by their age at the time of adoption. Analyses of variance were then done on the parenting variables. The means are presented in Table 20.4, and as can be seen, the one group primarily accountable for the negative responses is the younger group (age 18–32) who were adopted at a later age (over 20 weeks old).

Those who fell in the younger age adopted group perceived their parenting to be similar to that of their nonadopted peers in that there was a significant difference only for punishment by guilt.

Discussion

One of the purposes of this study was to validate an attributional perspective as a useful means of gaining insight into the differences between adopted and nonadopted persons. Findings from this sample, based on a normal, nonclinical population, indicated that adult adopted persons made significantly more favorable attributions about themselves and others and showed more confidence in their own

TABLE 20.3
Perceived Parenting Means for Adults

Parenting	Adopted	Nonadopted	"t"
Nurturance	2.83	3.35	3.46***
Protectively Concerned	2.50	1.91	3.81***
Affect, Nagging	2.48	1.83	4.66***
Predictable Discipline	3.28	3.05	1.89
Deprivation, Friends	1.61	1.16	1.92**
Punishment, Cold	1.96	1.08	4.77***
Affect, Yelling	2.33	1.75	4.34***
Predictable Standards	3.37	3.50	−1.15
Comforting	2.40	2.95	−3.27**
Punishment, Hurt	2.67	2.16	3.48***
Protective–Restrictive	1.90	1.49	2.74**
Officious Interference	1.56	1.09	3.06**
Deprivation, Things	1.26	.78	3.33***
Helpful Interference	1.69	2.10	−2.61**
Punishment, Guilt	2.43	1.35	6.00***

*p = .05
**p = .01
***p = .001

judgments than the nonadopted. They rated stimulus persons who are insiders, who are in control of their behavior, and who cause good things to happen as having more positive personal attributes; that is, as more independent, brave, calm, friendly, popular, secure, and normal. The fact that they made particularly positive attributions in the positive outcome condition demonstrates that a positive outcome is especially meaningful (see Table 20.1). This indicates that adopted persons expect people who effect positive outcomes to be especially acceptable. On the other hand the adopted subjects ascribed less responsibility to the story characters for the same positive outcome, or for any outcome. There is one exception: they felt a person was most responsible in the no-control/negative-outcome condition.

Adopted adults also tended to see themselves as lacking control over their own outcomes. This was evidenced by their tendency to consistently rate story characters in the no-control condition as similar to themselves (see Table 20.2). In other words they may see themselves in a position of having less control, but they still feel responsible if the outcome is negative. It seems that they are accepting responsibility only for negative outcomes.

TABLE 20.4
Means of Parenting for Adults by Age of Adoption/Nonadoption

	Analyses of Variance						
	Young Age Group (18–32)			Older Age Group (33–78)			
	Young Adoptees	Older Adoptees	Non-adopted	Young Adoptees	Older Adoptees	Non-adopted	HSD
Nurturance	3.15	2.46	3.25	2.91	2.73	3.41	.55
Protective Concern	2.56	2.70	2.13	2.63	2.13	1.76	.61
Nagging	2.27	3.02	1.88	2.41	2.29	1.79	.55
Predictable Discipline	3.27	3.44	3.05	3.03	3.31	3.05	.46
Deprivation, Friends	1.51	2.24	1.00	1.38	1.32	1.28	.60
Punishing Cold	1.51	2.46	1.10	1.78	2.18	1.07	.72
Yelling	2.09	2.95	1.95	2.19	2.16	1.60	.52
Predictive Standards	3.46	3.17	3.45	3.50	3.38	3.53	.46
Comforting	2.87	1.93	2.83	2.22	2.40	3.03	.66
Punishment, Hurt	2.44	3.02	2.21	2.91	2.47	2.12	.59
Protective Restrictive	1.91	2.15	1.53	2.00	1.60	1.47	.60
Officious Interference	1.58	1.63	1.08	1.78	1.33	1.10	.61
Deprivation, Things	1.18	1.81	.88	1.03	1.05	.71	.65
Helpful Interference	1.84	1.73	2.10	1.63	1.53	2.10	.63
Punishment, Guilt	2.02	2.81	1.23	2.59	2.44	1.43	.71

The responses on parenting (see Table 20.3) indicated that adopted adults perceived their parenting as more negative than did their nonadopted peers. The difference (see Table 20.4) is mostly due to the younger/low-age-adopt group (age 18–32) who were adopted at a later age (over 20 weeks old). Both groups were similar in parental predictable discipline and predictive behavior; however, the adoptees felt that their parents were more protectively concerned. Also, those who fell in the younger/low-age-adopt group perceived their parenting as being more similar to that of their nonadopted peers except in the area concerning punishment by guilt. In other words, the results suggest that if one is adopted at an early age, one is more likely to perceive one's parenting as similar to that perceived by the non-adopted.

COMPARISON OF THE YOUTH AND ADULT STUDIES

In attributions about others, both young and adult adopted groups make favorable attributions toward story characters who are

TABLE 20.5
Means of Descriptive Attributions for Youth Group by
Status by Outcome Interaction

Group	Positive	Negative
Adopted		
Insider	21.53	34.35
Outsider	28.97	33.62
Nonadopted		
Insider	31.69	38.06
Outsider	34.94	40.52

$F(1,138) = 4.20, p < .05)$
$(HSD = 7.84)$

insiders, who have control over their lives, and who effect positive outcomes. Also, both adopted samples demonstrated significantly more confidence in their own judgment than did their nonadopted peers.

However, the position of being an insider versus an outsider was an important issue to the adopted youth in that they viewed story characters in the insider/positive-interpersonal outcome situation significantly more favorably than they did in the outsider/positive-interpersonal outcome situation (see Table 20.5).

This was not the case with the adopted adults to whom any positive outcome was seen as good (see Table 20.1). However, it is interesting that when the adult group was divided by a median split according to age and age-at-adoption, the younger/low-age-adopted group showed the same pattern found in the youth study; they too made more positive attributions in the insider/positive-outcome situations than did the controls. This reinforces the notion that age-at-time-of-adoption may be an important factor.

In the matter of attributing responsibility, the youth group showed a trend to attribute more responsibility in the control situation and less in the no-control situation. The adults, on the other hand, attributed part of what happens to things outside the persons' control in most cases. There was one exception: adopted adults found story characters in the no-control situation more responsible for their negative outcomes and less responsible for their positive outcomes than

did the controls. So, like the adopted youths the matter of control was
an issue; but unlike the youths, the adopted adult took the blame for
a bad outcome.

This perceived control difference was also reflected on the similarity variable. Whereas the adopted youth rated their own similarity
to story characters significantly higher in the control situations and
significantly lower in the no-control situations, the adult group of
adopted reversed the pattern: they saw themselves as much more
similar to the story characters in all conditions of no-control.

Why is there this lack of congruence between the youth and adult
adopted persons in the issues of responsibility and similarity? Overall,
the adults attributed some responsibility for outcomes to things outside the person's control, with the exception of the no-control situation, with a negative outcome, and they consistently identified more
with persons in the no-control situation. However, they did not see
themselves as expecting to be less in control as indicated by their
almost identical locus-of-control score. They also tended to hold a
person in a no-control situation more responsible for a negative
outcome.

A number of explanations for this difference are possible. From
a historical point of view it could be said that these adult adoptees
are a product of their time in history—a time when there was little
knowledge of the effects of early maternal deprivation and a time
when it was not uncommon to place infants in foster homes for many
months, even years, prior to adoption. This probable loss of maternal
constancy existed in 50 percent of these adult adopted subjects and
may have left its mark on the child in inhibiting, to some degree, the
development of autonomy, thus leaving a residual of feeling not totally in control but still feeling responsible. A more plausible explanation, however, might be that they seem to be saying that although
there are forces outside one's control, they are not insurmountable
and one does not have to let bad things happen even if one does not
have complete control. Lawrence (1976), both a psychologist and an
adopted person, writes that young children have not grasped the full
meaning of adoption. Adoption is also an adult experience. It is very
possible that their identification with persons in the no-control condition is an undistorted healthy appraisal of their unique situation,
which should be different from the nonadopted persons who have
not had to forfeit some of their rights in exchange for a family. It is

also likely that this condition would be more salient to the adult adopted person than to the youth, especially in the United States where currently there is much emphasis on maintaining closed records.

The only obvious similarity between the adopted youths and the adopted adults to the perceived parenting questions was that the adults also rated their parenting as significantly more protective than did their nonadopted peers. However, when divided by a median split at age-at-adoption, where the low-age/low-age-adopt group of adults now share the early infancy placement, although there were no reversals, they did appear to perceive their parenting akin to the way the nonadopted perceived theirs, in that the only difference of significance was the perception of inculcation of guilt as a method of punishment.

In the youth study, the positive parenting was postulated as a possible antecedent to their positive world view. However, with the adults we have only protectiveness which was significantly more positive, and predictable standards and predictable behavior which were positive but not significantly more so, and there still existed the positive world view. Is it possible that having consistent parenting and feeling parental protection speaks to the adopted in terms of worthwhileness, and this sustains their self-esteem in the absence of sufficient nurturance?

Another possible explanation for the positive world view despite the predominantly negative parenting might be that these adopted adults had matured and worked through their adoptive experience, and/or because as maturing adults they had been able to experience and assimilate the changing social attitude toward adoptions; thus, they could make positive attributions. Societal attitude is a powerful influence and perhaps over time can assist in the repairing as well as the damaging of a world view.

CONCLUSIONS

Among the adopted we note a distinct difference in perceptions of parenting between the young and adult adopted groups; the adult adopted perceived their parenting as more controlling and intrusive than did their control group, while the adopted youth perceived their parenting as more nurturing and helpful than did their control group. It seems then that the emphasis should not be on some mystical factor related to whether or not one's genetic parents are physically present, as might seem to be the case when one reads so much about how being adopted means by definition that something is wrong, but rather the emphasis should be on the parenting one provides. Positive parenting is fostered by an open and honest, not an embarrassed hush-hush, set of societal and personal attitudes toward adoption, as well as by a thoughtful yet confident approach. Within the context of supportive parenting, one can expect the development of healthy attitudes toward oneself and others. Thus, even if knowledge-of-adoption at some point does cause psychological stress, there will be a positive and supportive environment within which to work through the issues—just as people who experience any sort of psychological stress do resolve the situation better and more easily within a supportive context, and in fact grow and become better persons because of it. Indeed, since the time of Moses, there are ample examples of persons who were adopted, raised in a positive and loving context, and who went on not only to make a contribution to this world, but who were apparently also psychologically healthy.

REFERENCES

Bowlby, J. (1951), *Maternal Care and Mental Health*. Geneva: World Health Organization.

Detweiler, R. A., & Marquis, K. S. (submitted), The adoptive experience: A positive view (1989).

Devereux, E. C., Bronfenbrenner, U., & Rodgers, R. R. (1969), A cross national comparison. *J. Marr. & Fam.*, 31:157–270.

Elonen, A., & Schwartz, E. M. (1969), A longitudinal study of emotional, social, and academic functioning of adopted children. *Child Welf.*, 48:72–78.

Gurin, P., Gurin, G., Lao, R. C., & Beattie, M. (1969), Internal–external control in the motivational dynamics of Negro youth. *J. Soc. Issues*, 25:29–53.

Kirk, H. D., Jonassohn, K., & Fish, A. D. (1966), Are adopted children vulnerable to stress? *Arch. Gen. Psychiat.*, 14:291–298.

Kirk, R. E. (1968), *Experimental Design: Procedures for the Behavioral Sciences*. Belmont, CA: Brooks/Cole.

Lawrence, M. M. (1976), Inside, looking out of adoption. Paper presented at the 84th Annual Convention of the American Psychological Association, Washington, DC.

MacDonald, A. P., Jr. (1971), Internal–external locus of control: Parental antecedents. *J. Consult. & Clin. Psychol.*, 37:141–147.

Marquis, K. S., & Detweiler, R. A. (1985), Does adopted mean different? An attributional analysis. *J. Personal. & Soc. Psychol.*, 48: 1054–1066.

Mech, E. V. (1965), Trends in adoption research. In: *Perspectives on Adoption Research*, ed. H. S. Maas. New York: Child Welfare League of America.

———— (1973), Adoption: A policy perspective. In: *Review of Child Development Research*, ed. B. Caldwell & H. Ricciuti, 3:467–507. Chicago, IL: University of Chicago Press.

Rotter, J. B. (1966), Generalized expectancies for internal versus external control of reinforcement. *Psychological Monographs*, 80: (Whole No. 1, pp. 609). Washington, DC: Psychological Association.

Shaver, K. G. (1975), *An Introduction to Attribution Processes*. Cambridge, MA: Winthrop Publishers.

Sorosky, A. D., Baran, A., & Pannor, R. (1978), *The Adoption Triangle*. Garden City, NY: Doubleday.

Toussieng, P. W. (1971), Realizing the potential in adoptions. *Child Welf.*, 50:322–327.

21

The Triangle of Fears:

Fallacies and Facts

Paul Sachdev, Ph.D.

Despite the recent indications of relaxed attitudes of adoptive parents toward unsealed adoption records, there is a general consensus among earlier writers that these parents feel threatened by such policy (Triseliotis, 1973; Burke, 1975; Pannor and Nerlove, 1977; Sorosky and Pannor, 1978; Lifton, 1979; Kadushin, 1980; Marcus, 1981; Tartanella, 1982; Geissinger, 1984; Sachdev, 1984, 1989). These studies suggest that adoptive parents seem to fear they may lose the love and loyalty of their children if the latter learn their origins, or establish reunion with birth parents. Adoptive parents also fear that openness in adoption might cause a confrontation with the biological mother and interference with the adoptive relationship. Birth mothers, too, are afraid that access to adoption files might result in unwanted intrusion by disgruntled adoptees in their newly formed lives and, thus, old and forgotten wounds would be opened. The above-mentioned authors also contend that discovery of genealogical facts could prove embarrassing to the adoptee and the opportunity

Acknowledgments. I wish to thank the Department of Social Services for its excellent cooperation in the conduct of the study. Funding support was provided by the Department of Health and Welfare, Canada, which is gratefully acknowledged.

to regain contact with birth parents would disrupt his or her identification with the adoptive family. It is very difficult to draw conclusions from these studies because they are largely based on small samples of volunteers or participants handpicked by social agencies. With a view to systematically examining these concerns and apprehensions we conducted two studies in Canada.

STUDY 1: THE DISCLOSURE STUDY

This investigation was designed to examine the attitudes of members of the adoption triad toward liberalizing current policy on the secrecy of the adoption records. It also explored potential conflicts of rights and interests that might result from the changes in the sealed record statuses. The study, the first of its kind, involved a combined total of 300 randomly selected subjects: adoptive parents (N = 152), birth mothers (N = 78), adoptees (N = 53), and adoption workers (N = 17) from the records of the provincial Department of Social Services in an Eastern Atlantic province. All the sample parents were Anglo-Saxon and had adopted a child one year old or younger through the department. Adoptions by relatives or by foster parents were excluded from the study because the participants in these adoptions have considerable prior knowledge of each other, which is not the case in nonrelative adoptions.

Adoptive parents and birth mothers were studied via a "time series" or "historical" method by selecting respondents from three different adoption periods: 1958, 1968, and 1978. The selection of birth mothers was confined to two adoption periods—1968 and 1978—because there was little or no identifying information on the birth mothers who relinquished children in 1958. This selection procedure permitted comparison of changes in attitudes over time, if any. It was assumed that the open records policy was likely to arouse the greatest anxiety and concerns among adoptive parents with older children and least among the parents of younger children. Children who had been adopted in the 1958 adoption period had attained adulthood at the time of the study, and their interest in genealogical information was likely to activate among their adoptive parents apprehension and fear of losing their allegiance; children adopted in 1968 had reached adolescence, a period when identity concerns are intensified which could trigger latent anxiety in adoptive parents; and, the

1978 adoptive parents were far removed from the issue and its implications since their children were still very young at the time of the interviews (1983–1984), and thus they would tend to intellectualize the phenomenon.

Adoptees who had been adopted in 1958 and were at least nineteen years old were contacted through their adoptive parents and interviewed. Social work personnel included eleven social workers employed in adoption services in the four regional offices of the Canadian Provincial Department of Social Service and six senior officials and administrators involved in policymaking. Given the sensitive nature of the subject, the secrecy surrounding the out-of-wedlock births in the 1960s, and the protracted time interval for follow-ups extending over twenty-five years since their last contact with the department, the rate of contact with the potential respondents was very high compared to earlier follow-up studies in adoption (Jaffee and Fanshel, 1970; Grown and Shapiro, 1974; Raynor, 1980; Simon and Alstein, 1981; MacDonnel, 1981). Fewer than twelve percent of the adoptive parents and birth mothers eligible for the study and 6 percent of the adoptees refused to participate. The high response rate was largely attributed to our persistent and imaginative outreach efforts. At times, in our efforts to trace eligible respondents we followed trails to other provinces in Canada. The information was gathered through in-depth interviews using semistructured interview schedules which were developed and pretested for the purpose of this study only, and contained 150 question items and subitems. The schedules combined open-ended and fixed alternative questions that permitted both a spontaneous response and specific uniform information. All interviews were tape recorded verbatim, and were about two to two-and-a-half hours long. The discursive interview material was converted in a book that provided preestablished coding categories. There was a concurrence in 81.2 percent of the categorized items between the interviewer/coder and the author, who was blind to the cases. The differences in the remaining 19 percent of the coded items were resolved by discussion with the interviewer and if necessary with an independent rater.

STUDY 2: THE REUNION STUDY

The second investigation involved 107 adoptees and 50 birth mothers who had accomplished reunions in the province of Ontario.

TABLE 21.1
Should the Department Release *Identifying* Information to Adoptees,
Upon Request?

Adoptive Parents By Year

	1958	1968	1978	All Adoptive Parents
N =	48	50	54	152
Degree of Agreement	%	%	%	%
Strongly Agree to Somewhat Agree	62.6	72.0	74.0	69.7
Strongly Disagree to Somewhat Disagree	37.5	28.0	25.9	30.3

The purpose of the investigation was to examine the reasons which drove the biological dyad to meet, the search process, doubts and fears prior to meetings, expectations, and actual reunion experiences. Questionnaires were mailed anonymously through Parent Finders of Ontario to all adoptees and birth mothers who had completed searches two to five years prior to the beginning of our investigation. The return to our questionnaires was 72.5 percent.

FINDINGS

Should the Department Release Identifying Information to Adoptees? The data in Table 21.1 reveals that a significant majority of all adoptive parents (69.7%) expressed their support for a disclosure policy. Support was even stronger among young parents with 72 to 74 percent in favor of such policy compared to their older counterparts, who constituted 62.6 percent.

However, probe questions revealed that the adoptive parents' support was more apparent than real. In other words, they acknowledged the rights of adopted people to information about and reunion with birth parents only when the issue was discussed on an impersonal level and in the context of social justice. They tended to manifest underlying apprehension and reservation once the issue was brought closer to home; that is, when adoptive parents were asked to view the disclosure policy in relation to their adopted children. A discrepancy between attitude and behavior has been well documented in the literature on women seeking abortion (Potts, Diggory, and Peel, 1977; Sachdev, 1981, 1985). For example, after each parent answered the simple for-and-against question referred to above, they were asked how they would feel if their children wanted to seek identifying information about or contact their birth parents. This 1978 adoptive mother's answer typifies these parents' feelings of discomfort.

> [Whether adoptees should be given identifying information.] If they want to know about their parents nobody should be allowed to keep that information from them. It's a natural desire and a part of growing up.
> [If your daughter wants the information or desires to meet.] I would probably end up being a little jealous and take tranquilizers. I raised her and she's always going to be mine. She can't look at a black stranger and fall in love with her because someone says that's the person who gave birth to her.

Furthermore, adoptive parents' support was not without equivocation. They wanted the disclosure to be contingent upon the criteria that:

1. Adoptees' desire for the information stems from their genuine need during the formation of their identity and does not reflect an idle curiosity.
2. Adoptees' desire is not an evanescent phase or a developmental crisis but represents sustained psychological and emotional distress.
3. Adoptees' motives are positive and they are not driven by the need to express negative feelings or to cause harm to the birth parents.
4. Adoptees possess an emotional strength to be able to cope with the experience.

Birth mothers, too, were supportive of releasing information about their identity to adoptees. As is shown in Table 21.2, nearly

TABLE 21.2
Should the Department Release *Identifying* Information to Adoptees,
Upon Request?

Birth Mothers by Year

	1968	1978	All Birth Mothers
N =	39	39	78
Degree of Agreement	%	%	%
Strongly Agree to Somewhat Agree	82.0	94.8	88.5
Strongly Disagree to Somewhat Disagree	18.0	5.2	11.5

88.5 (90%) of all birth mothers endorsed this step. But, like adoptive parents, their agreement was confidential. They wanted to be sure that the adoptee's decision is not precipitous and he or she is not motivated by a desire for vengeance or by resentment. They were afraid that the adoptee might make an indiscrete and unwanted appearance, and therefore a huge majority (75.4%) of the birth mothers favored the requirement of their consent before identifying information is released.

Should the Department Release Identifying Information Regarding Adoptees to Birth Mother? Response of the adoptees demonstrate that they were reticent in giving their support for a policy permitting the release of their identity to birth mothers, as shown in Table 21.3. Only a bare majority (56.6%) of all adoptees approved this measure.

Furthermore, a huge majority (80%) of adoptees supported this policy on the condition that their prior consent should be obtained. They were afraid that the birth mother might disrupt their happy home life or harass them. Their fear was typified by this male adoptee: "You might not want this woman chasing after you all over the place. You may never know when she might turn up."

TABLE 21.3
Should the Department Release *Identifying* Information Regarding
Adoptees to Birth Mothers

	Adoptees by Sex		
Degree of Agreement	Male N = 15	Female N = 38	All Adoptees N = 53
Strongly Agree to Somewhat Agree	46.7	60.5	56.6
Strongly Disagree to Somewhat Disagree	53.3	39.5	43.3

This female adoptee expressed a similar concern about a birth mother's insensitivity: "This woman may get to the point where she'll just go and knock on the door and say 'Hello, my name is Susan; the child you are caring for is mine.' She could throw people into an awful loop."

Adoptees who were opposed to the release of their identifying information were either not convinced about the reasons why a birth mother would have an interest in the child she relinquished or they were afraid of an unwanted intrusion in their lives. The following excerpts illustrate this point:

From what I can tell there is no definite reason why, aside from curiosity, the birth mother wants to find out about the adopted child. I don't see the birth mother gaining anything from information about the child that would be helpful to her the rest of her life. (Female adoptee)

She should not be given the information because she has the potential to cause disturbance and conflicts in the adoptee's life. She could walk into a perfectly happy family and create confusion. (Male adoptee)

Thus, we see that the above discussion supports the findings of the earlier authors in that fears and suspicions run deep among members of the triad about each other's motives. Each perceives the other

TABLE 21.4
Birth Mother's Reasons for Not Initiating Search

Reasons	Percent* n = 78
Dilemma About Her Rights	20.4
Concern for Adoptive Parents	26.5
Concern for Adopted Child	51.0
Effects on Birth Mother's Emotional State	12.2
Effects on Birth Mother's Family Relationship	4.1
Uncertain of Mechanism	20.4
Fear of Child's Negative Reaction	8.2

*Percentages exceed 100 because respondents selected more than one answer.

party as being insensitive to their feelings and needs. However, the examination of the data in both our studies on the attitudes of each toward the other members in the adoption triangle unequivocally shows that these assumptions and perceptions are unrealistic. Our results, presented below, provide ample evidence that members of the triad demonstrate a considerable concern for the other's interests and feelings.

Do Birth Mothers Disrupt the Adoptive Parent–Adoptee Relationship? Birth mothers were asked if they ever made or thought of making contact with the department of social services to meet the child since relinquishment. A little less than two-thirds (62.3%) desired to enquire, but only 38 percent of them actually visited the department. Lack of initiative by birth mothers was also reported in our "reunion study." Only about one-quarter (28%) of them undertook the search and almost seven out of ten (69.5%) said that despite their desire to meet they would not have taken the first step. The primary reason cited by them related to the consideration for the adoptee's or for the adoptive parents' feelings, evident in Table 21.4.

The following statements are illustrative of these birth mothers' sentiments.

> I had no right to interfere with the adoptive parents' home. I made my decision to give my daughter up and must live with it no matter how it hurts.

> I didn't want to upset anyone, especially the adoptive parents or the child. I think adoptive parents live in fear that the real mother will show up at their door at any time which would be a terrible shock. I feel I could cause more damage than good by disrupting a whole household.

Birth mothers feel a sense of gratitude for the care the child received from the adoptive parents. They regard them as real parents whose rights to the child supersede their own need to reunite with him or her, as this birth mother so eloquently put it. "It's not who gave birth to this child, but it's who raised it is the real parent. Any woman can go and have a child but that doesn't make her a mother."

Nevertheless, birth mothers reveal their loss and need for information about the relinquished child and the possibility for reunion when the child becomes an adult. But they want to avoid any impression of surreptitious involvement in the child's life. Thus, a comfortable majority of them (57.4%) favored mandatory adoptive parents' (parental) consent for releasing the identity of the adoptee, and another 40 percent were in favor of the department informing the adoptive parents, as a courtesy, about the birth mother's intent.

Do Birth Mothers Intrude in the Adoptee's Life? Almost all birth mothers had vivid memories of the relinquished children and often wondered what had become of them. They would like to have access to identifying information about the adoptee but only if it is accompanied by the adoptee's consent. They wanted to avoid an inadvertent disruption in the adoptee's life and therefore emphasized almost in monotony, "Not until I know my child's reaction"; "Only if my son wants to see me"; "If my daughter doesn't want to meet me I won't face her."

More significantly, birth mothers' interest in the well-being of the relinquished children is reflected in their heightened concern for the health and development of these children. All birth mothers, except one, agreed to the information on their medical history and hereditary diseases being provided to adoptees, preferably to adoptive parents at adoption. Almost half (49.3%) of them offered themselves for a periodic direct contact by the department of social services for an update on their health status or for consent to contact their family

TABLE 21.5

Manner in Which Department Should Update Records on Birth
Parent's Medical History

Department's Action	All Adoptive Parents (1958, 1968, 1978)	All Birth Mothers (1968, 1978)	All Adoptees
N =	(138)	(77)	(51)
	%	%	%
1. Birth parent should be required to file periodically	3.6	6.5	21.6
2. Birth parents should be left on their own to file periodically	8.7	23.4	27.5
3. Department should contact birth parent whenever needed	29.7	49.3	13.7
4. Department should not update	23.2	2.6	—
5. No suggestion or can't be done	34.8	18.2	37.3

physicians, and about one-quarter (23.4%) were willing to file medical information as it becomes relevant (see Table 21.5).

Realizing how vital the medical history is to the health of their birth child, these birth mothers were eager to cooperate with the department, as is illustrated by the following statements:

> If my daughter needs a kidney transplant or something that only her blood relatives can provide, the department should contact me.

> If my child is in a car accident and she needs a transfusion, the department should tell her my whereabouts so that my daughter can get my blood.

> If there is something wrong with my little girl and the adoptive parents want to find out if there is anything in my family, the department should come to me.

TABLE 21.6
Should the Department Release *Identifying* Information to Adoptees,
Upon Request?

	All Adoptive Parents (1958, 1968, 1978)	All Birth Mothers (1968, 1978)	All Adoptees
N =	152	78	53
	%	%	%
Degree of Agreement			
Strongly Agree to Somewhat Agree	69.7	88.5	81.1
Strongly Disagree to Somewhat Disagree	30.3	11.5	18.9

Contrary to popular belief, a huge majority (77%) of the sample birth mothers in our disclosure study admitted to having "very frequently" or "somewhat frequently" thought of the child they relinquished some fourteen years previously with considerable mixed guilt, pain, and loss. They expressed a longing for reunion and were agreeable to the release of information about their identity to adoptees. As we witness in Table 21.6, the level of support is the highest among birth mothers, with 88.5 percent endorsing such a measure compared to 69.3 percent and 81.1 percent for the adoptive parents and adoptees, respectively.

Actually, birth mothers' approval was not without condition in that they insisted that the disclosure of their identity was contingent upon their consent. However, the requirement of consent was not an indication of their resistance or their intent to add another bureaucratic impediment to restrict an adoptee from learning their identity. They said they would be willing to meet but would need time so that they could prepare themselves and the members of their family, should the adoptee resume contact. Typical of this sentiment was the statement made by a 1968 birth mother: "I definitely would like to see my child, but it's something that you can't come right out and say, 'Yes, it's all right.' You have to talk this over with your husband and children."

We noted in our reunion study that the initiative to meet was generally undertaken by adoptees in almost three-fourths (77%) of the reunions, and more than three-fourths (76.6%) of the birth mothers reacted to the contact with strong to moderate enthusiasm. Only 13.9% were either neutral or negative toward the adoptee's initiative.

Are Adoptees Unscrupulous, Self-Centered, and Inconsiderate Toward the Birth Mother? As was expected a massive proportion (81.1%) of adoptees in our disclosure study would support a policy permitting the release of information regarding the identity of their birth mothers. But they were opposed to a carte blanche right to the information so that their desire does not override the birth mother's need to remain anonymous. Almost seven out of ten adoptees (69.8%) favored the requirement of the birth mother's consent because they felt that some birth mothers might need protection against unwanted intrusion in their lives for fear of dredging up painful memories or revealing information that could be incriminating to her and to the adoptee. The example of this view was expressed by this female adoptee.

> The birth mother might feel that she signed away all her rights to that child so that she could go on with her life. For her it was a permanent arrangement and all of a sudden it's not permanent anymore. It could be a terrible shock because there may be something in that lady's past that she may not want reopened.

Adoptees also provided criteria to screen those adoptees who may be emotionally unstable or may have a malicious motive and, thus, prove disruptive to the birth mother's new family. They also stressed that sharing sensitive information, such as the identity of the birth mothers, should be handled with discretion and circumspection. An even more significant finding is that nine out of ten (90.7%) adoptees favored the age of majority, preferably in the twenties, as a condition for learning the identity of their birth parents. As shown in Table 21.7, the highest percentage of those recommending the legal age requirement were adoptees while 84 percent of the adoptive parents and 58 percent of the birth mothers recommended the legal age for providing identifying information.

Adoptees felt that their searching peers should be psychologically mature to make a well-considered, dispassionate decision and a minimum age of legal adulthood would make them realize the level of

TABLE 21.7
Should the Department Release *Identifying* Information to Adoptees,
Upon Request?

	All Adoptive Parents (1958, 1968, 1978)	All Birth Mothers (1968, 1978)	All Adoptees
N =	106	69	43
	%	%	%
AGE			
At Any Age	—	4.3	—
Only When Adoptee Is Mature	16.0	37.7	9.3
Of Legal Age	84.0	58.0	90.7

maturity needed to cope with the new relationship or with rejection by the birth mother.

Do Adoptees Change Their Allegiance and Affection Following Reunion with Biological Parents? The data from both studies dismiss the adoptive parents' belief that their adopted children are ungrateful if they manifest interest in birth parents and reject their fear that they will lose affection and allegiance if their children resume contact with birth parents. The studies show that adoptees recognize the significant role adoptive parents played in their life in providing them with a loving and secure home. They regard them as real parents who nurtured them and with whom the bond is irrevocable and much stronger than that with the biological parents. An illustration of their sense of allegiance was given by this twenty-four-year-old housewife. "I don't know if my parents can understand why I'm curious to know about my birth parents. They should know that I wouldn't run over to whoever came in the room and say, 'Oh mother' and wrap my arms around her. She is not and never will be my mother. She might have delivered me but that was it."

In the reunion study we asked respondents to characterize the nature of the relationship that developed between them and their biological mother. Table 21.8 shows that almost one-half (48.5%) developed a friendship, and more than one-third (37.6%) felt like a stranger or mere acquaintance. Fewer than one-fifth (19.8%) claimed a mother–child relationship.

TABLE 21.8
Nature of Relationship Between Birth Mother–Adoptee Post Reunion
By Adoptee's Perception

Nature of Relationship	Percent N = 107
Mother–child Relationship	19.8
Friendship	48.5
Acquaintance	16.8
Total Stranger	7.9
Other	6.9

Close to two-thirds (63.6%) of the sample adoptees in the disclosure study felt during the growing-up period that they might hurt their parents' feelings if they raised the subject or expressed niggling doubts about their origins, as is typified by this female adoptee: "The only thing that kept me from asking about my biological mother was my adoptive parents' feelings. They have been so caring and good and I was afraid it wouldn't be fair to them to ask." To avoid anguish for their parents, adoptees do not, generally, embark upon a search surreptitiously. In the reunion study, nearly two-thirds (61.8%) of the searching adoptees talked with either adoptive parent about their desire to meet their birth mothers. One-third (34.4%) did not confide in their parents primarily because they did not want to "hurt their feelings."

CONCLUSION

Clearly, the findings of our two studies point up the fallacies about the fears and apprehensions the members of adoption triads harbor regarding each other's motives. It seems likely that the inherent suspicions are largely responsible for the historical secrecy that has been the hallmark of the adoption practice. Adoption agencies have reinforced these beliefs among the triads partly because of the paucity of research evidence to the contrary, and partly owing to their need for control and monopolization of the service area. A case can also be made that the current dilemma in many jurisdictions in which the legislatures are striving for greater openness in the adoptive institution owes its existence largely to the mutual fears within the triad of the loss of familial privacy, unwanted intrusion, and/or disruption of relationships. As demonstrated by our two investigations, what is needed is an educational strategy that fosters a better understanding among activist groups of adoptees, adoptive parents, and birth parents, if reform of the adoptive institution is to succeed.

REFERENCES

Burke, C. (1975), The adult adoptee's constitutional right to know his origins. *S. Cal. Law Rev.*, 48:1196–1220.

Geissinger, S. (1984), Adoptive parents' attitudes toward open birth records. *Fam. Rel.*, Oct:579–585.

Grown, L. J., & Shapiro, D. (1974), *Black Children—White Families: A Study of Transactional Adoption*. New York: Child Welfare League of America.

Jaffee, B., & Fanshel, D. (1970), *How They Fared in Adoption: A Follow-Up Study*. New York: Columbia University Press.

Kadushin, A. (1980), *Child Welfare Services*, 3rd ed. Toronto: Macmillan.

Lifton, B. J. (1979), *Lost and Found: The Adoption Experience*. New York: Dial.

MacDonnel, S. (1981), *Vulnerable Mothers, Vulnerable Children*. Halifax, NS: Nova Scotia Department of Social Services.

Marcus, C. (1981), *Who Is My Mother?* Toronto: Macmillan.

Pannor, R., & Nerlove, E. A. (1977), Fostering understanding between adolescents and adoptive parents through group experiences. *Child Welf.*, 26:220–227.

Potts, M., Diggory, P., & Peel, J. (1977), *Abortion*. Cambridge, UK: Cambridge University Press.

Raynor, L. (1980), *The Adopted Child Comes of Age*. London: George Allen & Unwin.

Sachdev, P., ed. (1981), *Abortion: Readings and Research*. Toronto: Butterworths.

—— (1984), Unlocking the adoption files: A social and legal dilemma. *Adoption: Current Issues and Trends*, ed. P. Sachdev. Toronto: Butterworths.

—— ed. (1985), *Perspectives on Abortion*. Metuchen, NJ: Scarecrow Press.

—— (1989), *Unlocking the Adoption Files*. Lexington, MA: D. C. Heath.

Simon, R. J., & Alstein, H. (1981), *Transracial Adoption: A Follow-Up*. Toronto: Lexington Books.

Sorosky, A. D., & Pannor, R. (1978), *The Adoption Triangle*. Garden City, NY: Doubleday/Anchor Books.

Tartanella, P. J. (1982), Sealed adoption records and the constitutional right of privacy of the natural parent. *Rutgers Law Rev.*, 34:451–490.

Triseliotis, J. (1973), *In Search of Origins*. London: Routledge & Kegan Paul.

22

Understanding and Preventing "Failing Adoptions"

René A. C. Hoksbergen, Ph.D.

> For the basically deprived child his world is a jungle, a
> dangerous place, filled with incomprehensible emotions
> and expectations. The main task is to find him and help
> him to explore his real self, which is the central core, the
> deep source of growth and development.
>
> Prof. Dr. René A. C. Hoksbergen

Approximately 18,000 children from no less than sixty different countries had been adopted in the Netherlands as of January 1, 1989. In the 1960s and early 1970s a comparatively high number of the children (about 150 each year) came from European countries, most of them from Austria and the Metera Babies Center in Greece. Since the 1970s, this situation has gradually changed, first with the adoption of interracial children from Korea, and later with the adoption of children from India, Sri Lanka, Bangladesh, Colombia, and Brazil.

By the beginning of 1970, few Dutch children were available for adoption. This lack of adoptable children can be attributed to the

Acknowledgments. This study was granted, among others, by the Netherlands Committee voor Kinderpostzegels.

Many thanks to Berte Waardenburg and Jacqueline Spaan who have been instrumental in carrying out the research activities in a professional manner.

TABLE 22.1
Number of Children Born in the Netherlands and Number of Dutch
and Inter-country Adoptees

Year	Total Births in the Netherlands N	Dutch Children Placed in Adoption N	Inter-country Adoptees N	Percent of i-c Adoptees Total Births %	Total Adoptions per Year
1970	238,912	747	142	.06	889
1971	227,912	568	159	.07	727
1973	194,993	328	316	.16	644
1975	177,876	171	1018	.57	1189
1977	173,296	142	1105	.64	1247
1979	175,000	143	1287	.74	1430
1981	178,600	99	1161	.65	1260
1983	170,240	66	1365	.81	1431
1985	177,000	72	1137	.64	1209
1987	186,700	66	872	.47	938

following causes (Hoksbergen, Bunjes, Baarda, Nota, and Waarden-berg, 1982):

1. The introduction of sex education classes in Dutch schools which teach young people methods of birth control.
2. Easy access to birth control measures which help prevent unwanted pregnancies.
3. A more accepting attitude toward unwed mothers on the part of society.
4. The legalization of abortion.

Table 22.1 shows the total number of births in the Netherlands and the number of Dutch and foreign-born children placed in adoption, biennially 1970 to 1987.

In this study, we focused on inter-country (i-c) adopted children, who after a period of time (months or years) had to be removed from their adoptive homes and placed in children's homes, psychiatric clinics, or institutes for disturbed children in order to receive psychological treatment. In the Netherlands we call this placement "residential care," and we characterize these adoptions as "disrupted." We prefer to speak of disrupted rather than failed adoptions, because the term *disrupted* better describes the complete phenomenon. A lasting relationship between adoptive parents and adopted children continues to exist, regardless of its final outcome.

Because some of these children eventually return to live with their adoptive parents, or are placed with new parents, and others remain in institutional care, our definition is different from that used by the Child Welfare League of America. In their National Adoption Task Force (1987), the League defines "disruption" as: "A permanent return of the child to the agency at any time, for any reason, following adoptive placement and before legal adoption." In Holland, approximately 50 percent of the children return to their original adoptive families after treatment and no child ever returns to the adoption agencies—they are placed either by a child welfare organization or directly by the parents with a new adoptive family or in an institution for child care. Nearly all disruptions appear to occur after legal adoption has taken place, which usually materializes after one year of care in the adoptive family.

In Holland, we do not have data on the number of children who are transferred directly from one adoptive family to another without the intervention of a social welfare institution. Therefore, for the purpose of this survey we considered only those disruptions that made use of the services of a social welfare institution.

Disrupted adoptions are experienced as real family disasters for both the adults who wish to be parents and the children who need a stable environment in which to grow. Disruption is an especially painful experience and is accompanied by the feeling of failure and rejection. The purpose of this investigation was to examine some of the variables which may contribute to disruptive adoptions. Does the country of origin, age on arrival, or the behavioral characteristics of the child play a role in disrupted adoptions, or do the reasons lie with the characteristics of the adoptive parents, or a combination of all factors?

METHODOLOGY

Our investigation began in 1985 with a survey of the number of disruptions that had taken place since the late 1970s, when Dutch

TABLE 22.2

Inter-country Adoptees in Residential Care in Holland,
by Country of Origin and Year

Country of Origin	Total No. of i-c Adoptees at the Moment of Counting		i-c Adoptees in Residential Care	Percent
	Year	N		
Korea*	1978	1787	101	5.6
Indonesia	1979	1119	17	1.5
Colombia	1980	872	64	7.3
India	1980	718	14	2.0
Sri Lanka	1983	410	5	1.2
Bangladesh	1978	317	15	4.7
Lebanon	1978	216	13	6.0
Chile	1980	80	2	2.5
Europe	1978	2139	53	2.5
Others	1978	633	62	9.8
Unknown Origin	—	—	3	—
Totals		8291	349	5.7

*We took into account the average time that the Korean group lived in Holland (8 years), and counted only the adoptees who arrived before 1978 (1986 minus 8 years). The average time of stay is different for adoptees from different countries.

parents began adopting children from Asia and South America (see Table 22.2).

The data were obtained by sending questionnaires to 670 institutions involved in residential child care. The return rate was 93 percent, which was extremely high. The institutions were asked to give the following information about each i-c adopted child that had been a resident: birth date, sex, country of origin, date of arrival in Holland, and date of placement and/or length of stay in the institution.

Questionnaires were returned on 349 children, from which 145 were randomly selected for the study. In addition, the case workers responsible for each child were interviewed concerning the child's background, development, adjustment, and any psychological problems as reported by the adoptive family. If the child had stayed in several institutions, as some did, we used the information obtained from the last institution only. Though the data on the completed questionnaires was anonymous, we were able to trace those children who had stayed in more than one institution to ensure that each child was counted only once. We also examined the characteristics of those institutions which did not respond to our survey, and we ascertained that all institutions likely to be involved with i-c adoptees had responded.

RESULTS AND DISCUSSION

As stated earlier, we received data on 349 children, which was the total number of i-c adoptees who had lived, or were at the time of our investigation living, in residential care. This was 5.7 percent of all i-c adopted children in Holland, who had lived in the country for an average of 7.9 years. The number 7.9 years was used as a rectification on the total number of i-c adoptees as per January 1, 1986, which marks the end of our investigation. The rectification is based on the average time that the 349 children had stayed with the adoptive family before the first placement in residential care took place. We assumed that the number of children with disruption experience is distributed normally, with 7.9 years as the average time of stay in the family. We did not use the data on children who arrived in Holland after January 1, 1986, in our calculations, because that would have included children who had lived with their adoptive families for only a short time (some days or months) and one could have assumed that some could have experienced a disruption. This was not a real supposition according to our data. We were rather surprised by the large number of disruptions and compared the number of disruptions and year of arrival in order to determine if the latter could have been a significant factor in influencing disruption. We did not find a relationship between year of arrival and disruption (see Table 22.3). However, we found that the disruption rate was somewhat higher for boys than for girls. This finding allows the same trend found in the overall population in residential care which tends to be made up of more male than female children, a 3 to 2 ratio.

COUNTRY OF ORIGIN

To determine if there was a relation between the country of origin and need for residential treatment, we examined the data on

TABLE 22.3
Inter-country Adoptees in Holland and in Residential Care, by Year
of Arrival

Year of Arrival	i-c Adoptees in Holland	i-c Adoptees in Residential Care	Percent
1974	619	41	6.6
1975	1018	55	5.4
1976	1125	49	4.3
1977	1105	63	5.7
1978	1211	53	4.4

children from each country. We considered only data on those countries of origin for which we had sufficient information (Table 22.2). Next, we examined the average age on arrival, but could get this data on children from only five countries. We found that Korean and Colombian children seemed to have the highest percentage of residential placement and also, on average, to be older on arrival. Since it was not clear if country of origin or age on arrival were the determining factors for residential care, we performed a regression analysis which indicated a strong linear relation between age on arrival and residential treatment ($R = .85$).

The highest percentage of i-c adoptee subjects placed in residential care belonged in the group "other countries." This was due to the fact that most of these children were adopted privately and, generally, without a home study selection. Often these adoptions took place while the Dutch families were living in a foreign country or had a direct contact in that country. As a consequence they did not join an organization for adoptive parents, they did not have the benefit of preparatory courses, nor did they receive support from other adoptive parents or follow-up care from social workers, services which are offered by adoption organizations.

AGE ON ARRIVAL

In Table 22.4, we see that the older the child was on arrival, the higher were the chances that disruption would take place. The same results were also found by Winter-Stettin (1984) and Fitzgerald (1983).

TABLE 22.4
Distribution of Placements in Residential Care, by Age on Arrival

Age on Arrival in Months	Total Number of i-c Adoptees	i-c Adoptees in Residential Care	
		N	Percent
under 6	6828	47	.7
6–17	3255	43	1.3
18–29	1324	39	3.0
30–41	1267	43	3.4
42–53	1296	66	5.1
54–65	835	36	4.3
66–77	749	36	4.8
over 78	316	39	12.3
	15,871	349	

When we compared the younger and older groups, a relatively significant increase in numbers in residential care was found in the children who arrived in Holland as toddlers, at 1.6 to 2.6 years of age. This is undoubtedly a very abrupt transition for children at this age who are moved from one country to another, who break ties with the primary caretakers (if they have any) at a time when they need to build trust in others and themselves and to become autonomous while having a secure primary attachment. By changing the toddlers' milieu, smooth development is interrupted, and although the adoptive parents give them all the attention and love they so badly need, this age group will very often be at a loss when faced with these significant changes. Since only a very little can be explained to a toddler, large demands will be made on the adjustment capacity of both child and parents.

Further statistical analyses have indicated the following: in the three youngest age-on-arrival groups, the first significant problems (interpersonal difficulties and acting out) surface around the age of nine; in all adoptee age groups the highest rate of placement in residential care is reached around the age of twelve years (9 months earlier on average for boys than for girls); and children from Asia and South America who experience disruptions are three to four years younger than those from Europe.

BEHAVIORAL CHARACTERISTICS OF CHILDREN

We compared the collected data on the 145 children, who served as a control group, and who lived with their families. These were 116 children from Thailand who participated in our former investigations during 1985 and 1986 (Hoksbergen, Juffer, and Waardenburg, 1987). These Thai children arrived in Holland between the years 1974 and 1979, with an average age on arrival of ten months.

BACKGROUND OF THE CHILDREN

Seventy-eight (50%) of the children in the experimental group had lived mainly in children's homes in their country of origin, twelve (8%) had lived as waifs and strays, and the rest, fifty-five (38%), had lived mainly within a family. When we compared the study group children with the 116 from Thailand, the former group showed a more troubled past. Most of the waifs and strays came from South America and were in poorer physical health on arrival than were the children from Thailand. Physical condition was not linearly related to age on arrival. Forty-seven (60%) of the infants (ages 0–1) and 39 (52%) of the oldest children (ages 6–11) were in good physical condition on arrival, while only 82 (35%) of the toddlers (ages 2–3) were in good physical condition on arrival. Based on these findings we can presume that poor physical condition on arrival should be considered an important high-risk factor that warrants intervention. A process of "survival of the fittest" may have taken place in the case of adopted children, who, after a disadvantaged start, have managed to survive up to age six or older without expressing pathology. Living as a survivor, though, affects the general development of the personality, which in turn causes grief to the adoptive parents because they are not able to understand it and consequently feel frustrated and defeated in their efforts to help the child.

PSYCHOLOGICAL PROBLEMS

Two-thirds of the children in our study had serious adjustment problems immediately after their arrival. As could be expected, the older children encountered more immediate problems than the younger ones. Interpersonal problems, such as difficulty in relating and forming significant attachments, and eating problems, such as refusing food or bingeing, were often mentioned. It is significant that almost 75 percent of the children in our group continued to experience some type of adjustment problems after living several years with the adoptive family; while only 40 percent of the children from Thailand exhibited chronicity of adjustment. It is now evident that these seemingly temporary adjustment problems should be added to the list of high-risk factors.

An investigation of the problems exhibited by the children during the period prior to the disruption indicated that the most prevalent problem by far was difficulty in interpersonal relations between the child and the parents (especially the mother). Sixty-three (75%) of the girls seemed to suffer from interpersonal problems compared to eighty-two (61%) of the boys. Sixty-five (78%) of the Asian children also presented severe difficulties in relating compared to twenty-nine (44%) of the European ones. A similarly striking difference was found between the Asian and the European children in the area of withdrawn and/or anxious behavior in the child. These behaviors were more common among girls in general, while hot tempers and/or aggressive behaviors were more often encountered among boys (Table 22.5).

Other problem areas found in our study group children were school difficulties, lying and/or stealing, and inability in establishing contact with peers. Seldom did we encounter only one problem. From the very beginning the adoptive parents are confronted with a complicated child who exhibits many different behavioral and emotional problems. Under such circumstances, one would expect parents to seek professional help without delay. However, this has not been the case with the parents in our study group who waited an average of six years before seeking professional help.

We asked the social workers to indicate the parental complaints at the admission to residential treatment. Difficulties in interpersonal relations were mentioned in more than 50 percent of the group, especially the inability of the children to express their feelings. The neglect in earlier years may account for the scarcity of emotions in later years. Acting-out behavior was mentioned in 50 percent of the children, equally often for boys as for girls. The type of acting-out behavior, however, was very different: boys behaved aggressively,

TABLE 22.5
Complaints Reported to the Social Workers by the Adoptive Parents

	N	Percent
Interpersonal Difficulties of the Child	86	59
Acting Out	71	49
Interpersonal Problems within the Family	51	35
Anxiety, Depression, Loneliness	29	20
Problems at School	28	19
Child Mentally Retarded	16	11
Disorganized Behavior	8	6
Other Problems: Autistic-like Behavior, Mood Changes, Chronic Eating Problems (N = 145, more than one problem may be mentioned)	106	73

whereas girls more often resorted to sexually promiscuous behavior. The latter behavior may bring to light parental conflicts about their sexuality and infertility. Infertile couples who have tried to conceive a child for years, where for too long a time their sexual activities had to be functional for something (conception) that never happened, may have trouble understanding and accepting such promiscuous behavior from their daughter.

CHARACTERISTICS OF ADOPTIVE PARENTS

The adoptive fathers (N = 140) in our experimental group had a mean age of thirty-six years, while the mean age for the adoptive mothers was thirty-four. This group was, on average, two years older than the parents of the Thai group. Fourteen (10%) of the parents of our group were more than forty years older than their children. This is a high percentage, considering that the directives of the Dutch Ministry of Justice provide that no more than forty years should be allowed between parents and adopted child. And the divorce rate was 10 percent among our parents, double that of the Thai group (5%).

A salient finding was that the socioeconomic status of the parents of the experimental group was higher than that of other adoptive groups reported in the literature. This finding is in striking disagreement with the results of other investigations, where a higher socioeconomic status (SES) of the parents is considered a compensatory factor for all kinds of problems (Garmezy and Rutter, 1983). One explanation might be that high SES parents might be both practically and emotionally too demanding. Many children who have been neglected for a long period of time find it difficult from the very beginning to live up to such expectations, and parents with rigid demands have a hard time coping with children who don't fulfill their high hopes and dreams.

Another important finding that resulted from our investigation was that adoptive parents with biological offspring of their own more often encountered problems than those without biological children. No less than 66 percent of the children in our research group were adopted into families who also had biological children. This is a high percentage when compared to statistics for all adoptees in Holland, which showed that only 30 percent of all adopted children are placed in families with one or more children of their own. What could account for this?

First, there is the practice of choosing adoptive parents with biological children for somewhat older "hard-to-place" adoptees, because it is commonly believed that parents with previous childrearing experience may provide a better home for these children. Second, there is the motivation of adoptive parents in considering adoption. In our group, altruistic and idealistic motives were far more often given by parents with children of their own. They were very willing "to help a child in need" when they consider themselves in a position to do so, while "liking children" or "wish to have children" were more often given as reasons for wanting to adopt by people without children. The latter motives may be more valid and induce the parental strength and dedication required in coping with serious behavioral problems. Parents with biological children also have a more complicated family situation, and often compare their own less troublesome children with the adoptees. In addition, a small family may have fewer family problems than a larger family, or parents with children of their own may have less energy to deal with problems as they arise and, subsequently, may decide to place the adopted child under supervision in an institution sooner than would parents without other children.

The placement of the adopted child within the birth order of the already existing children in the adoptive family seems to be another factor for precipitating disruption. In our study group we found twice as many "inter" and "higher" placements than in the Thai group (an interplacement occurs between an older and a younger child, and a higher placement refers to the placement of an adopted child who becomes the oldest in the adoptive family). Also the age differences between the already existing children and the adoptees were relatively small—less than two years. It is easy to understand why adoption agencies try to take into consideration the natural logic of birth order, age differences, and placements whenever possible.

Finally, it is worth mentioning that, out of the 145 children in our study, 36 (25%) arrived in Holland with a sibling. For the entire population of adopted children in Holland, the sibling placement is only 12.5 percent.

CONCLUSION

The purpose of this investigation was to examine some of the factors that contributed to the disruption of adoptions. More than country of origin, we found that the child's age and health on arrival, and early adjustment difficulties were factors that contributed to the adoption disruption. The characteristics of the adoptive family most likely to relate to adoption disruption were: older age for parents, biological children in the family, and birth order. However, it is very difficult to separate the contributing factors, and we may assume that usually many variables are involved when disruption occurs.

The total number of disruptions we found in our study was rather high although it was comparable to the findings of other investigators (Fitzgerald, 1983). Still, we consider this number unacceptable for adoptive parents, adoptees, and society in general. One way to improve the situation would be to better prepare adoptive parents for behavioral problems to expect. We believe that by now we are increasingly able to understand the risk factors in adoptive families—the factors, behaviors, and attitudes that have a negative influence on the quality of the interactions. Based on the investigations conducted by others (Sach and Dale, 1982; Zimpfer, 1983) and by us, we are now able to better prepare parents seeking to adopt i-c children. Following are some areas we found to be of help when working with prospective adoptive parents:

1. Past traumatic experiences of the parents, such as the loss of significant persons and possibly a personal experience of neglect, abuse, or incest, must be sufficiently accepted, worked through, and incorporated.
2. Conflicts about infertility or loss of a child may lead to an extreme emotional dependence on the adopted child, who is not seen as a different person with needs of his own and with personal characteristics and limitations.
3. Adoptive parents may have unrealistic expectations about the degree of gratification and pleasure to be derived from parenthood, especially if they are involuntarily childless.
4. Older parents with biological children and high social and intellectual expectations based on previous experiences with these children may apply too rigid norms to the adopted child. In such cases the child is supposed to fit perfectly into a predetermined family pattern.
5. Acting as though the adopted child were a biological child, thus ignoring the reality of the adoption status, also presents a risk. The necessity of the acknowledgment-of-difference attitude (Kirk, 1981; Lifton, 1983) is important for both adoptive parent and adoptee.
6. Should the social environment give parents too little support, and they are not able to seek it elsewhere, for example, among other adoptive parents, the family may feel socially isolated.

Several Dutch organizations try to assist with preparatory help and follow-up care for adoptive families. We strongly subscribe to the Swedish approach, in which the preparation is organized in the form of adoption-study circles, which consist of about ten study evenings or some weekends where discussions, lectures by professionals, and film presentations are offered on the topic of adoption. Intensive preparation will not prevent all problems, but intensive preparation of child and parent may diminish the number of disruptions drastically, as will the regular exchange of ideas among adoptive parents, specialized social workers, and psychologists. For the i-c adopted children, overcoming the risk factors in adoption might give them their second chance in life—a second chance so badly needed by them.

REFERENCES

Child Welfare League (1987), *Report of the National Adoption Task Force*. Washington, DC: Child Welfare League of America.

Fitzgerald, J. (1983), *Understanding Disruption*. London: BAAF.

Garmezy, R., & Rutter, M. (1983), *Stress, Coping and Development*. New York: McGraw-Hill.

Hoksbergen, R. A. C., Bunjes, L. A. C., Baarda, B., Nota, J. A., & Waardenburg, B. C. (1982), *Adopted Children at Home and at School*. Lisse: Swets & Zeitlinger.

———— Juffer, F., & Waardenburg, B. C. (1987), *Adopteie uit de kinderschoenen* (Adoption from the beginning). Deventer: Van Loghum Slaterus.

Kirk, H. D. (1981), *Adoptive Kinship, a Modern Institution in Need of Reform*. Port Angeles, WA: Ben-Simon Publications, 1985.

Lifton, B. J. (1983), *Lost and Found: The Adoption Experience*. New York: Dial Press.

Rutter, M. (1972), *Maternal Deprivation Re-assessed*. Harmondsworth, UK: Penguin.

Sach, W. H., & Dale, D. (1982), Abuse and deprivation in failing adoption. *Child Abuse & Neg.*, 6:443–451.

Winter-Stettin, A. (1984), *Die bei Terre des Hommes Deutschland e.V. im Rahmen der Auslandsadoptionsarbeit vorkommenden Replacements, eine Aktenanalyse*. Unpublished manuscript.

Zimpfer, D. M. (1983), Indications of adoption breakdown. *Soç. Casework*, 64:169–177.

23

Born in the Third World: To School in the Netherlands

Lucile A. C. Bunjes, Ph.D.

For the past twenty years a number of non-European children have been adopted in the Netherlands, and today, about 1,000 children per year arrive from several countries. In all likelihood, these children would not have had a chance for a decent existence in their country of birth, since most of them arrive physically and emotionally deprived. In the Netherlands, they have been welcomed into families with parents who make great efforts to help them adapt to their new environment and seem eager to facilitate their development.

However, after a period of time—sometimes a few years, but often just a few months or weeks, depending upon their age on arrival—these children have to attend school and compete with their Dutch contemporaries. Is it possible for children to cope with this unexpected and incomprehensible change in their lives and at the same time adapt and perform well within the educational system in the Netherlands?

Age on arrival may play a major role in a child's ability to perform well at school, since a child who was adopted as a baby will have virtually an identical school career to that of a child born in the Netherlands, where children are allowed to enter primary school on their fourth birthday and must attend from their fifth birthday.

Earlier research by Winick, Meyer, and Harris (1976) indicated that after more than six years in the United States Korean girls were able to compete successfully with or even surpass their American classmates. In this study, we wanted to assess the intellectual development of foreign adopted children in the Netherlands. To accomplish this, we began a two-stage investigation starting in early 1980.

METHODS AND PROCEDURE

FIRST STAGE

The subjects were 144 adopted toddlers from Korea, India, Bangladesh, and Colombia (65 were males and 79 were females, with a mean age 58.8 months). The assessment consisted of the following:

1. An extensive interview with the adopted parents: all known past history of the children was gathered as well as information on their state of health at arrival, adoption difficulties, and later adjustment problems they may have exhibited.
2. An intellectual assessment of the children using the Utrechtse Korte Kleuter Intelligentietest (UKKI) (Utrecht's Short Intelligence Tests) [Baarda (1978)] based on the Vane (unpublished) Kindergarten Test. This test measures intellectual functioning using the vocabulary subjects, draw-a-person test, and geometric figures. In addition, the culture-free intelligence measure of Colored Progressive Matrices (CPM) (Raven, Court, and Raven, 1977) were administered.

We directly matched four classmates (2 males and 2 females) for each child to serve as a comparison. The choice of this large control group was based on the concern that adopted children are often singled out and receive more than their fair share of attention. By including more nonadopted, native-born Dutch children, we hoped to avoid drawing undue attention to the adopted population.

SECOND STAGE

Three years later we examined 118 children out of the 144 in the original sample in order to ascertain their intellectual functioning in the early grades of elementary school. We were not able to reach 26 of the original sample because some had moved with their new families or, for various reasons, were not able to participate. During the second stage we matched each of the adopted children with two classmates (1 male and 1 female), for a total of 107 males and 109 females in our control group.

During this assessment we administered the subtests of the WISC-R (van Haasen, 1976), Vocabulary, Similarities and Block Design; a Dutch Reading Test: Differentiele Zinnenleestest (Dommerholt, 1970); and a Standard Spelling Test (van der Wissel, unpublished) to assess linguistic abilities.

We interviewed the adoptive parents for information on the child's development, life events, and the state of the child's health at the time of the second observation.

RESULTS

CHILDREN'S STATUS ON ARRIVAL

An overview of the group's status at the time of arrival in the Netherlands is presented in Table 23.1. It appears that the Colombian children, on average, were older by two years at the time of arrival than those from other countries.

Previous studies (Bunjes, 1980; Hoksbergen, Bunjes, Baarda, and Nota, 1982; Kingma, Schulpen, and Wolters, 1983) reported that a great number of foreign adopted children were undernourished

TABLE 23.1
Age on Arrival by Country of Origin—First Observation

Age (in months)	India		Bangladesh		S. Korea		Colombia		Total	
	N	%	N	%	N	%	N	%	N	%
0–12	13	39.4	12	46.2	17	39.5	11	26.1	53	36.8
13–24	6	18.2	2	7.7	6	13.9	6	14.3	20	13.9
25–36	6	18.2	6	23.1	10	23.2	10	23.8	32	22.2
37	8	24.2	6	23.1	10	23.2	15	35.7	39	27.1
Total	33	100.0	26	100.0	43	100.0	42	100.0	144	100.0

TABLE 23.2

Degree of Undernourishment by Age on Arrival in the Netherlands
Numbers and Percentages

Age on Arrival (in months)	Severely Undernourished		Moderately Undernourished		Not Undernourished		Total	
	N	%	N	%	N	%	N	%
0–6	7	5	8	6	16	11	31	22
7–12	7	5	3	2	12	8	22	15
13–24	5	4	4	3	11	8	31	22
25–36	5	4	9	6	17	12	31	22
37–	5	4	9	6	25	18	39	27
Total	29	20	33	23	81	75	143	100

and/or ill at the time of arrival. For many adoptive families this presents a heavy burden and often a difficult beginning, more so when unknown infectious diseases are involved.

Undernourishment and signs of illness appeared also in quite a few of the children in our group (Table 23.2). Forty-three percent of our study population seemed to suffer from severe to moderate forms of undernourishment on arrival. Furthermore, nearly all (90%) of the children showed signs of ill health, such as diarrhea, intestinal disorders, infestations with worms, and ear infections. In addition to physical illnesses and disorders it appeared that many of these children may also have been deprived of a parental figure. This was determined by asking the adoptive parents about the previous home or other surroundings where the child lived before coming to the Netherlands. We surmised that parental deprivation had occurred if the child was in more than one living situation prior to adoption. Table 23.3 indicates that 73 percent of the study population had experienced parental deprivation. This was particularly true of the Colombian children, for thirty-six out of forty-two had been in more than one previous living situation.

RESULTS AND DISCUSSION OF THE FIRST OBSERVATION

The statistical analyses used to compare the test results of the adopted children to those of the comparison group were t-test, analysis of variance, and analysis of covariance. A comparison of the UKKI and CPM scores of the experimental and control groups indicated

TABLE 23.3
Number of Child Care Situations (Parents/Foster Care/Residential Care) by Country of Origin

Number of Child Care Situations	India/ Bangladesh		S. Korea		Colombia		Total	
	N	%	N	%	N	%	N	%
1 Situation	19	13	14	10	6	4	39	27
2 Situations	29	20	26	18	18	13	73	51
3 Situations	10	7	3	2	18	13	31	22
Total	58	41	43	30	42	29	143	100

that the foreign adopted children, as was expected, scored significantly lower as a group on the UKKI ($t = 2.54$, $p = .01$) but no significant differences were observed on the CPM scores. However, when we looked at the vocabulary results which emphasize language abilities, we noted that significant differences were present when the country groups were compared separately.

Notably the Korean children averaged best, even better than the Dutch children; the Colombian children, followed by the Indian, showed lowest scores on the Vocabulary subtest. On closer consideration of the influence of different variables it was found that there were significant differences between the average scores of children from different countries. The following variables seemed to have an influence on the UKKI-IQ, the Vocabulary of the UKKI, and the CPM of both groups (Table 23.4): (1) country of origin; (2) sex; (3)

TABLE 23.4
Variable Influencing UKKI-IQ, UKKI-Vocabulary, and CPM

Variables	UKKI-IQ		UKKI-Vocabulary		CPM	
	Statistic	P	Statistic	P	Statistic	P
A. Country	$F = 7.24$	$< .0001$	$F = 3.86$	$< .0001$	$F = 6.22$	$< .0001$
B. Sex	$t = 2.91$	$< .0001$		NS		NS
C. Age (when tested)	$V = -.15$	.05	$V = .29$	$< .0001$	$V = .29$	$< .0001$
D. Age on Arrival	$V = .30$	$< .0001$	$V = -.30$	$< .0001$		NS
E. State of Health	$F = 3.47$	.03		NS		NS

Based on results of testing children attending kindergarten

TABLE 23.5
CPM Analysis of Covariance

	F	sign. p.
All Covariates	4.48	< .0001
Sex	.69	.41
Age	18.35	< .0001
Age on Arrival	6.65	.01
Health	2.13	.41
Main Effect of Country of Origin	4.92	< .0001

age of testing; (4) age on arrival; and (5) state of health.

An analysis of covariance, when keeping constant the above-mentioned variables, indicated that the country of birth did have an effect on the UKKI-IQ. However, the state of health appeared to be the major factor, followed by the age on arrival and gender. It became clear that in the case of Vocabulary subtest significant differences were determined by the various ages at the time of the assessment and the ages on arrival. The effect of the country of birth bears on the score of the CPM (F = 4.92, p < .0001). Age seemed to have a decisive influence on the CPM score, but this was due to the fact that assessment was made on the strength of raw scores (Table 23.5).

RESULTS OF THE SECOND OBSERVATION

From our interviews with the adoptive parents it appeared that for most of the children life circumstances between the first and second observation were uneventful and their health was good.

To ascertain the children's intellectual development over the past three years, we compared the scores of the CPM of the first observation with those of the second observation for both the group and the control groups.

Using the Kendall and Pearson rank-correlation coefficient, the Dutch control group, which had a mean score of 15 (± 3.84) for the first observation, and 24.65 (± 5.0) for the second observation,

TABLE 23.6
Age on Arrival by Country of Origin—Second Observation

Age (in months)	India		Bangladesh		S. Korea		Colombia		Total	
	N	%	N	%	N	%	N	%	N	%
0–12	8	32.2	10	43.5	15	40.5	5	15.2	38	32.2
13–24	4	16.0	2	8.7	4	10.8	5	15.2	15	12.7
25–36	6	24.0	6	26.1	9	24.3	9	27.3	30	25.4
37–	7	28.0	5	21.7	9	24.3	14	42.1	35	29.7
Total	25	100.0	23	100.0	37	99.9	33	100.0	118	100.0

showed a significant balance. We found a similar trend with the foreign adopted children, indicating that the differences by age and country of origin faded (Table 23.6).

When compared separately by country groups, results no longer showed a contrast. This signifies a marked recovery growth for the Colombian children.

A comparison of the scores of the WISC-R-IQ subtest of the Vocabulary, Similarities and Block design of the two groups showed that the foreign adopted children have caught up in areas where they had been deficient. It was clearly shown that the foreign adopted children as a group averaged a higher score than the Dutch children on the Vocabulary subtest.

However, further analysis comparing individual country group scores indicated that age on arrival was still an influence on test results, as well as the country of birth, but to a much lesser extent. Gender did not seem to be of significance. In Table 23.6, we present the means and standard deviations of reading and spelling abilities, according to country of birth. We see that Korean children were the most advanced in reading ability, while Indian and Dutch children were better in spelling. The scores of the Colombian children differed significantly from those of the other groups. The spelling scores of the foreign adopted children and the control group were nearly identical.

SUMMARY

In the first observation we measured the intellectual development of the foreign adopted and Dutch children, using the Dutch IQ-test. We found some differences among toddlers, influenced by the country of origin. The Korean children showed a higher level of intellectual development than their Dutch contemporaries. The culture free test (CPM) showed, as was expected, no differences; but when we examined each country individually the children from India and Colombia showed a lag in intellectual development.

The effect of the variables of influence during the first observation seemed to have diminished considerably, with the most disadvantaged children showing a remarkable recovery. However, this phenomenon may be due to the regression to the mean, while the remaining children appeared to follow a regular pattern of development.

It is not surprising that child psychologists are frequently confronted with problems concerning foreign adopted children at school (Bunjes, 1986) since they arrived at different ages. From our studies, it became apparent, as it was from the investigation among Thai children in the Netherlands (Hoksbergen, Juffer, and Waardenburg, 1986), that arrival at different ages continued to affect the second observation.

A statement on the exact period of influence of this factor cannot yet be made on the basis of the data available from our investigation. Further research is needed to understand the effects of age on arrival and how to intervene.

REFERENCES

Baarda, D. B. (1978), *Utrechtse korte kleuter intelligentietest.* Handleiding. Lisse: Swets En Zeitlinger.

Bunjes, L. A. C. (1980), Ervaring in de kleuterschool. In: *Opgroeiende adotief-kinderen.* Deventer: Van Loghum Slaterus.

——— (1986), Adoptiekinderen. In: *Handboek Kinderen en Adolescenten,* afl. 3. Deventer: Van Loghum Slaterus.

Dommerholt, I. (1970), *Handleiding differentiele zinneenleestest,* NIPG/TNO. Groningen: Tjeenk, Willink.

Hoksbergen, R. A. C., Bunjes, L. A. C., Baarda, D. B., & Nota, J. (1982), *Adoptie van Kinderen uit verre landen,* 2nd ed. Deventer: Van Loghum Slaterus.

——— Juffer, F., & Waardenburg, B. C. (1986), *Adoptiekinderen thuis & op school.* Lisse: Swets & Zeitlinger.

Kingma, B. E., Schulpen, T. W. J., & Wolters, W. H. G. (1983), Medische aspecten van buitenlandse adoptiefkinderen. In: *Adoptie uit de Kinderschoenen*. Deventer: Van Loghum Slaterus.

Raven, J. C., Court, J. H., & Raven, J. (1977), The colored progressive matrices. In: *Manual for Raven's Progressive Matrices and Vocabulary Scales*. London: H. K. Lewis & Co., 1979.

Vane, J. (unpublished), *Kindergarten Test*, 1968.

van der Wissel, A. (unpublished), *Profdictees*, 1973.

van Haasen, P. P. (1976), WISC-R, Wechsler Intelligence Scale for Children (revised WISC-R, 1974). Nederlandse.

Winick, M., Meyer, K. K., & Harris, R. C. (1976), Malnutrition and environmental enrichment by early adoption. *Science*, 198:1173–1175.

Part IX

Adoption Outcome

24

Adoption Outcomes: A Review

John Triseliotis, Ph.D., O.B.E.

In this chapter I will present a brief review of some of the main studies in adoption carried out in recent years. It is not my intention, though, to discuss interracial or inter-country adoptions as those merit a separate paper.

Adoption has been a suitable ground for study by researchers of different persuasions and disciplines, albeit with different objectives in mind. Most studies seek answers to questions such as the policy and practice of adoption; the experience of adoption; who can successfully adopt and who can be adopted successfully; how to match parents and children; the development of predictive criteria of success or failure; the relative influence of heredity and environment; the importance of early childhood experiences for adult life and many other subsidiary questions.

All outcome studies involving human beings, and adoption is no exception, are difficult and complex to carry out. As a result, it is difficult to provide controls or to contrast like with like, such as children of similar age, background, and circumstances exposed to different types of care or rearing. The best that can be hoped for is approximations by exploiting the variations. Identifying outcome criteria and measuring tools is equally problematic. Judgments about "adjustment," "success," or "failure" are usually approached differently by

Acknowledgment. The influence of Anne Clarke's (1981) paper is warmly acknowledged.

291

different studies and so comparisons should be made with caution. Furthermore, different researchers have studied adopted children at different ages, for example, at ages five, seven, eleven, or sixteen, or three or five years following placement. Because of this, the studies have many limitations in terms of predictions about development. Some researchers have based their judgments on reports by adoptive parents and/or teachers, while others based theirs on a range of tests administered to adopted children. Very few studies indeed are based on the perceptions of adoptees, either as children or as adults. Longitudinal studies, such as Bohman's (1970) and Seglow, Pringle, and Wedge (1972), were of course excellent in that they followed adoptees at different ages into adult life and they provided comparisons with other separated and nonseparated children. Their main limitation was that they often relied on ratings by parents or teachers. Also, by the time a full cohort is studied the social conditions and research questions change. Retrospective studies of adult adoptees, such as Raynor (1980) and Triseliotis and Russell (1984), had to separate problems of outcome that were related to adoption from the rest of life's experiences, since there can be many events unconnected with adoption.

Except for some general guidelines, predictive factors of "success" and "failure" have been elusive. This is not difficult to understand. Because of variations in human personality, human reactions and behavior are difficult to predict. Unlike the natural sciences, the social sciences cannot be explained by natural laws based on firm empirical methods. People's customs, beliefs, and emotions cannot be studied and predicted in the same way as solid physical objects. Furthermore, people have a free will and the possibility of some choice in their lives. In spite of these reservations, reference will be made to those indicators that were supported by more than one study.

This paper separates the studies into those whose focus was early adoptions and those that were concerned with the adoption of special needs children, including reference to studies evaluating outcomes from the permanency movement of the last fifteen or so years.

EARLY ADOPTIONS

There is no shortage of these studies of early adoption and only selective reference will be made to them. A summary of a number of American follow-up studies covering a total of 2,236 adoptions provided by Kadushin (1971) found that success rates varied from 74 to 85 percent, depending on whether one included the intermediate groups in the success group. Some 15 percent were definitely unsuccessful.

Bohman's (1970, 1978) and Bohman and Sigvardsson's (1980) prospective longitudinal studies of a large cohort of unwanted male children in Sweden provides possibly the most consistent and interesting findings. This is probably the best documented study of its kind, except that again at no point were the subjects of the study interviewed, even when they were aged eighteen. Reliance was placed on official records, school grades, interviews with teachers, and questionnaires. The children in the study were born in 1956 and 1957, the pregnancies were unwanted, and at the time of their birth their mothers had reported to an adoption agency that they wished the children to be adopted. Out of these children, 168 were placed in adoptive homes before the age of one year, 208 were returned to their biological mothers, and 203 were placed in foster care, most of the latter before the age of one year. The adopted children were placed in homes which had been selected and thoroughly prepared. They were of higher educational and social status than the homes to which the other children went.

The children were assessed at ages eleven, fifteen, and eighteen. At the age of eleven, interviews with teachers showed that the adopted boys displayed a high rate of nervous and behavioral disturbance compared to the control children in their classrooms (the teachers were unaware which children were the subject of the study). Twenty-two percent were classified as problem children, compared to 12 percent among their class controls. There were, however, very few among either the subjects or the controls who could be classified as presenting conduct disorders, in comparison with the children who were reared by their mothers or who were fostered. The rate of disturbance was the same. Four years later at the age of fifteen, the differences between adopted children and their classmates were further diminished. There was still a slight tendency for the adopted children to have lower scores for adjustment and lower grades, but these differences were very small and only occasionally significant. By age eighteen, though, the few problems presented by the adopted group disappeared when compared to the rest of the class. Bohman comments that the "social prognosis of these children was not better or worse than with boys in general."

The National Children's Bureau cohort study covering children born in one week in Britain in 1958, some of whom were adopted, has yielded some useful material (Seglow et al., 1972). The children were studied at ages seven and eleven. At the age of seven, adopted children were generally as good, or slightly better in abilities, educational attainments, and social adjustment than other children, and significantly better than children who had been born illegitimate, but had not been adopted. As far as social adjustment at school and at home, the adopted children gave some indications of behavior difficulties when compared with other children, but not as many behavior difficulties as the illegitimate children. By the age of eleven, adopted children were significantly better at reading than other children, they were doing as well in math, and their social adjustment was not worse. However, the authors found that the achievements of the adopted group were associated not with their adoptive status as such, but with the exceptionally favorable environmental circumstances in which they were living. When environmental factors were taken into account, then the social adjustment of adopted children at eleven was poorer than that of the legitimate nonadopted ones.

As others have pointed out, if adopted children display somewhat more emotional problems in early adolescence, it may not be unrelated to the fact that this is the stage when they are beginning to grasp and integrate their adoptive status. Frisk (1964), Schonberg (1974), and others asserted that the chances of developing disturbances during adolescence are greater in the adopted child because of ego development, identification, and the forming of identity. Offer, Ostiv, and Howard (1981) and Stein and Hoopes (1985), on the other hand, have found no significant differences between adopted and nonadopted adolescents on overall measures of identity and adjustment. When Stein and Hoopes asked adolescents how their adoptive status impinged on different areas of their lives (i.e., family, peers, relations with opposite sex, self-esteem, and education), an overwhelming majority reported no significant effect. The adolescent adopted remarked that "it was not the adoptive status but other factors that tended to account for the difficulties in these spheres." Similarly Bohman (1970), Raynor (1980), and Triseliotis and Russell (1984) found no evidence that adoptees are more prone to psychological disorders compared to the rest of the population. A number of clinical studies in the 1960s purporting to show a higher rate of maladjustment among adopted children, have been shown to have been biased. Clinical studies are not reliable when it comes to issues such as rates of maladjustment between different groups (Schechter, 1960; Toussieg, 1962; Simon and Senturia, 1966).

One of the few studies available is that of Raynor (1980), who looked at adoption when the adoptees were twenty-one and over. Nearly all the children were placed with the adopters in their first year of life. This is possibly the only retrospective study where an attempt was made to match the perceptions of both adoptive parents and adoptees about the adoption experience. Sadly, it was possible to interview only 37 percent of the adoptees in the original sample, but nevertheless a very big achievement. The results showed that overall, 86 percent of the parents rated the experience of adoption as having been very satisfactory or reasonably satisfactory, leaving only 14 percent definitely dissatisfied. Among the adoptees, 70 percent were found to be making good or excellent life adjustment as adults, and 30 percent were either poorly adjusted or very much at risk. Though some of the children displayed a range of emotional and behavioral problems during childhood, by adulthood behaviors such as criminality or psychological disturbance were no higher than the average in the rest of the community.

When parents were asked what they liked least about their child, it was the child's poor academic record, or his lack of ambition at school. Poor schoolwork had often given rise to friction. Triseliotis and Russell (1984) also found that there was a correlation, though not amounting to full significance, between adoptive parents (mostly of a middle-class background) making many educational demands on children and dissatisfaction on the part of the adoptee. In Raynor's study, conflict over school was one of the main areas of contention even where the outcome was satisfactory. A major finding by Raynor not found by other studies was that successful outcomes were very significantly associated with a feeling of family likeness on the part of both parents and child. The adoptees and their adoptive parents were much more often satisfied when they were able to perceive or imagine likeness between them, and a major cause of dissatisfaction was an absence of this link—and the child's failure to acquire the family's value system. Raynor uses this finding to support the "matching" of children and adoptive parents by likeness, intelligence, and temperament. Ripple (1968), on the other hand, found no association between matching appearance and background with favorable outcome. Apart from the difficulty in identifying these in very young infants to "match" them with prospective adopters, there is a further issue of whether it is good practice to place the most promising children with the most promising families, or whether to go for a policy of "negative" placements. This would mean placing the more needy children with the more promising families. Another reasonable question to ask is whether the expectation of likeness is inherent in adoption or is fostered by agency practices. Also, does such a preference encourage a negation of the fact that adoption is different from biological parenthood?

EARLY ADOPTION AND INTELLECTUAL ABILITY

Studies generally suggest that the IQs of children correlate with the birth parents' IQ or educational status rather than with that of their adoptive parents, despite selective placement. Though there have been one or two exceptions to these studies, overall we have to accept that "genetic factors are a very significant cause of variation in IQ among adopted children, and therefore among children generally" (Clarke, 1981). Most studies suggest that favorable enviromental influences can help develop the child's potential to the full. There is still a lot to be learned about the interaction between nature and nurture in matters of intelligence. A French study (Schiff, Duyme, Dumoret, Stewart, Tomkiewicz, and Feingold, 1978) for example, which contrasted siblings who were adopted with those who stayed with their biological parents, has found that in terms of school attainment the two groups were typical of their rearing environments. The children reared by their biological parents had an average IQ of 94.5 and those adopted, 110.6. On another test the IQs were 95.4 and 106.9, respectively. The question that this study raises is the extent to which IQ is depressed by a poor environment and improved as a result of a favorable environment. A more recent French study of adopted children (Capron and Duyme, 1989) strengthens other findings that the home environment can improve IQ performance by up to 10 to 12 points. In an assessment of the research in the same journal, McGue (1989) says that the work shows clearly that IQ is influenced by both biological background and the circumstances of rearing. He also adds: "The most intriguing aspect of these results is that whereas the effects of nature and nurture are each significant on their own, there seems to be no interaction between the two factors" (p. 7).

TANGIBLE CHARACTERISTICS IN THE ADOPTIVE PARENTS

Characteristics such as age, religion, and years after marriage have not been found to be relevant to how adoption will work out. Triseliotis and Russell (1984), however, have found some evidence suggesting that placing young children with couples over forty-five carries certain risks. The presence of the couple's own children or of other children does not appear to influence outcome. More important seems to be the parenting qualities and attitudes of the adopting couple. Correlations between the socioeconomic background of adopters and adoption satisfaction are mixed. What seems to be happening is that some couples with higher socioeconomic status have expectations and make demands for academic education which lead to the children's negative attitude toward school and to poorer overall adjustment, a factor noted also by Hoopes, Sherman, Lowder, Andrews, and Lowe (1970).

In summary, research indicated that the vast majority of children adopted early in life seem to develop no differently, and do not present more social or personal problems when compared to children growing up with their biological parents. Any problems arising in childhood seem also to diminish with age. Overall, something like 70 percent of the children do well or very well, another 15 percent definitely do not do well, and the outcome of the remaining 15 percent is half and half.

Triseliotis' (1973) study "In Search of Origins" and subsequent studies in adoption and foster care, also dismissed the myth of the "blood tie" and established that the people who matter to children are those who care for them, rather than those who give birth to them.

PREDICTIVE FACTORS

When referring to the outcome of early adoptions, most studies put the emphasis on the circumstances and characteristics of the adopting parents rather than those of the child. Tangible characteristics such as age, religious persuasion, and economic situation have not on the whole been found to be predictive of outcome. With regard to intangible characteristics seen as desirable in would-be adopters, they include: being warm and accepting toward the child; a stable marital relationship and family; acceptance of the adopting role; accepting attitude toward the family of origin; the ability to help the adopted person develop his or her emerging personality on the concept of two sets of parents—biological and psychological. Knowledge about these attributes does not tell us how to recognize them among would-be adopters and substitute parents. This difficulty may account for the failure to find any differences between agency and independent placements (Witmer, Herzog, Weinstein, and Sullivan, 1963). Even if social workers' assessment skills of would-be adopters have not improved since then, there are many other reasons why independent or third-party adoptions should be banned, the paramount reason being that they do not always safeguard the best interests of the child.

THE ADOPTION OF SPECIAL NEEDS CHILDREN

In this section the emphasis will be on children who are at placement with their adoptive parents were considered as having special needs which placed them in the high risk category. By special needs we mean either older children who usually went through a number of "in care" experiences involving separations from parents and leading to the kind of deprivations described by Bowlby (1951) and others as irreversible, or children with handicaps or whose families had a history of psychiatric illness, criminality, or alcohol abuse, or sibling groups. Frequently these characteristics overlap. Prior to the permanency movement of the early 1970s, children with poor health, disabilities, those who were older, or whose parents exhibited deviant behavior were held back from adoption, and cared for mostly in institutions, thus increasing the children's negative early experiences.

It is to these studies that we turn to look at general outcomes, at possible genetic and other familial transmissions, as well as the extent to which early negative childhood experiences were later reversed and by what type of experiences. With the dramatic fall in baby adoptions in Western countries, and leaving aside international adoptions, adoption will increasingly be confined mostly to special needs children who go through the public care system. Future improvement of services to families and children in need should reduce this pool of adoptable children further. A new type of adoption that may become more popular is open or inclusive adoption.

The famous study by Skeels (1966) involved the placement of thirteen children from an institution who presented unmistakable signs of mental retardation and had inferior family histories. All thirteen were placed with adoptive families, while another twelve were left behind in the institution. The authors assured us that the ones placed for adoption were not particularly selected from the rest. The adoption of the children took place at about the age of three-and-a-half. The families are described as average and not expecting too much of these children. Twenty-five years later the fortunes of both groups were assessed. The differences were startling. The adopted group were normal adults; several had some professional training and most of them were happily married. In contrast, the children who were left behind in the institution, with one exception, had all done badly in their adult life. This study indicated that, given a favorable home, children can recover from early deprivations and that they are not held hostages to the histories of their biological families. Hereditary factors, however, were seen to be at play as the IQ of children still correlated with that of their birth parents. Placement in a good environment, though, had led to a major increase in the overall level of intelligence. In some cases, the children's IQ was 20 points above that of their natural mothers. Similarly, Witmer et al. (1963) found little difference in the adjustment of fifty-six children with poor histories as contrasted with other adoptees placed at a similar age and in similar adoptive homes.

Besides studies in adoption, there are a few well-documented case histories of children rescued from conditions of severe deprivation and subsequently reared by individual families. Clarke and Clarke (1976) in their book describe a number of such case studies. As Clarke (1981) points out case studies of this kind illustrate in a tragic but dramatic way the effect of physical and social deprivation on developing humans, together with later recovery, provided the child is removed from the depriving environment and placed in a nurturing, caring, and stimulating one.

One important investigation carried out in the United States by Kadushin (1971) attempted to determine the reversibility, or otherwise, of early psychological damage in children who are subsequently placed in adoptive homes. He followed up a group of ninety-one children who were in early adolescence at the time of the investigations. The children were placed for adoption when they were at least five years old or older and had suffered considerable deprivation experiences before adoptive placement, including a number of moves between various institutions. The children came from families living at a very low socioeconomic level. Kadushin based his findings on data obtained from the parents. Compared to studies of early adoptions, the success rate of these "higher risk," older children was similar; 74 percent successful, 15 percent unsuccessful, and 11 percent equivocal. In his view, "outcome was positively related to parents' acceptance of the child, in their perception of him as a member of the family, and negatively related to self-consciousness by parents regarding the adoptive status" (p. 210). He attributed the resilience of these children to the security of the home and the relationships within it. In addition, and very importantly, he suggested that the wider social context plays a significant part in the recovery process. Kadushin concluded that "there has been a tendency to overestimate the importance and power of the past. . . . Agencies can take risks in placing older children with a high probability of success" (p. 215).

A few years later, Tizard's study (1977) was to reinforce Kadushin's findings. She followed up a small sample of hard to place children who were two years or older by the time they left residential care, some were adopted, and others returned to their mothers. Tizard found that by the age of about seven, the adopted children had overcome the effects of the residential experience. She concluded that the subsequent development of the early institutionalized child depends upon the environment to which he is moved. Neither a below average IQ nor very difficult behavior prevent satisfaction with adoption, provided that mutual affection develops between parent and child. Similarly, Flint (1978), reporting on a follow-up study of twenty-five children aged about fifteen who were placed with adoptive parents directly from an institution, when less than three years old, showed that as "a group, the children have demonstrated a remarkable capacity for in-depth affiliation with their parents and families" (p. 163). Like Kadushin, Tizard, and Triseliotis and Russell, Flint concluded that "events which took place after placement in families were more powerful factors in the final outcome than were earlier experiences" (p. 190).

A more recent study involving high risk and older children was conducted by Triseliotis and Russell (1984). This study looked at three different groups of children in substitute care (i.e., adoption, long-term foster care, and upbringing in institutional groups), and examined the extent to which aspects of behavior, social handicaps, and other difficulties were transmitted from one generation to the next in situations where the children were separated and remained apart from their families from early life onward. The three groups of children had many common similarities and some differences. For example, the adopted children's group came from a somewhat more favorable social background compared to the other two groups. On the other hand, more of the adopted ones were considered high risk compared to the other two groups. The adopted group was placed with their adoptive parents when they were between three and eight years of age. They had experienced at least four institutional moves, physical and mental health problems were not uncommon, and their adoption had been held back because of queries concerning either their social background or physical or mental health. All the respondents were between twenty-one and thirty by the time of the investigation. The study was based exclusively on the perceptions of the sample group.

Over 80 percent of the adoptees felt very positive about their adoption experience. Adopted people enjoyed the feeling of belonging to a family, of being accepted for themselves and made to feel as one of the family. They generally enjoyed close and warm relationships with parental figures, with siblings and members of the extended family. They saw themselves as the children of their adoptive parents on whom they looked as their "real" parents. The less than one-fifth who experienced mixed feelings or dissatisfaction with their adoption linked their dissatisfaction mostly to pressures to fulfill parental ambitions or to the absence of closeness and emotional warmth in the adoptive relationship.

The age at which the children came into public care, the number of moves experienced before the final placement, past behavior, parental background, health risks, and age at placement did not affect the outcome of adoption. An element of risk, though, was associated with the placement of children with couples aged forty-five and over. The children experienced their parents as rather "too set in their ways," "rigid in expectations," and felt "embarrassed to be seen with them." Adoptees with "inferior" background histories, including those born to women described as suffering from a degree of mental handicap, did not function very differently from the rest. The adoptees' social and material circumstances, as well as their overall social and emotional adjustment, were superior to those of children who grew up in foster care and far superior to those reared in institutions. Like Bohman (1970) and Raynor (1980), the study also found that emotional or behavioral difficulties in childhood do not necessarily continue in adult life.

The adoption sample in this study also demonstrated discontinuities with the material, social, and personal circumstances of the natural family. Based on the available records on the natural family, adoptees were much more likely to resemble in circumstances their adoptive rather than their natural families. Also, no significant association could be established between individual forms of deviant social and personal behavior, such as crime, drink, psychiatric illness, relationship problems, and similar behavior and attributes in the biological family.

When single forms of behavior in the offspring were correlated with similar behavior in the parents of origin, no significant association could be established. Triseliotis and Russell (1984) concluded not only that the older age and high risk nature of the adopted group at placement achieved as good outcomes as those of young, healthy infants, but also that the social and personal attributes of the family of origin were irrelevant to the current social and personal behavior of the adoptees. This point is in agreement with Bohman and Sigvardsson (1980) who also concluded from their studies that the "social heritage" seems to have been by and large neutralized by the secure placement which a well-prepared adoption offers.

This brings us to such matters as the transmission of criminality, alcohol abuse, and psychiatric recovery. Transmissions can occur through genetic processes or, in the case of children who are separated when older, through learning processes. A small scale and rather poorly documented study by Crowe (1972), involving adopted children, showed that those with criminal parents were more likely to commit crime in later years than the rest. Similarly, Hutchings and Medwick (1974) claim to have found a significant correlation between criminality among adoptees and their biological parents. Bohman's (1978) more extensive studies, like Triseliotis and Russell's (1984), failed to establish such a connection.

In matters of alcohol abuse, and with the exception of Triseliotis and Russell, other studies claim to have found a significant correlation between alcohol abuse among biological parents and similar behavior among adoptees. For example, Goodwin, Schulsinger, Moller, Hermansen, Winokur, and Guze (1974) found from their Danish study a significantly higher rate of alcoholism among the adopted sons of alcoholic biological fathers than among control adoptees. If it is genetic transmissions that are operating, it is puzzling to explain why adopted daughters of alcoholic biological fathers did not have a higher rate of alcohol abuse than control adoptees. Bohman (1978) and Cadoret and Gath (1978) also suggest a link between alcohol abuse in biological parents and similar behavior in adopted offspring.

Psychiatric illness and its possible genetic transmission is mostly examined in relation to schizophrenic illness. The best known studies, involving identical twins, have been carried out in Scandinavia. Kety, Rosenthal, Wender, and Schulsinger (1968) and Rosenthal and Seymour (1968) concluded from their studies that heredity was a prominent factor in the etiology of schizophrenic disorder, adding at the same time that environmental variations were also of importance for the display of such behavior in adults. It does appear that adoptees with biological parents who are schizophrenic, alcoholic, or even criminal, are at somewhat greater risk for these problems than are other children (for a summary of studies, see Defries and Plomin [1978]). However, because adoptive families are selected and prepared, they offer "better than average opportunities for their children and almost certainly mitigating to an unknown extent risks which otherwise result in children becoming deviant in one way or another" (Clarke, 1981, p. 28). Similarly, Triseliotis and Russell (1984) concluded that even in situations where genetic factors seem to be at play, it does not follow that familial disorders will find expression. Properly arranged adoptions, in contrast to residential rearing, seems to have the capacity to neutralize certain hereditary influences. After all, genetic theory predicts parent–offspring differences as well as resemblances. Subsequent social stresses and the quality of care may determine to a large extent whether the resemblances will dominate.

OUTCOME STUDIES COVERING THE "PERMANENCY" MOVEMENT

Emerging studies monitoring the recent permanency movement, while providing somewhat contradictory results on the placement of special needs children, also demonstrate some consistency. The main differences concern the rate of disruptions, which is partly due to definitional problems of what constitutes a disruption or breakdown, and to how soon or late the studies took place following placement or adoption. There is broad agreement that breakdown rates for those under ten years old are around 9 percent; however, the rates for older children vary depending on the study viewed.

Breakdown rates for those over ten years old range from 15 to 50 percent for late adolescents. It is also becoming clearer that increased age, especially after about the age of ten, and increased disturbance in children are appearing as important variables in higher disruption rates. For example, Tremitiere (1984) reviewed around 2,500 adoptions from 1979 to 1983 and found that six- to twelve-year-old children had a disruption rate of 9.7 percent and twelve to eighteen-year-olds had a rate of 13.5 percent. Boyne, Denby, Kettering, and Wheeler (1984) identified a 23.2 percent disruption rate amongst 219 special needs children with disruption rates of 9, 15, 25, and 47 percent for age groups birth to five, six to eight, nine to eleven, and twelve to seventeen, respectively. Kagan and Reid (1986) reported around 50 percent adoption disruption of "emotionally disturbed" teenagers. In contrast, the Oregon Project's policy of aggressive adoption resulted in sixty-four adoptions and only two disruptions in the months following the end of the project, and two or more years after the placement for 75 percent of the children (Lahti, 1982). A review of nearly 500 adoptive placements in Britain showed a 9 percent disruption rate (Fitzgerald, 1983). Nelson (1985) also found that adoptions of only seven out of twenty-five children placed when eight years of age and over were disrupted within a year of the adoption order. Festinger (1985) and O'Hara and Hoggan (1988) report equally low rates of disruption.

Thoburn and Rowe's (1988) large survey of voluntary agencies in Britain covered 1,165 children placed by these agencies between 1979 and 1984. Overall breakdowns were 21 percent, but the rate for ten- to twelve-year-olds rose to 30 percent, and for those thirteen or more to 48 percent, which was similar to the findings of Kagan and Reid (1986). Lower breakdowns are found where children were first fostered and then adopted. This, of course, does not take into account those fostered and never placed for adoption because of age or other problems. Thoburn, Murdoch, and O'Brien (1986), for example, reported that two years following placement, a high percentage of adolescents had not yet been adopted, possibly because the families were still waiting for behavior and emotional problems to diminish.

It is still too early to say whether there is a critical age above which the breakdown rates are too high to be acceptable. Unlike infants and young children, adolescents and teenagers have a longer background history, a range of in-care experiences, and more definite views of what they want. In many respects older children and would-be adopters should have the chance to choose each other. Though some adolescents in public care would like to be adopted, others would like to do so only if links with their original families are maintained, while still others do not wish to be adopted. It also has to be recognized that at a time when adolescents are starting to establish greater independence in life, placement in an adoptive home places demands for close attachments.

Among the many innovative developments of the last ten years or so in the placement of hard to place children has been the finding of adoptive homes for Down's Syndrome children. In fact, one agency in London, Parents for Children, specializes in this kind of placement. Macaskill (1985) followed some twenty families who adopted mentally handicapped children from six different voluntary adoption agencies. The study took place from three months to four-and-a-half years after placement. Macaskill claims that overall the families were satisfied with the adoption experience. The children seemed to make progress on all fronts. Because of this progress, seventeen of the families wanted to adopt another handicapped child. Some difficulties were attributed to the child's former institutionalization rather than

to the handicap. Macaskill makes a strong plea for postadoption services to forestall difficulties and hardships from developing later on.

Macaskill's, and other yet unpublished studies, suggest that the
people who come forward to adopt special needs children do not have
the same background and characteristics as those formerly adopting
young infants. Such adopters come from all walks of life, and in many
respects are unusual compared to traditional adopters. For example,
many of those adopting mentally handicapped children had some
experience of handicap through their families or work. Clear criteria
of suitability for this form of adoption are yet to emerge.

PREDICTIVE FACTORS

Though some clues are beginning to emerge, it is still largely
unclear what family and child characteristics contribute to stability
and adjustment in the adoption of special needs children. The following characteristics in children and adopting families have been identified by at least more than one of the studies quoted earlier as contributory to placement stability.

CHILD FACTORS CONTRIBUTORY TO STABILITY

- At least under ten years of age at placement and not too problematic. Breakdown increases with age and with increasing
  emotional behavior problems;
- Forming an attachment with his or her new family within the
  first fifteen months or so;
- Knowledge about his or her origins, in-care situation, and circumstances of placement or adoption;
- Placement with a sibling (supported by the majority but not all
  studies);
- Strong motivation on the part of the older child, with adoption
  being a positive choice;
- Had not been subjected to physical or sexual abuse before the
  placement;
- Had been well prepared before placement.

ADOPTIVE PARENT FACTORS CONTRIBUTORY TO STABILITY

- Marital stability, a degree of warmth, empathy, and security; tolerance of differences, flexible roles and rules, and an open communication system; acceptance of the child and its membership in the family;
- Parents expect and accept behavior and emotional problems in the child. Studies tend to show that the period fifteen to eighteen months following placement is a critical one during which more breakdowns take place. There is a view that after the first twelve to fifteen months adoptive parents begin to give up if they can see no improvement in the child's behavior and no attachments are being formed. In other words, some positive emotional response from the child is necessary;
- Parents are open and receptive to seeking and accepting support and help from outside;
- Acceptance of the family of origin, the child's background, and his past links;
- Have been well prepared by the agency and have access to postadoption support services. Postplacement support needs to continue until after the critical period of fifteen to eighteen months is passed.

SUMMARY

It can now be accepted that children adopted up to about the age of nine can settle well in their adoptive families and become indistinguishable from the rest of the population. Some negative early experiences may influence subsequent development but their importance has been exaggerated. Rutter (1981) makes the point that undue emphasis has been placed on the mother–child relationship, that the experience of multiple caretakers is not necessarily problematic, provided the standard of care is good and the caretakers do not change, and that separation as such is not usually the critical variable which causes distress or developmental problems. Problems following separation are not related to a breaking of relationships but to an initial failure to form new bonds and attachments. Finally, as the new studies suggest, difficulties may emerge throughout childhood and be ameliorated by a return to an environment in which the damaging factors no longer operate. Single isolated chronic stresses need not cause later disorders. More stresses, however, increase the possibility of disturbance. Overall, the studies demonstrate the vital importance and centrality of relationships and their quality to how adoptions work out.

In spite of the many studies quoted, it is still difficult to link particular types of social work practice to specific outcomes except in terms of preparation and postplacement. Group preparation and support also seem to have been found more helpful in preparing for adoption and postplacement compared to individual methods (Triseliotis, 1988). There have virtually been no studies of the extent of agency variations, agency selection processes, different preparation, and introductory methods, and the impact of organizational variable on outcome. The studies are not yet subtle enough to discriminate between different placements and particularly which families can do well for which type of child. The current view is that different families bring different qualities which suit different children. What these qualities are is not yet clear. The suggestion is that more importance should be placed on the preparation of families and children and the provision of postadoption support services, rather than trying to identify the ideal family.

REFERENCES

Bohman, M. (1970), *Adopted Children and Their Families*. Stockholm: Proprios.
——— (1978), Some genetic aspects of alcoholism and criminality. *Arch. Gen. Psychiat.*, 35:269–276.
——— Sigvardsson, S. (1980), Negative social heritage. *Adopt. & Foster.*, 101:25–31.
Bowlby, J. (1951), *Maternal Care and Mental Health*. Geneva: WHO.
Boyne, J., Denby, L., Kettering, J. R., & Wheeler, W. (1984), *The Shadow of Success*. Unpublished Research Report. Westfield: Spaulding for Children.
Cadoret, J., & Gath, A. (1978), Inheritance of alcoholism in adoptees. *Brit. J. Psychiat.*, 132:258–259.
Capron, C., & Duyme, M. (1989), Assessment of effects of socio-economic status on IQ in a full cross-fostering study. *Nature*, 340:552–554.
Clarke, A. (1981), Adoption studies. *Adopt. & Foster.*, 104:17–29.
Clarke, A. M., & Clarke, A. D. B., eds. (1976), *Early Experience: Myth and Evidence*. London: Open Books.

Crowe, R. R. (1972), The adopted offspring of women criminal offenders. *Arch. Gen. Psychiat.,* 126:534–559.

Defries, J. C., & Plomin, R. (1978), Behavioral genetics. *Ann. Rev. Psychol.,* 29:473–515.

Festinger, T. (1985), *Necessary Risk.* New York: CWLA.

Fitzgerald, J. (1983), *Understanding Disruption.* London: BAAF.

Flint, B. M. (1978), *New Hope for Deprived Children.* Toronto: University of Toronto Press.

Frisk, M. (1964), Identity problems and confused conceptions of the genetic ego in adopted children during adolescence. *Acta Psychiat.,* 31:6–12.

Goodwin, D. W., Schulsinger, E., Moller, N., Hermansen, L., Winokur, C., & Guze, S. B. (1974), Drinking problems in adopted and non-adopted sons of alcoholics. *Arch. Gen. Psychiat.,* 31:164–169.

Hoopes, J., Sherman, E., Lowder, A., Andrews, R., & Lowe, K. (1970), *A Follow-Up Study of Adoptions: Post-Placement Functioning of Adoptive Children,* Vol 2. London: CWLA.

Hutchings, B., & Medwick, S. (1974), Registered criminality in the adoptive and biological parents of registered male criminal adoptees. In: *Genetics and Psychopathology,* ed. R. R. Feeve & D. A. Zubin. Baltimore: Johns Hopkins University Press.

Kadushin, A. (1971), *Adopting Older Children,* 2nd ed. New York: Columbia University Press.

Kagan, M. R., & Reid, J. W. (1986), Critical factors in the adoption of emotionally disturbed youths. *Child Welf.,* 50:63–73.

Kety, S. S., Rosenthal, D., Wender, P. H., & Schulsinger, F. (1968), The types and prevalence of mental illness in the biological and adoptive families of adopted schizophrenics. In: *The Transmission of Schizophrenia,* ed. D. Rosenthal & S. S. Kety. Oxford: Pergamon Press.

Lahti, J. (1982), A follow-up study of foster children in permanent placement. *Soc. Serv. Rev.,* 56:556–571.

McGue, M. (1989), Nature-nurture and intelligence. *Nature,* 340: 506–507.

Macaskill, C. (1985), *Against the Odds.* London: BAAF.

Mai, F. M., Munday, R. N., & Rump, E. D. (1972), Psychiatric interview comparisons between infertile and fertile couples. *Psychosom. Med.,* 34:431–440.

Nelson, K. A. (1985), *On the Frontier of Adoption.* New York: CWLA.

Offer, D., Ostiv, E., & Howard, K. I. (1981), *The Adolescent: A Psychological Self-Portrait.* New York: Basic Books.

O'Hara, G., & Hoggan, K. I. (1988), Permanent substitute family care in Lothian: Placement outcomes. *Adopt. & Foster.,* 12:35–39.

Raynor, L. (1980), *The Adopted Child Comes of Age.* London: Allen & Unwin.

Ripple, L. (1968), A follow-up study of adopted children. *Soc. Serv. Rev.,* 42:479–499.

Rosenthal, D., & Seymour, S. K. (1968), *The Transmission of Schizophrenia.* Oxford: Pergamon Press.

Rutter, M. (1981), *Maternal Deprivation Re-assessed,* 2nd ed. London: Penguin.

Schechter, M. D. (1960), Observations on adopted children. *Arch. Gen. Psychiat.*, 3:45–56.

———— Carlson, P. V., Simmons, J. Q., & Work, H. H. (1964), Emotional problems in the adoptee. *Arch. Gen. Psychiat.*, 10:109–118.

Schiff, M., Duyme, M., Dumoret, A., Stewart, J., Tomkiewicz, S., & Feingold, J. (1978), Intellectual status of working class children adopted early into upper-middle-class families. *Science*, 200: 1503–1504.

Schonberg, C. (1974), On adoption and identity. *Child Welf.*, 53:549–555.

Seglow, J., Pringle, M. L., & Wedge, P. (1972), *Growing Up Adopted*. London: National Foundation for Educational Research in England and Wales.

Simon, N. M., & Senturia, A. G. (1966), Adoption and psychiatric illness. *Amer. J. Psychiat.*, 122:858–868.

Skeels, H. M. (1966), Adult Status of Children with Contrasting Early Life Experience: A Follow-Up Study. *Monographs of the Society for Research in Child Development*, Vol. 31, No. 105, p. 3. Chicago.

Stein, L. M., & Hoopes, J. L. (1985), Identity formation in the adopted adolescent. New York: CWLA.

Thoburn, J., Murdoch, A., & O'Brien, A. (1986), *Permanence in Child Care*. Oxford: Basil Blackwell.

———— Rowe, J. (1988), A snapshot of permanent family placement. *Adopt. & Foster.*, 12:29–34.

Tizard, B. (1977), *Adoption: A Second Chance*. London: Open Books.

Toussieg, P. W. (1962), Thoughts regarding the etiology of psychological difficulties in adopted children. *Child Welf.*, 41:59–65.

Tremitiere, B. T. (1984), Adoption of children with special needs in the client central approach. *Child Welf.*, 58:681–685.

Triseliotis, J. (1973), *In Search of Origins*. London: RKP.

———— ed. (1980), *New Developments in Foster Care and Adoption*. London: RKP.

———— ed. (1988), *Group Work in Adoption and Foster Care*. London: Batsford.

———— Russell, J. (1984), *Hard to Place*. London: Gower.

Witmer, H. L., Herzog, E., Weinstein, E. A., & Sullivan, M. E. (1963), *Independent Adoptions: A Follow-Up Study*. New York: Russell Sage Foundation.

Name Index

311

Subject Index

315